Letters to
GARDEN LOVERS

1937

Letters to

GARDEN LOVERS

Edna Walling

NH
NEW
HOLLAND

1948

ABOUT THE AUTHOR

Edna Walling was one of Australia's finest garden designers. Dressed in jodphurs, gaiters and boots, she created hundreds of gardens throughout Australia, integrating native plants with stonework and aspects of light and shade to create different moods in the garden. She also became known as a distinguished photographer, popular garden writer and environmentalist during her illustrious career. Her reputation continues to survive thanks to her marvellous watercolour garden illustrations that have now become collectors' items.

Edna gained acclaim for her landscape designs after her first commission—to construct the gardens at Melbourne Zoo in 1927. From this time until the 1940s she was in great demand for her ingenious landscaping, and was involved in the development of Bickleigh Vale village, as well as promoting her garden nursery at Sonning, the simple stone cottage she lived in from the early 1920s, at Mooroolbark, near Melbourne. She also began her popular 'Letters to Garden Lovers' column for the *Australian Home Beautiful* magazine, in which she'd talk about her landscapes, her favourite plants (she adored crabapples and thyme lawns), and the importance of caring for the environment.

Whilst her career and reputation flourished, Edna continued to live at Sonning surrounded by old-fashioned flowers and bushland. Sonning would be the centrepiece of her work, always evolving in harmony with its bush surrounds. It was here that Edna developed her passion for Australian native flora, a love affair evident in her work throughout the late 1940s and the 1950s. In 1967, her sojourn at Sonning ended and Edna moved to Buderim in Queensland to escape the encroaching suburbia and to improve her increasingly poor health. After several strokes she died on 8 August 1973.

Edna's philosophies undoubtedly influenced Australian gardening and are still relevant to landscape design today. An abundance of her writings, plans and photographs remain for future garden lovers to explore, a testament to her creativity and enormous talent. However, despite the acclaim, for Edna gardening was always a simple joy.

'Dear Gardeners, I'm the luckiest person in the world! I have just been asked to design a garden where lovely birches and other treasures already exist! A long time ago I planted this piece of ground when it was the lower part of a large garden, and now a house has been built upon this block, and, as luck would have it, the trees are in the happiest positions possible, and it is only a matter of a restraining hand and the most careful introduction of some very large weathered boulders, and we shall have a piece of restful landscape that should prove much of a joy to the owner and those who will share it with her.'

First published in Australia in 2000 by
New Holland Publishers (Australia) Pty Ltd
Sydney • Auckland • London • Cape Town

14 Aquatic Drive Frenchs Forest NSW 2086 Australia
218 Lake Road Northcote Auckland New Zealand
24 Nutford Place London W1H 6DQ United Kingdom
80 McKenzie Street Cape Town 8001 South Africa

National Library of Australia Cataloguing-in-Publication Data:

Walling, Edna, 1895–1973
    Letters to garden lovers.

    ISBN 1 86436 621 4

    1. Landscape gardening - Australia. 2. Gardens - Australia -
    Design. I. Title. II. Title: Australian home beautiful

    712.60994

Project Manager: Monica Ban
Designer: Nanette Backhouse
Cover and internal illustrations: Helen McCosker
Reproduction: DNL Resources
Printer: Griffin Press
Picture credits: Front flap—Mitchell Library,
                              State Library of New South Wales
                Back flap—Sue Burston

CONTENTS

PREFACE

Fifty years on, Edna Walling's writing still bubbles with her infectious enthusiasm for gardening. Her columns in the *Australian Home Beautiful*, written throughout the 1930s and 1940s, inspired several generations of Australians to view gardening afresh.

Edna managed to be instructive (in fact she was sometimes downright bossy!), but her gardening advice was never dry. Edna's columns were more like letters to dear friends than lectures from a brilliant enthusiast to an audience of amateurs.

This book has reproduced Edna's original letters to garden lovers. The botanical names of the period (the current name has been added in square brackets), the imperial measurements, and the comments made by the *Australian Home Beautiful's* editor at the time, all remain. Edna often contributed photographs to the column, however while not reproduced here, reference to them remains in the text to maintain the charm of Edna's writing.

Without doubt, what made Edna Walling one of our finest gardeners was the sheer pleasure and amusement she derived from gardening. Anyone who reads her column is forced to look at gardening from a new perspective. Even half a century later, her columns still challenge the reader not to be as utterly delighted with the joy of gardening as Edna found herself. Alas, there is no peer for Edna today, but her vision, which aspires to a sense of tranquility and creating a spiritual haven within our own backyards, has never been more relevant.

Andrea Jones,
Editor, *Australian Home Beautiful*

Dear Gardeners,

A little while ago it was suggested that I should write a monthly letter to the gardening readers of the *Home Beautiful*, and the Editor has kindly fallen in with the suggestion, and so here we are! I can see that the chief difficulty is going to be to keep within the allotted space, for gardening is such a broad subject, taking it from the tiny cottage garden full of Old World flowers, to the spacious grounds where large trees and constructional features are appropriate.

A NEW TREE

And talking of trees, there is one that I feel you would like to know about, and that is the pyramid birch. This tree grows just like a Lombardy poplar, which means that we can now have that effect so many of us long to have close to our houses without the hopeless disadvantages produced by the root system of the poplars. It is indeed one of the greatest acquisitions in the plant world and is one of the daintiest trees I know.

I wonder why more of us do not grow Japanese irises, for they thrive in ordinary garden conditions and are such wonderful things for an early summer effect. The tremendous floodings sometimes advocated for these plants have been found to be quite unnecessary. You can treat them as ordinary herbaceous perennials and get splendid blooms; we have them growing in one part of the garden where we never water at all, and they are as good here as where the ground is watered in any weather. When we have it to spare they are given a top dressing of cow manure in the spring which helps to keep them from drying out as well as nourishing them. They will not tolerate cutting off the leaves before they have died right off, or being moved before the winter, so do not imagine that because the germanicas—commonly called 'flags'—can be moved with safety the whole year around, that it applies to the whole family of irises.

FLOWERS FOR INDOORS

Perennial lupins are an excellent foil for Japanese irises and aren't they just the loveliest and easiest of perennials to grow? They are so prolific for cutting for indoor decoration, too. I always feel that these *Lupinus polyphyllus* are among the most useful flowers to grow for this purpose. They bloom over a long period, the colours are sufficiently varied to suit almost any colour scheme, and seedlings planted out so quickly develop into lusty flowering plants.

What a very dainty little shrub is the pale pink *Escallonia donard* seedling and the brighter pink *E. edinburghii*. They both make the most delightful wall shrubs and for those mixed bowls of flowers that so many women favour for table decoration nowadays the blooms are invaluable. You will find these escallonias most useful summer blooming shrubs for a rather hot, dry position.

A RANDOM RAMBLER

Just at present there are cascades of the most delightful pale pink blossoms of a climbing rose spilling out of clumps of tea-tree, and scrambling over old sheds. It is a rambler type (I think) which I fancy was purchased under the name of 'Wedding Bells' many years ago, since when someone has told me it is 'Apple Blossom'. We have adopted this name until all shadow of doubt has been removed, because we like it best! It is a rampant grower but is really never a nuisance and everyone is enthralled with it.

The intoxicating fragrance of the Italian honeysuckle *Lonicera caprifolium* fills the air and is proving a delightful companion to the 'Apple Blossom' rose. The perfume of this honeysuckle is quite distinct from most of the other varieties, suggestive of *Lilium auratum* perhaps. The blooms are in bunches and are an exquisite shade of biscuit and rose.

COUNTRY GARDENS

What a marvellous summer it has been, so far, for country gardeners. Here we are just over the doorstep of January as I write, with bright green grass all about and everything else looking wonderfully fresh. Of course the refreshing rains have not always come peacefully. Last Sunday there was a storm that was terrifying in its ferocity: it destroyed all the fuses in everyone's telephones, snapped the top of an elm tree, making a large hole in the roof of a neighbour of mine. It swept through another house, sending a miscellaneous collection of articles through the windows, including a loaf of bread!—later retrieved an incredibly long distance away. And many other and worse calamities befell all in the path of the hurricane. We hurried down to 'Winty', the latest little cottage at Bickleigh Vale, hardly daring to hope that all would be well, for the windows and doors were not yet in, and the new roof completed only the day before. But there she stood quite intact and just beginning to look rather sweet with her white walls and her little rough plastered chimney. 'Winty' will probably be the subject of a further instalment of 'Adventures in Landscape Gardening', two of which have already appeared in the *Home Beautiful*, telling the story of the Bickleigh Vale Village at Mooroolbark.

I'm just off to visit a very lovely rock garden in the mountains, and am hoping to get some good photographs of it because it is one of the few examples of a really artistic rock garden, so perhaps I will have some pictures that the Editor will think clear enough to print in a future issue of the *Home Beautiful*.

Until next month, goodbye and good gardening!

Yours deciduously,

Edna Walling

M A R C H   1 ,   1 9 3 7

Dear Gardeners,

I expect that quite a number of you possess a narrow strip of ground between the house and one of the boundaries which is more often than not quite useless, and a source of irritation as well, because if we have any pride in our property at all we cannot bear to have any part of it that is not presentable, and the unsatisfactory growing conditions in these draughty alleyways certainly present many difficulties. You may therefore be interested in the treatment of such a problem that came my way a little while ago. Two windows in the principal room in the house looked out upon a paling fence—that was the first problem and it was agreed that a wall finished with the same texture and colour as the house would be infinitely preferable. Existing trees were hard up against the fence, so there was no room for a brick wall of even a single brick in width, so we extended the fence posts to the height that we required, nailed expanded metal to them, and gave it three coats of plaster. The square pillar is for a little bronze figure that is now in place (I'm sorry it was not there when I took the picture). This makes a picture immediately outside one of the windows, and opposite the other window, which is about nine feet away, there is a wall fountain. The water falls from a lead mask on the wall to an oblong pool, which is retained by a little wall 10 inches high faced with blue tiles of all shapes and sizes, giving the appearance of a strip of blue mosaic. The ground is entirely paved with slate paving stones which have transformed this narrow strip of ground into quite a pleasing courtyard, where hydrangeas bloom in summer, and in the spring there will be azaleas and the smaller growing rhododendrons—all in tubs, of course. In this way it is possible to keep the little courtyard in perfect trim, because it is so easy to remove any plant that is not looking particularly attractive, and replace it with one from the workshop of your garden, where such things are kept in readiness for display. Oh! And I must remember to

tell you about some of those smaller growing rhododendrons some time, they're fascinating! There's one about an inch high, did you know?

THE OSAGE ORANGE

Just out of Lilydale last autumn I noticed a rather charming old hedge that had turned such a beautiful clear yellow that I was prompted to pull up and see what it was. It was Osage orange—*Maclura aurantiaca* [*Maclura pomifera*]. It is thorny and quite hardy and makes a delightful country garden hedge and breakwind. The late Doctor Bird stopped me in the Botanic Gardens one day to tell me a vivid story about a very sedate person whose bowler hat had been suddenly bashed in by the falling of a large hard Osage orange from a big maclura under which he was unsuspectingly strolling. And this is the reason why one hesitates to use it as a lawn specimen, although it is tempting at times.

FOUNDATION PLANTING

I suppose that some of you have a little difficulty in getting just the right evergreen shrubs for planting the foundations of your houses sometimes, I know I do. The various varieties of cistus are, of course, indispensable for such positions, for so often the conditions are hot and dry, and these little plants revel in such a spot. A plant that is very useful for this purpose is *Hebe ligustrifolia*. It is very rarely catalogued, but will be more often in the near future I fancy. Sometimes it is listed under the veronicas, which it closely resembles. It is not long since I secured it, but I think it came to me under the name of *Veronica buxifolia*.

There is a rather lovely showing of bloom on the purple-leafed Catalpa just now, the mauve-tinged flowers are in loose panicles. For large gardens it is useful for its summer blooming habit, but the large, rather coarse leaves make it inappropriate for the small garden.

ROCK GARDENING

In the rock garden *Prunella grandiflora* is covered with its rather coarse purple-like blue flowers, the colour is good and the heavy effect of the blooms can be softened down with *Thymus huta harma*, with its mauve pink flowers and soft grey foliage. The soft blue stars of *Campanula istriaca* will aid the picture, too. I do not think we sufficiently appreciate the need for turf in our rock gardens—observe the closely nibbled grass that butts right up to some lovely outcrop of stone and go home and try introducing a similar effect into your own rock gardens. The fescues are the best grasses for the purpose. Whatever you do avoid the creeping bents for they creep so quickly into the pockets where your precious plants are growing, and there is sufficient to combat without planting trouble. I secured *Thymus serphyllum albus* a few days ago, to my great joy: it is one of the most attractive varieties of the creeping thymes. Nothing can be lovelier for the pathways through the rock garden with some big flat stones to step on. *Thymus serphyllum coccineus* is a mass of brilliance softened down by the close proximity of a grey-leafed thyme secured as *T. lanuginosus*, but it isn't! The Sonning rock garden is as yet just a poorly stocked museum, part of which resembles a plum pudding that has sagged rather badly. However, time will cure this.

For a hedge that is evergreen and summer-blooming—always a good point because there are so many things flowering in the spring—has it ever occurred to you to use *Abelia rupestris*? I think you would like it because the foliage is such a good, dark, somewhat shiny bronze-green. It grows very quickly and yet three at most cuttings in the year will keep it sufficiently shapely. The flowers are a delicate shell pink and white, and when they have fallen the ducky red bracts, which remains right through the winter, are as effective as the flowers. We have found it most useful for indoor decoration mixed with autumn foliage.

All the best gardening writers know all about pests, but personally I am very inclined to agree with Mr Sellar and Mr Yeatman in *Garden Rubbish* when they say,

> *... ever since horticulture became a science, scientists have been joyously discovering so many varieties of pests and breeding so many species of counter-pests that there are now probably more pests than scientists! ...*

Under the heading 'Their Nature and Treatment', they give much helpful advice which appeals to my lazy instincts where such things are concerned. Take for instance pest No. IV, WEEVILS: Ignore them—remember to the old warning, 'hear no weevil, see no weevil, speak no weevil', and cut them dead.

I'll try and be more helpful next time ... these holidays are so distracting.

Yours deciduously,

Edna Walling

APRIL   1,   1 9 3 7

Dear Gardeners,

This is 'Winty' of whom I spoke in a previous letter. Lots of nice things will be planted about her when she acquires an owner, but if she does not do this by winter she will, of course, have some hardy plants tucked around her—a vine on the pergola-covered piazza, and some shade trees planted about. When she was being built we used to go down much more often than was really necessary because she developed into such a lovesome little cot; some cottages grow like that, don't they? And others that may have received just as much thought somehow never get an atmosphere about them. It is only very tiny, of course, with a recess for a kitchenette with lots of shelves in it, and a shower room off the living room—that's all. I always feel it would be a marvellous place to write a book. And now it looks as though 'Winty' will have to be left out of the 'Further Adventures'—she can't expect to appear *everywhere*.

A SWEET HONEYSUCKLE

On seeing the Burmese honeysuckle for the first time the other day a friend of mine remarked 'There's no such animal!' It is somewhat grotesque, for although it is just like the honeysuckles with which we are all familiar, the flower is about six sizes larger, and it certainly does make you rub your eyes and wonder if you are dreaming. The fragrance is delicious and rather like some lilies, and the colouring deep buff, cream, and mauve on the outside of the long tube-like petals. The foliage is large and a little coarse but quite effective on a pergola post or trellis.

TREATING THE LAWN

Before I forget, the Editor has asked for an opinion upon the following suggestion which he has received:

Here is a simple and effective device for garden enthusiasts for keeping the lawn free from creeping weeds and grasses. Sharpen the outer edge of a brush or reaping hook, and lightly tap the grass at intervals of half an inch or so with the edge of this blade. In this way the creeping grasses which defy the lawn-mower are cut, all coarser grasses and weeds are discouraged, and the finer grasses at once triumph over their competitors. The process, of course, does not kill some of the non-creeping weeds, but it gives space for the grass in their immediate neighbourhood. This device is also in accord with the general faith of lawn keepers that the more you 'savage' a rebellious lawn the better it will grow.

With so many creeping grasses (many of which are varieties of the creeping bent) now being used in the lawns of today this method would probably not be at all suitable. Then again, the patent weedicides prepared for the eradication of weeds in lawns are so much more expeditious that I doubt if many would be prepared to spend the time involved by the suggested method, though its efficacy in discouraging weeds in a lawn of upright growing grasses such as the fescues would, I should think, be undoubted, and the treatment would certainly have the effect of cultivation, which is an advantage to any lawn since it aerates the ground. However, this is done most effectively by pricking the lawn with a fork, and does the least amount of damage to the roots and appearance of the lawn. An advantage of the patent weedicides is that they contain fertilizers that bring on the growth of the desirable grasses whilst discouraging the weeds.

I am sorry to say that the photographs of the Rock Garden were not sharp enough even to submit for the Editor's opinion—I knew just how 'His Highness' would throw up his hands, so kept them out of sight! Garden subjects are not easy, are they? There must be plenty of white flowers, and some clear-cut piece of construction to make a success of a garden photograph, unless, of course, one is very expert and possessed of light filters and other gadgets that do help with difficult pictures.

What is it that makes a garden doorway so enthralling? Is it, do you think, the air of mystery that always lies beyond a closed door? Anyway, it is an excellent illustration of the fact that seclusion is a very important thing to be remembered when you are designing your garden. That was a very nice dictionary that interpreted the word 'garden' as a place of seclusion. When it is not secluded it always seems to be just plain 'grounds'!

What a sweet note a little closely clipped hedge gives to a garden. I know everyone 'falls' for our little rosemary hedge that runs around the back of the herbaceous borders. It is in the winter, perhaps, that it shows to the best advantage, for when there is no luxuriant growth of flowers and foliage the design is more obvious, and these little hedges play quite an important part in the general design of the garden. Italian lavender is the most delightful thing when kept well-clipped, and is just a ribbon of purple in the spring. Both rosemary and Italian lavender resent being cut hard back, so be warned never to neglect the regular clipping of these two little fellows, or you may have to start afresh.

And now goodbye until I return from Tasmania; perhaps I shall have better luck with garden photographs over there, and I hope to have some exciting things to tell you about their gardens next month.

Yours deciduously,

Edna Walling

MAY 1, 1937

Dear Gardeners,

Looking back over our recent visit to Tasmania, most vivid in my memory of the flowers we saw is the sight of great drifts of *Campanula* 'Miss Wilmott' (fairies' thimbles) and a tall mauve Penstemon which grew in quite a number of gardens that we visited. I am wondering if it is *Penstemon glaucus stenosepalus*, but I shall not be able to tell you until we get the seed up, for even Mr St John of the Botanic Gardens could hardly be expected to name the seed, and the specimen was unrecognised by the time we reached Melbourne. I can imagine nothing lovelier for a summer picture than a group of this luminous Penstemon carpeted with fairies' thimbles, a dash of shasta daisy 'chiffon', and a spot of yellow milfoil (*Achillea eupatorium*).

In the Government House rock garden, which is most attractively constructed in an old quarry, they have achieved summer colour with drifts of a pale blue lobelia and groups of blue godetia, and the effect is quite pleasing. This introducing of annuals into the rock gardens is a thing to be most carefully considered. I know of one rock garden not far out of Melbourne where literally thousands must have been spent in its construction and planting of rock plants from all over the world; hundreds of plants of bonfire

salvia, dwarf zinnias and many other equally incongruous annuals were planted because of the owner's demand for 'a mass of colour in midsummer'. I wonder what happened to some of the treasures that suffered this invasion.

Felecia berengiana is a delightful little blue-flowered annual, and *Brachycome iberidifolia* with its teeny, weeny cineraria-like flowers of blue, white and pink, are both admirable summer flowering annuals for the rock garden because their foliage is not heavy. They can be made to serve a very useful purpose, too, in casting a light shade over some of the perennial plants that resent the scorching rays of the midsummer sun; they must be carefully watched so that they [the annuals] do not encroach upon them [the perennials] at all.

It was rather funny about the Government House rock garden in Hobart. We were driving along to the Botanic Gardens when we suddenly remembered having been told that 'you can see the rock garden from the road'. We pulled up at the entrance gates, and there through the shrubs we glimpsed the rock garden beyond! We peered, and we peered, and we peered, and when we were satisfied that nothing further could be gained by any more peering, we boarded the car and drove on and had hardly changed into top gear when there before us lay the rock garden in full view over the top of a low hedge! From here we were able to study the construction with ease, and heavens, what conditions! Enormous masses of sandstone were obviously already there, and the additions that have been made to the existing conditions have been done with more understanding than is customary. At the bottom of the quarry there is closely clipped turf and a pool set into the side of the stone-faced hillside.

Springtime in the rock garden of the two dear people who so graciously showed us all over their garden about half-way up Mount Wellington must be too intoxicating for words. This garden was commenced about 20 years ago, when the owners were around about 60 years of age, and they still do a considerable amount of the work of keeping it in order themselves. There were millions of fairies' thimbles everywhere, and although it runs riot in these cool mountain gardens it is not considered a 'weed' by those who know the value of having at least one or two plants that colonise freely.

Sutera grandiflora was in flower in one of the nurseries we visited, and being a low-growing, blue-flowering shrub of but three feet (so I am told, I have no personal experience of it as yet), it should prove rather useful beneath taller-growing shrubs.

Was it, I wonder, the fact that the silver birch is so generally known as 'The Lady of the Forest' among tree lovers, that was responsible for the slip of the paint brush on the label in the Launceston Botanic Gardens, 'Bitula alba'? Oh! But those marvellous sequoias, and that heavenly beech! And congratulations to the Curator upon his conservatory. It was certainly a wonderful show. I haven't been so aware of the little double lobelia in Melbourne as in Hobart, and to make sure of it, I brought back some plants. One grows it from cuttings, of course. And it should also prove useful in the rock garden—but do be careful not to overdo this 'planting for summer effect', for it is apt to leave gaps in your rock garden.

Shall I ever forget the wonder of being on top of Mount Wellington? In some ways it is so like Scotland (they tell—and I believe them). In a snapshot we took of it the lass is in a plaid frock, and somehow even the dog looks Scotch. (I'm sorry, old fellow; yes of course, I know you are pure bred spaniel.) But all this is not very horticultural—I had better tell you about the little creeping tea-tree that scrambles all over the rocks on this mountain, namely *Leptospermum rupestre*, according to Mr St John. It was in full bloom, with its creamy white, somewhat leathery flowers, and we were fascinated by it and thrilled to find some seed. In sheltered places on the mount we found the Tasmanian laurel—*Anopterus glandulosa*. Now this is a treasure of an evergreen, with dark, glossy green foliage and cream flowers, sometimes tinged with rose, in terminal racemes. Those of you who have Bean's third volume of *Trees and Hardy Shrubs in the British Isles* will be able to read a description of it that will make you want to order it at once. And it is procurable.

And so until next month, goodbye.

Yours deciduously,

Edna Walling

PS—In self-defence, I must explain the line in my letter of the March issue, referring to the Sonning rock garden, 'Time will cure this' should read, 'The time to reconstruct will cure this'—E.W.

JUNE 1, 1937

... and lifting up her voice, silver with the green and white beauty of ten thousand leaves, tender and plashing and cool as crisp water over a fall, in the absolute, holy stillness, in the hush of heaven, she sang.

Dear Gardeners,

Of all the lovely foliage trees that have thrilled us again this year the aspen continues to hold a front rank position in one's affection. At present it glows with many shades of amber red and pale yellow. And in spring how beautiful she is too ... When you read the last few lines of 'Populus Tremula' in Mary Webb's book *Poems and the Spring of Joy* that I have quoted above, can't you see it through her eyes?

Last year when the dry weather divested the garden of many of its accustomed autumn pictures, the aspens held their own and were so beautiful that we missed the colouring of these plants whose leaves had shrivelled not at all. It is not a tree for a small garden because (please, Mr Editor, will you put this in *very* small print?) so exquisite are they at the moment I hate to have to say—they do sucker a little!

WHEN BUYING TREES

I have just been down to the nursery to look through some of the trees that have been planted there awaiting their permanent positions. How anyone ever manages without a nursery I don't know, for here we row out all the plants that are purchased whilst the ground is being prepared for their reception. This gives us the whole of the summer to decide upon their positions, and by winter we have trees, with splendid fibrous root systems, that go right ahead because they have had one growing season to recover from the shock of having their roots cut back, as they must to a certain extent, in the nursery. But before I forget do study the roots as well as the top when you are purchasing your trees this season. So often I hear people say what marvellous trees can be had from such and such a nursery, and when they get them home they find they are all top! Height is not much good unless there is sufficient root to support it.

AN AMERICAN FAVOURITE

But I had nearly forgotten to tell you about the plants that particularly attracted me in the nursery this morning. There was the American hornbeam, *Carpinus americana*, looking exquisite in its autumn gown; the branchlets are almost wiry in their slenderness, and the autumn colouring is simply delightful—some of the leaves are yellow, some bright red, and others varying shades of these two colours. Oh! I should mention that though it is most often listed here as *C. americana*, it is, I believe more correctly named *C. caroliniana*. It is not a very large tree and is quite appropriate to the medium-sized garden.

For a clear yellow the English maple, *Acer campestris*, is one of the loveliest in autumn, and I adore the shape of its little leaves. I do hope we shall see it more often now that the summers are kinder to such trees. I have one planted right out in the open, where it gets all the north winds that blow, and it is a beautiful little specimen now; but I would advise a more sheltered position when available.

Sorbus sambucifolia has a brilliant red berry; it seems very similar to the better known rowan berry, *Sorbus aucuparia*, except that the leaves are a little more pointed, and I believe it is more pyramidal in habit.

ORNAMENTAL AND BEAUTIFUL

One of the best late autumn trees of my acquaintance is an ornamental pear, *Pyrus ussuriensis*; it is only just beginning to turn whilst I write (25/4/37), and soon it will be a vivid splash of colour. Some of the leaves are a rich mahogany and rather leathery in texture. This pear is a rich picture in the autumn landscape with its shapely crown that should never be pruned if you would not destroy its natural beauty. Even the removal of branches for interior decoration should be done with the utmost care so as not to spoil the balance or reveal where the cut has been made.

. The glossiness, the heavy texture, and the rich red colouring of the foliage of *Viburnum nudum* make me glad we have it in our collection. (Yes, I'm afraid I 'collect' viburnums.) It seems a little sparse of foliage, which gives it a rather thin appearance, but when one sees the soft wine red of the foliage at this time of the year it makes one feel 'it's worth it'. *Viburnum davidii* is going to be a useful low-growing evergreen. The flowers are a dull white, of no great attractiveness, but the blue fruit is, I believe, quite interesting, and judging from the plant in this garden it will be nice and compact.

How very nice and understanding some people are. A year or two ago I drew a garden plan for two enthusiastic gardeners whom I met again quite recently. In talking of the garden they said, 'We never know whether to give you credit for our garden or to protect you from our mistakes!' My heart warmed to them, for quite often silence on the part of the owner automatically gives the designer credit for his (the owner's) mistakes!

I suppose we will be in the throes of planting by the next time I am writing to you and that will be a suitable occasion to say a few words about the planting of trees and shrubs ... 'Planting Don'ts by One Who Did' sort of thing.

Goodbye and good planting.

Yours deciduously,

Edna Walling

JULY 1, 1937

Dear Gardeners,

If any small flowering tree deserves to be 'decorated' it should surely be that exquisite little flowering apple (*Malus angustifolia*), the last of the apples to come into flower in the spring. The blooms are large and of the most delicate shade of flesh pink one could imagine. When the tree is in bud it appears to be covered with small pink balls, for the buds are the fattest little fellows that look almost as though they have been blown up before they break open. The flowers have a fragrance strongly suggestive of sweet peas. I have observed that the ground becomes quite tramped around my tree in spring—everyone puts his nose into it! You will notice the shape of the leaves in the photograph and see that they are quite distinct from the other flowering apples with which we are familiar; they are also of a more greyish green. I have told you of the exquisite blooms on this little tree, but that is not all—in autumn the foliage is wont to turn to shades of vivid reds and orange-yellow, and so you can place this tree with the utmost confidence in the most prominent position in your garden, for verily it is a 'dual-purpose' tree. But there's always a catch; it is not very easily procurable. Apparently it is not as simple to propagate as most other malus; it is, in fact, frequently grafted on to hawthorn. This should prove simple enough, but presumably even then the percentage of 'takes' is low. Otherwise, surely, they would be easier to procure.

PLANTING TIME

By the time this goes to press, you will be in the very midst of the planting season. Most of you will be past the stage of poring over catalogues in the evenings and probably will be studying the gardening books and periodicals which help us to remember all that must be done before the close of the planting season at the end of August.

Are you sure that you have all the trees and shrubs that help to give the succession of blooms, so important a matter in the intelligent planting of one's garden? It is nice, of course, to have a sort of grand slam in spring, but such a system leaves a very unsatisfactory gap for many months of the year. And so for the small grower the 'one of everything' idea is not to be despised. After all it is a matter of scale in planting, and it is in the large garden where the effect produced by 'one of this and one of that' is so spotty and unsatisfactory.

The blossom trees we must hurry about getting in are the flowering apricots and flowering almonds (*Prunus mume* and *Prunus pollardii*, respectively), for they come into bloom whilst winter is still with us.

Spirea thunbergii is also a very early bloomer, and should be in as soon as possible. There is an improved form that is well worth trying to secure, for it is slightly broader in the leaf and in consequence gives a better effect in autumn. This four-foot high shrub groups marvellously with silver birches, giving two pictures in the year. In spring the masses of tiny white flowers are like a cloud over the plant, and are exquisitely lovely with the silvery-white stems of the birches; and in late autumn one can always rely upon it growing well and making a good foil for the last golden leaves of the birches.

What an extremely useful little plant is the prostrate rosemary. Often when a grass verge is not just what you want at the side of a path or driveway this will serve the purpose and give a mat of green that is not quite so formal and does not need any attention but an occasional weeding. It is covered with its silvery-mauve flowers at the moment and will be all the winter. In fact, it is longer in flower than out of flower in this garden.

FLOWERING APPLES

When talking of flowering apples, I meant to mention that lovely double-flowered pale pink flowering apple called *Malus tenora carnea*. It is one of the best and is very suitable to the small garden because it does not run up too much and remains well-furnished on the lower branches. Of course, *Malus floribunda* and the varieties of it, *M. f. atrosanguinea*, and *lemoinei*, will always remain the most delightful of small trees for the small garden. They are shapely unless you start pruning them unwisely, and have autumn fruits as well as masses of flowers in spring.

A seedling from *Malus floribunda purpurea*, which has been named 'Sonning', is a wonderful wine red and has exceptionally good foliage which is positively red when it first bursts forth. The colour of the blooms of this variety shows out much more than the other red-flowered varieties. We have been very interested to notice how everyone is attracted to this tree when it is in full bloom and yet will take less notice of *purpurea*, which is usually in bloom at the same time. Small wonder that apples have become almost the most popular of the blossom trees, for they are the most presentable the whole year around.

Get as many trees in as you can, for they take up little ground space— not as much as shrubs—and there are many delightful things to grow beneath them.

Yours deciduously,

Edna Walling

AUGUST 2, 1937

Dear Gardeners,
Were I to embark upon the writing of a book entitled *Gardening Without Tears*, it would, I think, commence with a chapter upon pruning, for not only

does the drastic pruning of some much-loved plant bring forth weeping and gnashing of the teeth of the owners, but a lack of knowledge and experience often makes one wonder what to do until you are almost in tears whilst hovering around the plant that has outgrown its bounds, or its strength. One of the worst things that happens sometimes is that, having once started in with a good pair of secateurs, you simply cannot stop, until there is nothing left to clip! Then, too late, you find that the plant that you have waited for so many years is nothing more than an object of pity. MORAL: Don't let it develop beyond the finger and thumb stage. Yes, I can hear you say, 'What on earth do you mean?' Well, when a shoot is beginning to extend beyond the proportions you wish it to assume, why on earth don't you pinch it back? This is horticulturally known as 'stopping', and it has the advantage of keeping the plant compact and preventing legginess because it encourages the development of the lower buds. Being soft, the tips can easily be pinched off with the finger and thumb, and surely this is better than the hard pruning back that one is forced to do because this simple operation has been neglected. Even in the infancy of plants a judicious pinching back results in shrubs that are much more shapely and well-furnished right to the ground. I proved this for myself once again this year with some young *Escallonia edinensis* and *Escallonia donaro* seedlings, both of which are inclined to be a little thin in appearance without this 'stopping' of the long, straggling shoots it throws out.

WALL SHRUBS

This method of training—and if we would only study the training of plants there would be less pruning necessary—enables one to grow many fascinating shrubs as wall shrubs, and I don't think there is any garden sight more pleasing than a well-trained wall shrub. As a wall plant, flowering shrubs seem to show off their blooms to the best possible advantage, and it really is all so easy. You just place the plant hard against a wall or fence and discourage all the shoots that grow outwards—more finger and thumb work! The upright shoots will then quickly develop and grow like a fan against the wall. *Ceanothis edwardsii* is delightful grown in this way; its beautiful little powder-blue flowers will cover the branches in spring and the fresh evergreen foliage covers the wall in winter. The pyracanthas are good evergreens for the purpose, too, and will be smothered with bright red and yellow berries in the autumn. Japonica is delightful as a wall shrub against a cream painted wall, but don't stick to the red one and forget the dainty pink and white *Cydonia moerloosii*. I always think *Buddleia salvifolia*, that honey-scented winter flowerer, is more manageable as a wall shrub, although it does keep one busy with its lusty growth. *Cotoneaster franchetii* is another evergreen for autumn berry effect, and is admirably suited for training as a wall shrub, whilst *Escallonia fretheyii* will clothe your wall with its shell pink blooms all the summer.

I am enclosing a photograph of *Campanula isophylla alba* which I took the other day—oh, no, that's one of the pictures my friend took. I've been gloating over it thinking, 'Well, the Editor won't say that won't reproduce surely!' and now I have to admit 'she' took it. It was a rotten old camera anyway. It is all just luck, of course, with photography! We went forth around the garden together one morning with our cameras, and I altered my stop and my speed occasionally, just to humour her, and I think the light must have been particularly good that morning, for somehow my pictures were really much better than usual! Next month I shall be able to illustrate my letter with a 'perfectly charming' one I took of some pots on a wall. *Campanula isophylla alba* is one of the easiest of the rock campanulas, and its lovely clear white blooms in summer are a joy to behold. (Observe them above!)

It is very irritating to be told of the beauties of a plant that is unprocurable, I know, but if it is inquired for often enough the demand usually produces the supply in time, and *Rhododendron glaucum* is worthy of the effort. It is a small shrub with aromatic foliage and flowers of an old rose colour that are about an inch long. Like many of the other small-leaved rhododendrons, it is one of the most beautiful small evergreen flowering shrubs. One certainly could wish the nurseryman would hurry up and catalogue some of the very interesting and delightful low-growing species of the rhododendron family. Here is an extract from the May number of *My Garden* that will interest you:

'How to Improve Rhododendron Flowering.'
Loosely fork the soil beneath the spread of branches and over it lay a mulch of this mixture: four inches of leaf mould or peat, one bucket of rotted manure or 3 handfuls of hop manure. Finish by giving each bush two gallons of water through the mulch. The annual mulching of rhododendrons is very essential to the success of these beautiful evergreens.

Good planting.

Yours deciduously,

Edna Walling

S E P T E M B E R   1 ,   1 9 3 7

Dear Gardeners,
Although the process of getting this letter to you is by a long and devious route absorbing much time, as you will see by the date at the top, there will

still be time to do much good planting after it reaches you. And the planting season has been greatly lengthened for us by nurserymen who now pot up lots of trees, so that we may not lose the season.

POTTED TREES

There are, of course, some disadvantages in these potted trees, for instance, it does not need much imagination to know what happens to the roots to get them into a smallish flower pot. You will, too, sometimes get potted trees that have been carried over from last season. These need particular attention as regards the roots, for they will have become so twisted and will be growing round and round. In the case of the fibrous roots it will be easy to disentangle them and comb them right out until they extend straight out from the butt of the tree, but when the roots have enlarged and become rigid and are encircling the young tree it is better to sacrifice them by cutting them off with a sharp pair of secateurs right back to the spot where they begin to turn. If this is not done, the root gets fatter and fatter, and tighter and tighter until in time it strangles the tree. And that is often the reason why some trees grow quite healthily and vigorously for some years and then suddenly die. So do comb the roots out well when you plant your trees, and remember that some of the little fibrous roots become big roots one day.

Two other points about planting trees: have the hole dug square and not round, this makes it easier to spread the roots out, enabling you to take the longest of them into the four corners. Also, if the surrounding ground is at all firm or hard there is not the danger that exists when planting in a round hole of the roots growing out to the hard ground and then growing round and round instead of penetrating the hard ground. The bottom of the hole should be slightly deeper and wider at the edges so that the tree sits on a little hill, thus giving the roots a downward trend. Oh, those awful bowl-shaped holes that some people 'stuff' their trees into! Forgive me if I reiterate by saying DON'T make the holes round, smaller at the bottom and deeper in the centre, but DO make them square, slightly larger at the bottom and higher in the centre. Finally, if a stake is imperative put the stake in first and plant the tree up against it.

I simply cannot understand the popularity of camellia 'The Czar'. When asked to place one of this variety I find myself wandering about the garden with the darn thing in one hand until I am nearly dizzy. Ah well, every man to his taste; but give me the pink czar. It's a delicious pink without any of the harshness of the red czar. And the sasanqua camellias—isn't 'Apple Blossom' the daintiest thing to brighten the winter days, with its pink and white single blooms, and its small glistening foliage?

That charming winter flowering tea-tree *Leptospermum sandersii* is delightful grouped with these single camellias, and the white stems of birches seem to give an airy grace to the group and make of it an elusive winter picture that will gladden the heart of many who have not previously realised how joyous the garden can be in winter.

Is This a New Broom to You?

If you have a suitable position for *Cytisus purpurea*, one of the dwarf brooms that has light purple blooms, you will enjoy this little treasure I am sure. It is at its best high up above a large boulder; for one thing it appreciates the perfect drainage and for another it needs to be able to hang its drooping branches over some height to be seen to the best advantage. *Cytisus kewensis* is another broom of similar habits to *C. purpurea*, with cream flowers. It is capable of covering many yards of ground and is a marvellous picture on top of a retaining wall, where some of the branches can spill over.

But aren't there lots of lovely things one can do with a retaining wall? Given some good soil on the top of a wall facing south, there are hundreds of delightful effects to be created. But why must it be facing south? Well, the conditions always seem to be so ideal, both aesthetically and culturally. A raised border that is retained by a wall facing south with a planting of trees and shrubs to shelter it from the north winds that are so hot in summer and so cold in winter, affords ideal growing conditions for numbers of plants. Being raised, good drainage is assured; and being sheltered, the moisture content is more equable—the ground is not subjected to the quick drying out that takes place in a border facing north.

And now for the aesthetic value of such a border. It is, of course, the soft light coming from the south which makes the effects produced on these borders so much more pleasing than those facing north. It is such a pleasure to plant ground sheltered from the north, for one is all the time conscious that no tearing winds will harass the plants or tear the blooms to pieces here. For the northern aspects one must choose tough things like the cistus, lavenders, rosemary and rock spray—*Cotoneaster horizontalis* and *C. hor. pupissilla*.

PLANTING TIME

I must go and plant more trees. Don't forget, when you are planting shrubs out of pots, to remove the crocks from the bottom and tease out the roots just a little at the sides; if you just run your finger up and down the sides it will fray out the little fibrous roots and start them off outwards instead of continuing to go round and round as they did in the pot. Alternatively, if you crush the ball when it comes out of the pot just a little it will have the same effect. They come out of the pots extremely easily if you turn them upside down and knock the edge on the handle of a spade stuck in the ground.

Support the plant by placing the pot plant upside down on your hand, with the first finger on one side of the stem and the second finger on the other side; then knock the top of the pot, which is resting on your hand, on the top of the handle of the spade. One sees so many people making futile efforts to remove a plant from a pot by tapping the *bottom* of the pot, that I thought there may be some who might like to know just how easy it really is.

Yours deciduously,

Edna Walling

N O V E M B E R   1 ,   1 9 3 7

Dear Gardeners,

Someone remarked to me the other day that he was afraid that they had planted everything too deeply in their garden, and that in all his horticultural readings he had not come across a warning about not planting too deeply. There are many trees and shrubs that will not resent it but there are also many that receive a setback if the original nursery level is not observed. Silver birches are a particular case in point. These trees are very shallow-rooted and they do object to having soil around that part of the bark that should be out of the ground. There is one thing one does plant quite deeply, though, and that is a lilac that has been grafted on privet. It should be planted deeply enough to bury the graft two or three inches; this encourages the growth of roots from the lilac itself, which is desirable since it tends to make the plant shed the privet stock in time, therefore eliminating the troublesome suckers that sometimes arise from this stock. Conscientious nurserymen do all they can to avoid suckering by cutting out the buds in the privet stock, but in spite of this, trouble still arises with some plants. It is much better to have the lilacs on their own roots, but commercially it is more profitable to graft them on to something quicker-growing.

Folks who do not like white flowers must be in a quandary over their rock plants, for so many of the loveliest of them are white. At the moment *Phlox nelsonii* is giving us the greatest joy. It's like a drift of snow, and that darling little *Alyssum* 'Carpet of snow' is another white-flowered treasure I would find it hard to manage without. Although it seeds itself freely, it is never a trial in that respect; on the contrary it seems nearly always to come up in the right places, and often in spots where we would never have thought of planting it. It is these little accidental bits of planting that give charm to our gardens more than almost anything else.

It will be November before you receive this letter, but there will still be time to plant out things from pots and as that is the time when so many plants will be in flower you will have the opportunity of judging for yourselves instead of relying upon catalogue descriptions.

How rarely one sees that charming little rambling rose 'Golden Showers', and yet it is almost worth growing for the foliage effect alone. It is dark and shiny, and with us it is quite evergreen; and then just when you will be reading this it will be covered with wee little roses like 'Cecile Brunner', only an apricot colour. It is most useful on houses and walls that are too deep a cream to stand the pinks of other ramblers.

By the way, don't forget to prune your Himalayan rhododendrons after flowering.

They set seed rather freely and this exhausts the plants a great deal. Their habit is a little leggy, too; particularly is this noticeable in *R. fragrantissima*, which will be the variety you are likely to be most familiar with. They will stand quite hard pruning but this is not very often necessary and is inclined to destroy the loose habit that is one of the charms of these fragrant and delicately hued rhododendrons.

I am beginning to think that we do not realise fully the great benefit of mulching. All good gardeners put on a mulch of some sort as the summer approaches, but not before many a hot spring wind has made premature watering a necessity—not to mention the constant hoeing and forking of the surface to keep the top soil open and the weeds from growing.

Apart from the labor and water that early mulching saves at the time of the year when there is so much to be done in the garden, we all know that the sudden drying up of the soil is definitely detrimental to plant growth. This year we have been so impressed with the reduced number of weeds resulting from the hay mulch that covered the garden last year that we are putting it on immediately the plants are planted.

Another illustration of the value of a continuous mulch is that of some rock plants received from Tasmania during the winter. Fearing that some of them might damp off in our rather heavy ground, we top-dressed them with limestone toppings, the result being that they have remained perfectly clean and are looking extremely happy.

'More mulching and less hoeing' would seem to be better mulch for trees and shrubs than their own leaves and I cannot see the benefit of digging them in when by so doing you destroy so many of the fibrous feeding roots. A permanent mulch of leaves about the roots of rhododendrons is absolutely essential to their successful growth and there is no reason to suppose that the majority of trees and shrubs would not be equally benefited by a similar mulch. With seedlings the simplest way is to mulch your borders first, and then make a little hole in the mulch, and plant the seedling in the soil beneath. This saves a tremendous amount of time, since mulching around seedlings is one of the most tedious of jobs in the garden; the moisture content of the soil is kept even and the plants receive a mild dose of liquid manure during every rain.

Goodbye and good mulching.

Yours deciduously,

Edna Walling

DECEMBER 1, 1937

Dear Gardeners,
Ground covers are tremendously important, aren't they? I expect you dislike the bare ground beneath trees and shrubs as much as I do. It is quite a problem, too, to get low-growing plants to grow when once the trees and shrubs have become established. Of course, I know that some gardeners achieve quite noble displays of annuals right up to the butts of trees, but the periodic removal of the fibrous feeding roots from the area required for the annuals is decidedly harmful to the trees, and a big price to pay for a temporary splash of colour.

It is, of course, much better to grow some permanent ground cover, and amongst those who like their gardens to be as self-supporting as possible, annuals are out of the question. Three plants most useful for the purpose, I have come to regard as the Good Companions, because they are all in flower at the same time, and they all grow happily where few other plants will thrive. Here they are: the Italian lavender (*Lavendula staechis*), baby's tears (*Erigeron mucronatus*), and *Ajuga reptans*, which Reginald Farrer has described with his usual aptitude:

The most useful coverer of dishonourable ground, which throws out runners in every direction with feverish rapidity, and is profuse in spring with its shining leafy columns a-twinkle with blue dragons.

I did not take to this little plant very readily—it seemed a little coarse, but when I saw a brave row of little blue soldiers growing quite happily in some of *my* 'dishonourable' ground, close to some pines, my heart warmed to it at once, and every available offshoot has been gathered to cover more difficult patches in other parts of the garden.

If baby's tears was dispossessed of its extraordinary hardiness and capacity for growing in arid or shady places, and if it made demands upon one's patience to rear it, I think I would still grow it, so delightful are the masses of little white and pink daisy-like flowers. It bears pink and white flowers separately on the same plant, a characteristic which probably helps to make it so charming. It covers the ground fairly rapidly by means of self-sowing, and it really isn't safe to plant it close to anything smaller growing that it may smother.

I must not absorb much space on the Italian lavender for it seems to crop up in almost every one of my letters—there is such a diversity of uses to which it may be put. I first saw it flowering like a purple carpet under an enormous old cypress tree! That was good enough for me. Here surely was one of the most useful and delightful of ground covers. Just at the moment (25/10/37) it is in full bloom—a mass of rich purple flowers, so you see it flowers ever so much earlier that the other lavenders.

Have you ever noticed how a garden that needs very little attention is so often much more charming and restful than one in which much labour is expended in its upkeep? And yet how these tree- and shrub-shaded retreats irritate the energetic horticulturist, who longs to get at them and 'clean them up'. Do be sure before you let anyone clean up your shady retreat that they know just which plants can be cut back with safety, and which will resent the treatment so much that they will eventually have to be removed. Otherwise you too will be saying, 'It used to look so sweet, there was an old rosemary bush just here, and that corner was filled with a huge Russian olive; that dry hot bank was smothered with a magnificent echium (Pride of Madeira), and different varieties of cistus.' And now I have told you of some, at least, of the plants that simply will not stand hard cutting back.

Have you ever heard of Prince von Puckler-Muskau? I do wish everyone would read his *Hints on Landscape Gardening*, for his contribution to the art of landscape architecture is large and permanent. Hear what he has to say about the grouping of trees:

With regard to the art of their grouping, frequently several may be planted close together in one and the same hole, some fork-like: sometimes five or six should be placed in almost straight lines, etc.; for groups symmetrically rounded off become as monotonous in the end as do regular alleys.

He deplores the 'ugly fashion of planting the pleasure grounds with single trees and shrubs, placed at a considerable distance apart, giving the grass plots the air of nursery grounds'.

There is so much ill-informed criticism in the matter of picturesque tree planting, and it seems such a pity that these uneducated opinions are so blindly accepted instead of those of great landscape gardeners such as Prince von Puckler.

Yours deciduously,

Edna Walling

JANUARY 1, 1938

Dear Gardeners,

Always one must turn back to Farrer for the perfect description where rock plants are concerned. Of *Nierembergia rivularis*, which we see all too seldom, he says:

> *... it comes from the River Plate where it sheets the damp, muddy banks with its packed masses of small heart shaped dark-green leaves, which emit an unimaginable profusion of very large and lovely pearl-pale cups or wide bells, like those of some exquisite* convolvulus *dropped from heaven.*

Apparently it likes a very rich but light and open loam, well watered from beneath.

I have just received a bound copy of Vol. 1 of the *Bulletin of the Alpine Garden Society*, and what a treasure it is! And what a happy part it will take in one's summer vacation. Under the heading 'Farreriana', there is a delightful page of quotations from Farrer's works. Here is one:

ON PLANTING: I believe in firm planting and in very firm planting; in dealing with a shrub I execute a sort of war-dance round it on one foot, which must wear a more than eccentric appearance in the eyes of an onlooker. And with an Alpine, I pursue the same policy on its lessened scale with a slamming fist.

The blue cups of *Nierembergia hippomanica* smothering this little shrublet at the moment (25/11/37) make it difficult to tear oneself away from the subject of rock plants. *N. azurea*, which is more frequently stocked by local nurserymen, will not do as a substitute at all, for it is much taller though still only a low-growing shrub, and more straggly in habit. *N. hippomanica* is delightful in the foreground of a herbaceous border or as a carpet beneath taller shrubs where it is in the sun and in rich soil. I do hope it will soon be more easily procurable.

I do love that little creeping forget-me-not, *Myosotis palustris*, sometimes known as the swamp forget-me-not: it clings so closely to the ground, forming an exquisite little carpet of blue. It has sown itself in the crevices of the stone paving outside the cabin door, and is creeping about unobtrusively to the delight of everyone who beholds it. This paved area is a veritable fairies' garden this year: foxgloves and baby's tears, pale blue lobelia, and a little pale pink daisy (*Belis rotundifolia*, I think) have all sprung up from heaven knows where. What a lot of truth there is in those words of gardening wisdom:

So often if you move a prospering plant from difficult surroundings into easy ones it will immediately cease to prosper. Another high matter for meditation and moralising.

No, I am not going to tell you who wrote them—I think you can guess!

Do you think we take into sufficient consideration the matter of texture in dealing with the soil of our gardens? I was amazed at the growth of the trees and shrubs in a garden planted only last winter, and in poking in a few lesser (in stature) plants, particularly noticed the gritty nature of the soil. Certainly the ground is very fertile, but richness is not everything, by any means; the coarse grit no doubt gave the roots a very free root run, enabling the plants to quickly send out new roots in search of nourishment immediately they were planted. It made me want to secure tons and tons of coarse river sand and spread it all over my garden to work into the soil. That and a plentiful mulch should give one wonderful growing conditions.

Today is simply scorching and the suddenness of the heat is so very hard on plants whose roots are close to the surface. If we had been able to achieve the complete 'mulchification' (I've just coined that one) of all the plants at Sonning, there would be no cause for anxiety at all.

The little white spires of *Hebe ligustrifolia* are covering this useful and attractive low-growing evergreen shrub at the moment; everyone admires it, for the effect of it in bloom is so soft and misty, with a very slight tinge of mauve given by the stamens of the freshly opened florets. I still find these hebe cum veronicas rather confusing: one looks up hebe in Rehder's manual of cultivated plants, and turning to that page, one is confronted with nothing but '*Veronicas*'. I was once told that all the shrubby veronicas are really hebes and all the herbaceous species are veronicas, for example *Veronica cupressoides*, listed as *Hebe cupressoides*. This is quite an unusual little evergreen with light green cypress-like foliage as its name implies. It does not fit in very harmoniously with many tree and shrub groups but with *Buddleia salvifolia* and *B. alternifolia* it groups fairly well. I have never found that it flowers consistently but this year it is covered with its tiny white flowers just now. The fact that it is low-growing and a help in covering the

ground is its chief attraction. There are masses of little veronicas for the rock garden and path edge, and amongst those easy to procure *V. repens* can always be relied upon to give a mass of blue flowers born in delightful little spires from four to six inches high—it's a treasure.

New Zealand, the home of so many of these veronicas, must be a marvellous place to wander through in search of plants. I long to go back there now that a keener love of plants has sharpened my observation, and with any luck will be there next year to do some work and some plant hunting.

One of the treasures we brought back from Tasmania last summer, *Euphrasia collina*, has just flowered. It is a little rosette of rich green leaves from which rise on nine-inch stems, mauve daisy flowers; it should prove a very useful little plant for tucking into some crevice of the rock garden or at the edge of a stone paved path. Oh! And our seed of *Leptospermum rupestre*, the creeping tea-tree that thrilled us so much, is coming up! Goodbye; this letter is getting far too lengthy. It's so hard to stop when one once gets started.

Yours deciduously,

Edna Walling

FEBRUARY 1, 1938

Dear Gardeners,

I have just noticed that the fairies' thimbles are in bloom. It is always such a delight to observe the excited enjoyment of children on seeing them for the first time. I have told you how this little campanula roamed all over the rock gardens in Tasmania, and yet could never be accounted a nuisance. Nurserymen frequently list it as *Camp. pusilla*, 'Miss Wilmott', but it is really *Camp. cochlearifolia*. From one plant many little seedlings will spring up, and you will soon have a dear little drift of this treasure—if you do the weeding yourself! Heaven knows, a self-sown plant gets little quarter in some gardens too assiduously cultivated. Oh! What an art is this maintenance of a garden; many years ago in student days I listened to a lecture in which we were told that 'a weed is any plant that is out of place'. Even before I fully appreciated how charming these self-sown pictures can be, I never felt inclined to accept this hard dictum, and later read, with joy, Gertrude Jekyll's chapter 'On when to leave well alone'.

One of the trees that gives me a tremendous amount of satisfaction is one that is very rarely planted now—the Chinese mulberry, *Morus alba*. Many of you will probably know it as the chosen food of silkworms. It was not for this purpose, however, that I secured my specimen, but because the clear yellow of the autumn foliage was so appealing, and the fresh bright green of the summer foliage so refreshing. It surely should prove one of the most delightful shade trees for the lawn, for to lie beneath it looking up through the foliage on a hot day is unimagined ease to the eye and mind. The fruit is white and should not become troublesome in the matter of staining one's garments.

The Osage orange, *Toxylon pomiferumi* (synonymous with *Maclura auranticum*) [*Maclura pomifera*] is another lovely tree, glorious in its lustrous foliage. It is certainly very spiny, and it is perhaps ill-advised to plant it on the lawn, where one may receive a good sharp crack from one of its falling fruit, which are as hard and as large as a cricket ball.

At this time of the year a shadeless garden is a dreadful thing with which to be afflicted, and that one is only renting a place is no reason why one should suffer summer after summer of blistering heat, or continue 'keeping' tidy ground that you really are not the slightest little bit interested in. There are quite a lot of quick-growing trees and shrubs that will give you a shady retreat which you may use instead of an area which you abuse! Take for instance, *Virgilia capensis*. In a remarkably short space of time you will find yourselves in possession of a shade tree under which you may take afternoon tea instead of sweltering in the house. Robinias are also very rapid-growing trees and are excellent for planting on the north and western boundaries to cut off the glaring summer sun. And we all know what a golden poplar will do when it is watered in summer. For the rented garden use plenty of ceanothus, because they race away into large shrubs in an amazingly short time, and so do psoralias, weigelias, abelias and spireas. And so if you have a friend who is likely to be living in a house for two years at least do persuade him to get to work immediately to make the garden habitable and attractive during their tenancy, and incidentally, when they leave they will leave behind a legacy for which they will be blessed indeed.

At one time my parents occupied a flat in Melbourne where there was quite a large piece of ground at the rear. In this there was a lawn, a canna or two and a few red geraniums. Well, we planted two or three golden willows in the north and west corner and some shrubs round about; they were still occupying the flat when the trees were big enough for two or three cars to run underneath to shelter from the blazing sun. I used to feel a little sore sometimes when there was no room for mine, but mostly we squeezed in somewhere.

Verbascum thapsus is a noble plant for the back of the herbaceous border, isn't it? It comes in a lovely rich yellow and a marvellous velvety cream, and they flower on and on right through the summer. Much daintier is the little mauve *Verbascum wiedmanniana*—it's the sweetest little spire; we have tried this and *V. phoeniceum* hybrids, and as far as we can see there is very little difference, except, perhaps, that *wiedmanniana* is mauve and the *phoeniceums* are mauve, white or pink. Very few of the *wiedmannianas* have flowered yet, and so if any of them come out white or pink we shall suppose that they are one and the same thing. At all events they are very dainty and charming little plants.

A charming blue annual which you may not yet know is *Helliophila leptophylla*. It is an exquisite sky blue, and the form is light and airy, growing to a height of nine inches to a foot. It would be a most useful annual for the rock garden or the front of the herbaceous border.

I am sending a sketch of a tiny little informal garden that might help you over an odd corner you don't know what to do with. This was built for a little girl, who has now gone to boarding school, so it is not what it might be, the grown-ups do not seem to love it, and it is little plants and lots of love that such wee gardens need.

Goodbye until March,

Yours deciduously,

Edna Walling

M A R C H   1,   1 9 3 8

Dear Gardeners,

I have been to Canberra for the first time since last writing to you, and my first and most lasting impression was of the good tree planting. They are so well-grouped and massed—and it is, of course, the massing that receives the most criticism. Mr Weston, the man who did this wonderful job, is now dead, and one trembles to think of what might happen to his work one day in the hands of others who may think differently from him. One thing we can be almost sure of, and that is that they will all be drastically thinned out so that no thickets remain, and in their place will be 'specimens' until one's eyes become weary of the monotony of them. Quite by accident we discovered that this man did this marvellous piece of work on £100 per annum! One would like to see a bronze tablet to his memory telling all who go to Canberra just how they got the majority of the thousands of trees of which they are justly so proud. Compared with some of the areas around Melbourne that have been planted in recent years—King's Domain, for instance—one is conscious at once that here was a man who understood the job and a man with vision. How badly we needed Mr Weston in Melbourne—and how the 'pansy-minded citizens' (this is not my own) would have criticised him!

What an excellent summer-flowering shrub is *Vitex agnus-castus*—it is similar to a Buddleia, but better. I saw it for the first time in the State nursery at Canberra, which is in the charge of Mr Hobday, and never have I seen a better kept nursery. It was charming, too, surrounded by shelter trees, which not only broke the wind, but gave it a background and a frame. We were extremely interested to see that the large specimens of the Chinese elm, *Ulmus parvifolia*, they transplant successfully. They evidently think it is worthwhile as a street tree. It is certainly a delightful evergreen shade tree.

One of the most satisfactory plants in the herbaceous borders that is blooming at the moment (25/1/38) and has been in bloom for two or three weeks is *Campanula primulifolia*—it grows to about two to three feet, and is a delightful pale powder blue in colour. It is a biennial that seeds freely, and if you are careful not to disturb them they will come up in the most unexpected places. There is nearly always one or two that sow themselves on the edge of the pathway amongst the low-growing thymes and other little plants we use to clothe the front of the borders. Here they look particularly charming as one brushes past them when walking down the path. *Campanula latifolia* is another excellent plant blooming now with spikes of sky blue cups from two to three feet high; this one is a perennial. Of all the perennial asters I do not think a perennial border is complete without *Aster cordifolius* and its varieties: it's the daintiest little thing which softens one's floral groupings so beautifully. The *cordifolius* varieties are nice and stiff in the stem; 'Diana' is positively wiry and the most rigid of all the varieties I know. It is quite tall and merely needs a short stake at the base to steady it in heavy winds or against overhead watering.

The staking of perennials is quite an art. If they are going to be bunched up to one stake it is really hardly worth growing them, for they look so ugly and uncomfortable. Staking should be done in the early stages of their growth, using several stakes around the plant, which allows the plant to spread out naturally, but not to sprawl on the ground. Forked tea-tree sticks can sometimes be used very effectually. The great thing is not to allow any stakes to be visible when the plant is developed, otherwise the effect of your borders will be quite ruined.

If you want to make your little rock plants happy give them a mulch of limestone 'toppings'—they are a little finer than screenings, and the thymes and other creeping things seem to love rooting down amongst the tiny chips of stone. Very coarse clean sand would do as well, no doubt. This mulch prevents the ground from caking around the little plants—helps to keep the soil cool, and discourages the growth of weeds. We covered the whole ground with these toppings where we are making a little thyme lawn, and it is most encouraging to see the growth that all the different varieties have made, although it was not planted until early summer. When it is watered it just soaks quickly through the 'mulch', and there is no tedious cultivating to do—only an occasional hand weeding.

Some of the roses that have conspicuous fruits are looking brilliant at the moment. I was very attracted to *Rosa* 'Coral Drops', *R. venosa* and *R. sweginzowii* yesterday in a mountain nursery. *Sweginzowii* has the longest and most slender 'hips' I have ever seen. They are certainly an asset for a summer effect in the shrub borders. And now until next month, goodbye.

Yours deciduously,

Edna Walling

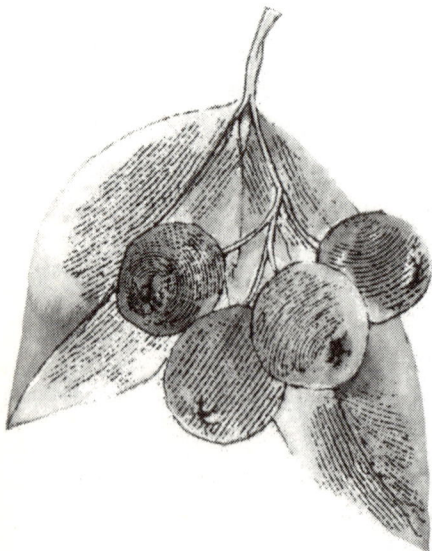

APRIL 1, 1938

Dear Gardeners,

Let's talk about Australian trees and shrubs! It is a pity that so many of them are unsuitable for the average suburban garden, and that even those that are suitable grow straggly if they are not regularly pruned at the right time. Yet what could be more beautiful and more satisfactory than the lilly pilly. Who in the world ever gave it such a name! The light of recognition so often comes into the eyes of those who greet the botanic name Eugenia with a blank expression, that one reluctantly adopts this appellative. This really is one of the most useful evergreen trees I know, it remains such a beautiful shape, demands nothing more than ordinary garden conditions, and grows to a height of 15 to 20 feet without absorbing a great amount of space. For hiding tall and unsightly neighbouring buildings I know of nothing better.

Let us see what there is in the local catalogues that we could plant with a reasonable hope of enjoyment. There is that adorable little shrublet *Baeckia plicata* (synonymous with *Micromyrtus microphylla*) with its tiny pink and white flowers. It is at its best in the rock garden—never did a little plant grace an outcrop of stone more delightfully. The foliage has a bronze tinge that is an excellent complement to the pink-tinged flowers. And, of course, for fragrance the boronia 'can't be beat!' I'm not impressed with it for landscape effect, and yet given a drift of a dozen or so plants placed near some lovely browny rocks the effect would probably be devastating. I must try it. Oh, but not that pink variety! But there, how often must one remember not to decry any plant (aspidistras and such like excluded), for one day you may discover just the right position for it. It is so hard to warm towards the bottlebrushes, and yet it should not be—they look so hot! On the mountainside amongst the massive rocks they are right and delightful, but in the small garden they never seem sufficiently clothed. (How contradictory this all reads.)

I'm tempted to mention callitris, the cypress pines: they are not quite suitable for small estates, but for landscape effects they are superb, giving the impression of rather fat Roman cypresses.

Eriostemon myoporoides is one of the most shapely native plants we have, as you probably know and, being low-growing, is a most useful plant for covering the ground beneath taller shrubs and trees. For sheer abundance of bloom there surely could be no other native shrub more prolific; in spring it is literally smothered with its white star-shaped flowers. The buds have a pink tinge which greatly enhances this plant, and relieves the whiteness of the fully-opened blooms.

I have often been criticised for using the coastal tea-tree, *Leptospermum laevigatum*, but where there is sufficient space it presents a very soft and pleasing effect, and is at its best when growing out of the lawn in a natural group, that is, several planted quite closely together, one or two being but a foot or two apart. Such a planting will give you a charming sheltered corner where the sun will filter through the tea-tree branches fitfully.

It would be hard to imagine anything more lovely than the Victorian beech on the south side of a tall building. The tracery of their exquisite small, dark green foliage against a white plastered house is a thing not readily forgotten. Here is its botanic name, *Nothofagus cunninghamii*.

And now we come to the Prostantheras ... I'm skipping lots of things, of course, because at the moment we are only concerned with plants that are fit for close inspection. Well, these mint bushes are the most charming flowering shrubs one could wish to possess, and *Prostanthera ovalifolia* is perhaps the best for general garden purposes. One cannot help being amused at the catalogue description of this dainty, soft, mauve-flowered gem, which is described as 'a very handsome variety!' Do you also think of something red and large when the word handsome is used to describe it? This plant grows like the very devil when it likes its spot, so keep going with the pinching back if you would have it well-clothed at the base, and do cut it back lightly immediately after flowering every year. Pinching back the strong-growing branches all through the growing season is ever so much better than resorting to heavy pruning once a year—the plants don't like it.

Tristania laurina is an evergreen tree about which I should like to know much more than I do. I have never yet seen a full-grown specimen, but the beautiful green of the foliage, and the fascinating effect of the mottled white bark is sufficient to justify the recommendation. I cannot even find any information about it so may be quite wrong in believing it to be a native of Australia.

I wish we could claim the Tasmanian laurel *Anoptenus glandulosa* as a native of Australia, too. Isn't it a lovely evergreen and are not those cream cup-shaped flowers exquisite? I am so glad to see it appearing in the catalogues here, for in sheltered positions it will be invaluable, and by the time this goes to press it will be a good time to plant most of the things we have discussed. So hurry up and look around your gardens for suitable positions.

Yours deciduously,

Edna Walling

MAY 2, 1938

Dear Gardeners,

The last time I came down from Hamilton by plane I thought to myself, 'Must tell the Garden Lovers of the excellence of flying from the point of view of landscape gardening.' Especially would one recommend it to those who would become proficient in the drawing of landscape plans, for from a few thousand feet up there is laid out beneath a perfect guide the little round blobs that are trees with dense shade on one side. How infinitely interesting it is to observe the green tinge of the ground on the southeast side of the trees. It would seem that there is wisdom in planting and preserving trees from more points of view than that of creating shade and shelter for the cattle. 'Trees take so much out of the ground', say gardener and farmer alike. Yes, but ... well you can think it out for yourselves, certainly there was no doubt about that green patch on the shady side of every tree in an otherwise burnt-up pasture.

The alpine lawn! Does that stir your imagination? and just what is an alpine lawn? Well here is the perfect description—I have just found it:

Translated to garden use, it becomes a far more practical method of domesticating a touch of elusive mountain charm than rock gardens have proved to many suburban home owners. It is a rock garden with few or no rocks, a brilliantly colored lawn without grass. Its remote ideal is not the rocky architecture of the peaks, but the flowering alpine meadows that stretch among the high, sparse timber or surround the mountain lakelets. It is exceedingly useful in covering wide expanses of ground and lessening upkeep, since it does away with the heavy chore of mowing grass.

That is so, but never, never may you let up on the weeding of an alpine lawn. It is a gentle and sweet task (and so good for the figure!), but there will be many times when you won't be able to find just the right person to whom to entrust such a task. And so think well on this before taking unto yourselves such a delightful responsibility.

We are all getting very keen on the various bents for lawns, but I'm afraid they are not going to be very satisfactory by themselves. The first year they are simply marvellous, and then they seem to go off in patches, if some other species has not been sown with the bent. The safest and best recommended seed mixture for fine lawns seems to be one kind of fescue and one kind of bent, and a lawn of Chewing's fescue and New Zealand brown top—both New Zealand grasses—would keep anyone at home! No, not to mow it, for it compares quite favourably with other grasses for low upkeep, but to enjoy it. There is many a lawn one would leave home for. One is a buffalo lawn, another is of rye grass. Oh yes, I know we must have buffalo by the sea, but do let us consign rye to the cattle pastures, once and for all. (I wonder if I know what I am talking about? I'm not so sure!) Anyway let's talk about trees! Oh, but before I forget—found a plant in a nursery the other day that attracted me by its bright autumn colouring. I paused and thought, suppose it's only because it is pot-bound that it is colouring so beautifully ... plants have a way of tricking one like that ... as soon as I get it out into a bit of good ground it will probably grow into a dull little shrub with washy greeny-white flowers and foliage that remains green for ever. However, the cost was not great, so I brought it home and hurried off to Mr Bailey's *Encyclopedia* to learn that '*Itea virginica* is a low, upright, somewhat coarse shrub ...' (there, I knew it!), but I read on, wading through this sort of thing:

... a shrub not usually more than 2–3 feet high: is deciduous, alternate oblong, pointed, minutely serrate, smooth green above, pale and slightly pubescent below, petioled, without stipules, 1–3 inches long: flower fragrant, white in solitary, erect, hairy, simple, dense, terminal racemes 2–6 inches long ... Its somewhat coarse character does not favour its approach to more refined objects ...

And then I read on: 'In autumn it becomes a brilliant red.' Oh! How could they have said such rude things about it! For evidently it was running true to type in the pot, and the colouring is certainly lovely.

An American Friend

Crataegus durobrivensis! In spite of his name what an adorable little American tree it is. The fruit is a pinkish red and of a shape that is like a dear little apple. They are about half an inch across and hung in clusters. There are such a lot of these American hawthorns and they are all so fascinating. The best-known one is the Washington thorn, and even that brilliantly autumn-coloured little tree is not as well known as one would imagine. The fruits of the Washington thorn are much smaller than *C. durobrivensis*, about the size of the ordinary hawthorn, but much more brilliant red in colour. *Crataegus splendens* colours wonderfully, too, and like all the others is a most shapely little tree. I know the nurserymen do sell lots and lots of *Crataegus mexicana*, but I wonder where on earth they are, one sees so few about, and isn't it just too wonderful in the winter when it is covered with those deep yellow little 'apples'? Small wonder it is often mistaken for a crab apple.

One really should be more careful, it is so easy to be carried away by small gardening successes in one's own domain, and then one day someone comes (they did today!) to see 'this thyme lawn' or 'that shrub group', and instantly that little thyme lawn becomes so very small, and the group is past its best! 'You should have been here last week' is repressed with much difficulty.

You will be very busy people preparing for your winter plantings by the time this reaches you. I do hope some of you have a smack at the alpine lawn.

Yours, With good wishes for a Happy Maytime,

Edna Walling

JULY 1, 1938

Dear Gardeners,
Since writing to you last month, Mr John King of Dromana very kindly wrote to me giving quite a lot of interesting information about *Tristania laurina*. Here is what he has to say about it:

It is commonly called 'Kanooka', I had a lot of it up a creek called Back Creek, which runs through my property at Buchan. Tristania lurina grows in the middle of the Buchan River but only in a stunted form, always bending in the direction of the river's flow. In Back Creek, however, where the current was much more sluggish even in flood, it grew into beautiful shady trees with a butt diameter of 18 inches to nearly two feet. I felled one, and put it over my saw bench and still have some of the timber cut 33 years ago. It is close grained and heavy, blood red when first cut and full of water, which makes it hard to season. They grow in the Nicholson River near Bairnsdale. J. H. Maiden in his book, Useful Native Timbers, *called it water gum, and says that it grows to 50–60 feet in height, diameter 12–24 inches. Habitat, Victoria, New South Wales, Queensland.*

There now, hasn't he told us a lot about this attractive evergreen? I was planting a regular sheet of *Thruptomene mitchellii* yesterday, and intend to group lots and lots of prostantheras behind and adjacent to them. Then we shall have clumps of the lemon scented tea-tree, *Leptospurmum citratum*, and *Eriostemon neriifolium* in the foreground of the tea-trees. Oh! And we shall have masses of eriostemon in front of the coastal tea-tree (*Leptospermum laevitgatum*) in the dry spots with *Callitris cupressiformis* at the very back. Here is to be none of your collection of 'Australian Plants', Oh no, this will be a lovely native garden, and once and for all let us hope it will help to lay the ghost that frightens people and makes them look so depressed when one mentions native plants. You really cannot wonder. Take the border of Australian plants in the Botanic Gardens. Could anything be more uninspiring?

The great thing seems to be to get the ground well covered with low-growing shrubs, and as there are plenty of low-growing natives that will grow under gum trees, there is no reason why we should have dust instead of verdure.

Another important point to remember is that to every tree that is planted you will probably need at least a dozen low-growing shrubs—a dozen of one kind, not 'one of this and one of that'; that is what is so often wrong. However, such plantings are not, of course, appropriate to the small garden, but many a half-acre could be delightfully treated in this way, and be extremely easy to maintain when it is once established.

Roadside Planting

Talking of native plants tempts me to mention roadside planting—a subject very dear to my heart. There are such infinite possibilities in the planting of country roadsides, but as I see it, it does not mean the destruction of what exists and the introduction of exotic species. Of all the places where we *should* display the beauty of our native plants surely the country roadside is the most fitting, and yet when tree planting is indulged in by various Progress Associations it is generally along formal lines, and all too often natural growth is destroyed to make way for some exotic trees evenly spaced at 30 feet apart. We have better examples in plenty all about us—the richness of the roadside growth in the vicinity of Warburton, for instance, to guide us in the planting of the roadsides that have been denuded of natural growth, and one day perhaps we shall see trucks going forth loaded with small plants of leptospernums, kunzeas, eucalypts, bursaria, callitris and acacias and lots and lots of the lower-growing ground covers to clothe the ground beneath. When one thinks of the comparatively low initial cost of planting natives, and the almost negligible maintenance required it does seem that we are lagging behind rather badly in this matter. I know someone who takes with him into the country bundles of eugenia seedlings every time he sets forth. What a lovely idea! Much could be done with seed, too. We are going to scatter seed of the woolly tea-tree and that broader-leaved silky textured variety I am told is also called *Leptospurmum lanigerum* (it's very confusing) in moistest spots, and the coastal tea-tree *Leptospurmum laevigatum* in the most arid places. One can generally find a little leaf mould to scatter over the seed—very, very lightly, of course, and with this encouragement they should be established by spring.

From roadside planting it is a far cry to gardening, and yet is it so very far? If in our peregrinations we would sometimes pull up at the ugly spots and drop a few seeds of native plants we should soon increase the miles of natural beauty.

Every year I get a fresh thrill from cascade chrysanthemums. We have them growing just as ordinary herbaceous perennials and they have the appearance of large-flowered perennial asters from the distance. What darling little flowers there are, and how hardy!

THE TREE IMPERIAL

Don't forget the shingle oak when you are considering trees for this winter's planting. It is one of the Americans and of great beauty. The leaves are willow or peach shaped, and for this reason many people are surprised when they hear it is an oak. It grows to 50 feet or more, nevertheless, it does not require such a very large garden because it is rather pyramid shaped in the young stage, becoming round-headed when it gets up a little. The summer beauty of the tree is sufficient

to commend it, but in spring it is covered with pink and silver which is the young leaves expanding, and in autumn the foliage changes to rich reds.

Except for the English oak, which is a little subject to scale and red spider, the oaks are the most desirable of trees; their deep root systems make growing conditions beneath them so much easier than with many other trees, and they ask so little in the matter of soil conditions. Let us, therefore, plant more oaks—lots more oaks! But don't be tempted to purchase very big trees; if you do it is really best to cut them almost level with the ground, and let them spring up afresh, you will be amazed at the rapid growth you will get and you will have a much better tree—but you won't do it! Whilst you are still unconscious I will say farewell until July.

Hoping it will be oak with you, yours,

Edna Walling

PS—Forgot to tell you the botanical name of the shingle oak—it is *Quercus imbricaria*.

SEPTEMBER 1, 1938

Dear Gardeners,
I have just found a picture of that indispensable little plant botanically known as *Erigeron mucronatus*, and much more euphoniously known as 'baby's tears'. It's a plant one must be cautious with when smaller fry are about, for it does walk over them a little, but what one would do without it I don't know. That a plant so charming will grow in spots where few other plants will thrive never ceases to thrill me, and once established it will begin

to pop up in all sorts of unexpected places and grace many a corner previously unclothed with beauty.

I know this habit of 'popping up' does not appeal to some gardeners, they simply cannot stand anything that seeds itself and comes up in a spot that has not been carefully allotted for it. They *like* to go through all the processes of sowing their seed, pricking them off into little boxes and finally planting them out in neat little rows, and my word!, if anything dares to come up amongst these precious seedlings off comes its head with that ever-active hoe. The policy is, 'if it hasn't been planted it's a weed', and what dull gardens result from such a policy!

Recently, with a kindred spirit I was taken over a vast garden, and neither of us managed to bring any realism into our expostulations of wonder at the magnificence of the specimens until we came to a little gate that lead us through a little old garden, sweet with carpets of forget-me-nots. We were being hurried through this property recently acquired by 'the octopus' to form a short cut to another part of his wonderland; but we paused, and from us both came forth the one honest exclamation of delight!

I always like to make quite sure that anyone I set to weed my humble plot knows the difference between a weed and a self-sown flower, and I like to know that they have no secateurs concealed about them—it's so much better to be sure than sorry.

Writing of gardens in winter makes one realise how important it is to plan and plant them so that they will be interesting and not dull in winter. A garden that has some stone work, in the form of walls, rock gardens or stone paving will always be more interesting in winter than one that entirely relies upon its planting. The colour and texture of the stone will be more noticeable, and the design that such features bring into the garden is of great value to the winter pictures you may have. I shall not readily forget the picture made by a pale pink *Camellia sasanqua* growing at the foot of a high stone wall. The camellia was lovely in itself, but it was the wall that completed the picture.

The pink-and-red flowering tea-trees do not seem to be long-lived, which makes them difficult to place, since the sudden collapse of a shrub may utterly upset one's grouping or leave a spot denuded just as one has become accustomed to its inhabitant. However, they are far too attractive to ban them for that, and the winter-flowering varieties are much too useful, too. This new one, *Leptospermum keatleyi* is an exquisite little plant and should form a perfect foreground for *Prunus mume* and *Prunus pollardii*, with *Camellia sasanqua* somewhere in the offing. *Leptospermum sandersii* we are, of course, more familiar with, and a very satisfactory winter-flowering little shrub it is, too.

We shall soon be planting our lawns by the yard! There came to me a few days ago a sample of this new method of lawn-making, known as 'pre-sown lawn'. Between two sheets of paper the seed is sown in rows about three-eighths of an inch apart. This is simply laid down on the prepare surface and sprinkled with fine soil, resulting in a growth of grass appearing with mathematical precision at predetermined distances apart, ensuring even and correct distribution in the soil. I must say that this 'mathematical precision' does appeal to me when it comes to lawns, and I am all for extracting all but the grasses I have sown from lawns. This new method would seem to eliminate the bird problem, since it would be well nigh impossible to wrest the seed from its paper covering before it had sprung into a less palatable grass plant.

Do you know the story of the meek little man reading his paper in the train? Fellow passengers were all having their three h'aporth of his news, some even turning the corners back to see the other side when he peered out from behind the paper and asked, 'Please may I turn over?' A friend of mine has been reading over my shoulder and has just said, 'Well you do leave them in mid-air, why don't you tell them more about winter grouping', but I tell her they know all about silver birches carpeted with prostrate rosemary with a misty background of grey tea-tree, and winter jasmine somewhere in the picture, and a little clump of crocuses just beginning to thrust up their little golden chalices, and not far away the first tiny flowers of *Spirea thunbergii* wreathing the slender branches of this fairy-like shrub ... they know all about winter sweet, with its exquisitely fragrant butter-coloured flowers tightly clinging to the bare grey branches, and the thrill and the fragrance of the winter-flowering apricots

... how they fill the air with their sweetness and make one momentarily forget the rest of the winter to come. Since they are quite small trees one looks for at least one in almost every garden.

There now, this has developed into what is so often a tiresome thing—a long letter. And it all started from my finding that photograph—felt I had to send it to you. Goodbye, and put in lots of trees.

Edna Walling

PS—Thanks W.A.S for the photograph of the fish pond with azolla floating on the surface and the rock garden behind it.

OCTOBER 1, 1938

Dear Gardeners,
Last week I was privileged (that sounds so trite) ... Last week I was thrilled (that's much better) to meet Mr Toop, of the Ballarat Gardens, for the first time. Quite a long time ago I heard him speak, and remember thinking at the

time, 'I like that man, he's less horticultural, and more arboricultural than most curators'. And if one needed to be convinced of this impression only one thing could be more convincing than walking amongst those magnificent trees that he cares for so tenderly, and that would be to walk amongst them with him.

One was almost tempted to be frivolous and say, 'You call yourself a curator and yet you let these trees grown naturally like this! See here, some of them are even touching each other. Why, they are even looking charming and picturesque because you have neglected to interfere with them! How do you retain this curatorship without thinning them out, and doing a spot of hacking occasionally? Why in Melbourne, when the poplar Dame Nellie Melba planted in the Botanic Gardens was sweeping gracefully to the ground, we did not merely remove sufficient branches to give comfortable head room; oh no, we made a thorough job of it, and denied it of branches so high up that it resembles a gum tree!' What a superb specimen of the English maple, *Acer campestris* these gardens possess; its winter form is so enthralling and the clear golden yellow of the autumn foliage so very lovely that it seems a great pity that they are not more generally planted.

I gasped when we came to the *Magnolia kobus*, towering up 20 feet or so: a few of its white, floppy little flowers were already in bloom, making an exquisite picture against the bare, grey branches. With sadness one remembers the slaughtering of a whole bed of magnolias at the Melbourne Botanic Gardens—the curator thought azaleas would be better! How fortunate are the people of Ballarat. The attitude of this man would have been: 'Yes, I think azaleas would have been better, but I would not take the magnolias away now.' If only such a policy were adopted in Melbourne in the matter of street trees, how much better it would be than the 'policy of the city council', which is used as an excuse for the destruction of so much arboreal beauty.

LILAC TIME

Since lilacs are still sent out from the nurseries grafted upon privet stocks (with rare exceptions), it is as well to know that as the lilac is always a better bush when it is on its own roots something must be done to induce these grafted plants to produce their own roots, and become independent of the privet in time. And the only thing to do is to plant the lilac so that the graft is about two inches below the soil. This generally means a rather deep hole, as the privet stock is usually fairly long, and the thing you will have to guard against is bad drainage. Therefore, if you have to break into hard ground to get the plant deep enough to have the graft below the surface, be sure to see that the hard ground is loosened to the same depth for some distance away from the hole, thus enabling the underground water to escape. So many plants suffer from being planted in potholes, subjecting them to wet feet every winter, until so many of the roots rot that the plants eventually give up the struggle and die.

THE GARDEN POOL

The little niceties about pools need a little more careful observance, I think, and the informal pool in a landscape garden is perhaps the most difficult type to deal with so that it will look quite natural. In a formal scheme, it is almost invariably surrounded by paving, sometimes by a coping. A frequent mistake with formal pools is the use of a coping where it would be better to run the paving level right to the water's edge. In some cases the coping is desirable, but if the sole reason for its existence is that it makes the pool less dangerous, I do not think it is a good solution of the problem, especially since it only achieves so small a degree of improvement of the problem. It is much better not to spoil the appearance of the pool and effect a complete measure of safety by placing a lightly-made grating just below the surface of the water, say two inches. This will not be visible except when one is quite close to the water, and it is, of course, entirely safe.

And now the informal pool. You have probably noticed that it is never quite successful to have any form of margin between the water and the turf in places where the grass runs right up to the pool; unless the grass rolls right into the water, and so often the reason that the margin is there at all is that there is a four-inch wall of concrete that is rather puzzling. If the top of this wall is bevelled back towards the lawn instead of being finished level, the grass will grow right to the water's edged. Big, flat boulders placed with restraint and artistry can be as delightful as a row of stones can be hideous for the parts where the shrub border butts on to the pool. We may learn so much from the Japanese in these matters, for surely no other people know the art of placing boulders as they do. And I will close with this little Japanese sonnet:

The years go by;
Age and its evils crowd upon me;
But be this as it may,
While flowers are here to see I cannot grieve.

(I found it in Gwendolyn Arley's 'Japanese Interlude', in the *Alpine Garden Society Bulletin.*)

Edna Walling

NOVEMBER 1, 1938

Dear Gardeners,
I am so late with my letter to you this month that it may miss the mail (shall be frightfully disappointed if it does, because there is so much to tell you), however it shall go forth and perhaps the Editor will not be as exacting as the postal authorities, and at the last minute find a little niche for it somewhere in the *Home Beautiful*. (Well, here it is— Ed *H.B.*)

What a lucky season it has been for the flowering apples; the gales came just a few days before they were fully open, and consequently we have been spared the heart-breaking sight of last year when the wind never ceased until it had stripped almost every petal from the trees.

ANOTHER APPLE STORY

Oh: I'm immensely proud of *Malus* 'Sonning'. This year it is more than ever evident that it is the clearest of all the wine-red varieties. *Malus floribunda purpurea* pales into insignificance beside it. There is, of course, no justification for my pride, for it was just one of those flukes of Nature! Indeed I was very nearly instrumental in the destruction of the original plant. Here is its history. A seedling came up beneath one of the *Malus fl. purpurea*s, and at that time there were not many plants available for the development of the landscape at Sonning, and it was planted out on an important point. Years went by and the tree grew and grew, but never flowered. The foliage was conspicuously fine, being a luscious reddish bronze, but thinking how foolish it was to plant a seedling in such a position, it was decided to replace it with something that *would* flower, and be worthy of the position. However, like many another job, there 'never was time', and so it remained until the year it surprised us with a small crop of blooms of a clear rich colour. Not daring to hope that something better had eventuated so easily, it was propagated so that we could grow it in different positions to determine whether it was the soil in which the original plant had been planted that had produced the clearness of colour. And now we feel confident in declaring it to be infinitely superior to *purpurea*, and earlier than *Aldenhamensis*.

I do think these darker flowering apples are much more attractive in the company of the pale pink varieties, and the taller and more upright growing *spectabilis* and *schideckerii* are particularly lovely in the group, and if you know anything more enthralling than *Rhododendron virgatum* as a ground cover to these apples, do please write and tell me by return!

This year we have *Malus eleyii* carpeted with that very satisfactory little pale pink primrose that increases so readily. With us it does so much better than the yellow English primrose, which is lost again and again. Mr Toop, of the Ballarat Gardens, tells me that he finds it better to raise the blue primroses from seed than to continually divide the roots. I won't be happy until there are a million of them at Sonning, so much do I adore the exquisite blueness of these little primroses!

Precious Dwarf Shrubs

That little pale blue veronica (*formosa*) is a most useful little shrub. It is smothered with its little star-shaped flowers at present, and is, I think, going to be most satisfactory as a substitute for *Felicia augustifolia*, which is dying out such a lot in some places. One literally leaps upon any low-growing shrub that is at all attractive and hardy, for there seems to be a dearth of hardy shrubs that do not exceed three feet in height. I suppose that one of the sweetest of all dwarf shrubs is *Baeckia plicata*, a little native plant with pink and white flowers in spring. It is such a lovable little fellow that I like to grow it in a pot, so that it can be moved around as a companion. But don't forget it is a native, and like many another native, it heartily dislikes being pot-bound, and so, soon after the roots begin to fill the pot it must be moved on to the next size pot or tub. Don't think you can jump it up to a very large pot and skip the work of potting it on from size to size, and don't ask me why some small plants hate being put into large containers ... I DON'T KNOW! No doubt someone will have some theory for you, but there is no doubt about the fact that with very few exceptions a small plant does not thrive in a large tub or pot unless it is grown on in successive containers. (There may be a moral for ministers in this—Ed.) I almost forgot a promise to give readers a list of plants that will grow in a dry district, and as it is so near the end of my letter now I shall have to tell you more about them in a future epistle. Anyway for a shade tree there is one beautiful tree you can plant instead of a pepper tree, and that is the Cape Chestnut, *Calodendrum capense*. It is a tree that sheds its leaves for just about three weeks only in the spring just before the new foliage appears, and so it is considered an evergreen. The cone-shaped bunches of pale pink flowers are very lovely in summer, and it really makes a very beautifully shaped shade tree.

Here's hoping for rain.

Yours deciduously,

Edna Walling

D E C E M B E R   1 ,   1 9 3 8

Dear Gardeners,

If our *Crataegus smithiana* has as many berries in the autumn as it has blooms at the present, it is going to be a wonderful sight. Do you know it by any chance? It is becoming fairly well-known now and its orange-scarlet fruits, which are a little larger than those of the English hawthorn, make a brilliant picture in late autumn. In habit and leaf it somewhat resembles the English hawthorn and it is equally indifferent as to soil and situation. A valuable smallish tree indeed.

HAWTHORNS AND HONEYSUCKLES

What an atmosphere of rural restfulness these hawthorns give to a garden. It is, perhaps, that they remind us of the quiet English countryside. I know that when I awake in the morning and look out upon the double pink hawthorn laden with bloom at the moment, my thoughts are always of the luscious meadows of England, and a peacefulness pervades the mind.

And that loveliest of all the honeysuckles, *Lonicera japonica* with its almost bronze-green foliage that has a flush of red behind the leaves, adding such richness to the foliage: how well it harmonises with the hawthorns, making the late spring a joyous time indeed. The flowers are the richest in colouring of all the honeysuckles that I know, and more varied in the tonings. It flowers in double pairs all the way up the long trailing branches, and whilst one bunch of four flowers will be a lovely soft rosy red with an almost pure white throat (it is the red back to the petals that gives it just that faint tinge of pink to the whiteness) the next set of blooms will be a more russet red with a distinctly apricot interior. It is this variation that seems to make this climbing plant one of the most interesting of the species.

It is a great pity to refrain from using some climbing plants because of their vigorous growth when regular and judicious pruning will make them not only quite safe, but will produce much better flowers and foliage. I can hear many of you saying—'But when should we prune them?' and the answer is immediately after flowering. That's easy isn't it?

A Landscape in Miniature

I happen to know that the Editor has a particularly good photograph of the little woodland scene we made at the Arts and Crafts Exhibition this month, and am hoping he will find space to place it somewhere in the offing of this letter, because I think you might like it. Of particular interest to you will be the new way to stake your birches. Cut off the tops of the trees and tie a wad of crepe rubber to the top and wedge them to the ceiling—if any. With this method you will find that within the space of an hour you may place and stake dozens of birches! There's only one trouble, of course, there's never a ceiling in one's garden.

Before I go any further with this fooling, you must know that these trees, cut down with such apparent ruthlessness, came from a patch where they were soon to be cut into firewood. They were actually the overgrown stock in a large nursery, where the ground was needed for other plants.

Ellis Stones, who did the 'outcrop,' certainly excelled himself. The little mountain track which wandered up amongst the large boulders gave Gwynnyth Crouch and myself some exciting spots to plant, and whilst I busied myself with the trees and shrubs, Gwynnyth tucked in her beloved rock plants, and hey presto, the landscape was complete.

It is a rare thing, this gift for placing stones, and strange that a man possessing it should bear the name Stones—it should be easy to memorise. Lovely as formal gardens can be, it is these informal schemes, in which boulders form so important a part, that appeal so tremendously for the reason, perhaps, that they give us the atmosphere of the country, and the refreshment of mind derived from such.

The Worth of a Garden

Gardens mean more and more to people in these troubled times, and it is in them alone that lies hope for the mental rest so vitally necessary to us all. The joy of growing flowers, with all the physical exertion necessary, provides mental relaxation to some, but there are many who need the type of garden where one may lie flat on one's back on the grass, under the trees, storing up fresh resources so vital to imaginative work. For these people one must design gardens within [which] lies the least amount of maintenance, for any evidence of the amount of work that must be done to maintain order is disturbing to the mind. I have wandered right away from the description of the Exhibition, and as the limit of space has been reached, I must content myself to let the picture tell the rest.

Until next month,

Yours, etc.,

Edna Walling

Dear Gardeners,

THE ESCALLONIAS

Three of the prettiest little flowering shrubs in bloom at the moment are the three escallonias, *E. edinensis*, *E. donard* seedling, and *E. slieve donard*. Each variety is such a happy complement to the others that they certainly seem to be at their best when they are all planted side by side. *Donard* seedling is the palest of the three, and then comes *edinensis*, and *slieve donard* most satisfactorily completes a most charming pink and white picture. There is a slightly deeper tinge of pink to *slieve donard* that declares it an improved form of *edinensis*, but it seems to me to be a desirable addition to the group rather than that it should be considered as a variety to displace *edinensis*.

These escallonias, which are much thinner in habit than *macrantha*, *ingramii roses*, and other coarser foliaged and more compact varieties, are

77

at their best as wall shrubs where they are seen to much better advantage than when their sometimes straggly form is seen in the foreground of other shrubs. Their hardiness is unquestioned, for they will thrive and cover themselves with bloom in the hottest and driest positions, if they have been given a good start so that they may establish themselves properly after transplanting.

THE HERBACEOUS BORDER

The plant that has given me the greatest thrill in the herbaceous borders this year is *Penstemon ovatus*, a tall mauve and blue spike. The pale *Penstemon gentianoides* is very desirable, too, in spite of its extreme paleness. I cannot see sufficient difference between *Penstemon gentianoides* and *Penstemon* 'Hot Springs' to justify growing both varieties, but what a charming little fellow is *Penstemon secundiflorus* with its pinkish-mauve spikes two feet tall. It is very stiff, erect and prim, and should be most useful for a midway position in the herbaceous border.

The spires of *Antirrhinum crassifolium* are almost invisible, so small are the individual flowers, and so soft a blue, but its very daintiness makes it desirable.

Thymus serphyllum var. 'Lang Hall' is smothered with its almost stemless pink flowers set amongst the grey-green foliage, and with *Nierembergia hippomancia* as an intermediate plant between these penstemons and this thyme you should have a very attractive picture for either your herbaceous borders or your rock garden.

THE VALUE OF MULCHING

My goodness, if this year does not teach us once and for all how imperative to good results is mulching, surely we shall never learn! To rake aside the grass mulch and see the wonderful moisture beneath on ground that was mulched in late winter makes one almost ashamed to possess any cultivated ground that has not been mulched. The difference is just this: one may see plants thriving with luscious green leaves, and within a yard or two one may see others shrivelling up and dying in the scorched up ground. In the following winter those who have mulched will have a mat of half-rotted material to turn under, thus giving the roots a sponge-like mass of humus to draw their moisture from in summer.

Don't be Too Crazy

What a good thing it is that 'crazy paving' is becoming less and less prevalent. It seems that we are realising that we can get the informal note into paving without being studiously crazy, and are consequently achieving much more restful effects than with those sharp angular patterns which give one such a jolt when you walk into a garden. The secret is to have the joints running across the path (not too meticulously, of course) and not to have the stones of too even a size.

Here's hoping for good gardening in 1939!

Edna Walling

FEBRUARY 1, 1939

Dear Gardeners,
The Editor has supplied me with a close-up picture, taken by a *Home Beautiful* photographer, of the rock garden shown at the Arts and Crafts Exhibition last month so that you may be told something about the little plants that appeared therein.

In the foreground, on the left, the little spires are the purple flowers of *Ajuga reptans atropurpurea*, a very familiar rock plant which is extremely useful for covering inhospitable ground, and you will recognise the English primrose in close proximity. Immediately below the little toadstool which Gwynnyth, 'the head gardener,' made there is a clump of the dwarf form of white thrift, and nestling into the rock on the right of the gravel path there is a drift of thyme which is one of the Westmoreland hybrids. The two little spikes that look like small foxgloves to the right of the birches come from a plant of adenaphora—very like a campanula and rather despised by some gardeners for its propensity for increasing so rapidly, but this and columbines and foxgloves are all very desirable woodland plants: in this instance we tried to suggest a rock garden drifting into woodland.

The gravel for little pathways such as this should be rather like coarse sand instead of one that binds into a hard mass so that the little creeping plants may run freely into it and it will resemble the rock in crumbled form; and certainly it should not be screened. You will notice the little pieces of stone in the path in the picture.

Luxuries of luxuries! I've been lying on my own thyme lawn, there was just enough room to turn over without landing onto the surrounding rock plants, and when I go forth to join the others they will (I hope) say, 'What a lovely smell', and if they don't I shall say, 'If you 'mell a 'mell it's me'.

But you haven't lived if you have not lain flat on your middle on a thyme lawn. The bees don't seem to mind a bit either, but just go on busily exploring the possibilities of each thyme flower. How cool and fresh to the touch are these lovely little plants, how exquisitely dusky the colouring of the various varieties, both in foliage and flower.

From ground level the rock garden becomes the most enchanting place—it's like another world; *Aquilegia longissima* almost towered above me, and the little flat faces of *Aquilegia clematifolia* looked down at me with surprised expressions. How utterly dissimilar are these two columbines, the one so haughtily graceful with its long sweeping spurs, and the other so plain Jane, and yet so quaint, with its plate-like flowers. *Penstemon secundiflorus* looked like a prim little old maid—a little disapproving—with its very stiff spikes of rosy mauve flowers, and *gentianoides* stood by, softly mauve, persuading *secundiflorus* to 'let her be'. The profusion of blue-mauve cups on *Nierembergia hippomanica* gave me a cheery greeting, as only this little treasure may; somehow one never seems to have enough of him, and yet it is easy enough to grow. (Avoid *Nierembergia azurea*, if you are looking for this little cup flower, for 'tis a very different thing and a poor substitute.)

I've been having such a lovely party with a bale of peat moss, almost every treasure has been top-dressed with it! What a mulch! Here is humus, my friends, and you all know how essential that is to the well-being of your plants, and here is a short cut to green manuring. Of course you get nothing for nothing in this world, but you do save many months and a lot of labour; compare the difference, one digs the ground, sows the peas, or some other leguminous crop, adds a fertiliser to encourage the crop, waters the crop in a season such as this, and after two or three months one turns it in. In another few months it has decomposed and become humus.

And here is the other method of adding humus. Spread two inches of peat moss over the ground and turn it in, that is all—no that is not all, you have the humus but what of the nitrogen that the leguminous plants have extracted for the air and stored in little bags on the roots? You do know of course that it is when the peas are in flower that the nitrogen is at its highest content, and that if you allow them to go to seed the pods use it up.

Whilst there is not much we may do at the moment in the matter of planting out permanent plants it is nevertheless an excellent time to divide and plant out the Germanica irises, for it gives them a chance to develop before they flower in spring. Unlike so many other species of iris such as the Japanese (*Kaemferi*)[*Iris Kaemferi*], these Germanicas may be lifted with perfect safety at any time of the year, and it is one job that may be done now to relieve the strain of all the activities that go on in the garden in winter.

Yours for good gardening,

Edna Walling

M A R C H   1 ,   1 9 3 9

Dear Gardeners,

I am enclosing a photograph that might interest you for in it you will see what we have done with two Roman cypress trees that stood at either side of a pathway. One shot ahead luxuriantly whilst the other was hampered by some cause we were unable to discover. We decided therefore to bend the tall one over and tie it to the weak one, for whilst neither the 'head gardener' nor myself are partial to arches we thought it would be better than the effect of the uneven pair, and now we are quite pleased with it. The top must of course receive an occasional trimming because the bending over has induced it to sprout quite freely there. The hedge through which the little gateway passes is of *Abelia rupestris*, and you will see it is quite nice and compact. It really is one of the prettiest of hedges.

Next year I am looking forward to having a good batch of *Trachelium caeruleum* in the garden for it is the most fascinating plant. Its common name is throatwort, which is a biennial or perennial with fluffy heads of mauve flowers growing to a foot or 18 inches high. It is splendid for the front of the herbaceous border and for certain spots in the rock garden, and although it may live for years, it is wise to have seedlings coming on every year to keep up the supply of plants for it is not a long-lived perennial, and sometimes is only a biennial.

The 'head gardener' has gone to the Baw Baws looking for native rock plants, and she has the right eyes for such work, so I may have something to tell you about her finds next month, but it would be better for her to tell you herself in her own words. We will see what the Editor has to say about it! (And we'll see what the 'head gardener' has to say about it before committing ourselves, says cautious Editor.)

Our gardens seem to be of such little moment just now, at a time when so many have been bereft of all they possess, and so much native beauty has been so tragically destroyed, that it is difficult to write in cheerful strain of things horticultural ... However, looking around the garden after a week of devastating heat and winds, one feels impelled to write of those plants that have survived and still remain fresh in the face of such conditions.

Pistacia chinensis, which so closely resembles *Rhus succedanea*, is in excellent nick, though it has not had one drop of water, other than that the heavens have sent it, this summer; it has, of course, many weeks of probable dryness to go before we can be sure of the glories of the autumn foliage of which it is capable, but so long as no 'kind' person comes along and gives it a can of water it looks as though it might survive even more dryness yet.

It is a strange thing isn't it, that if a plant is battling along without water and showing no signs of flagging how fatal it is to water it, unless you are prepared to go on pouring the water on until the autumn rains do it for you; that is why we are always a little terrified when anyone offers to do the watering for us, for fear they will dash a little on some plant that is not used to such luxuries, and miss those that we have had to start watering because they had shown signs of succumbing to the dryness. It must sound rather odd to overhear such remarks as these rapped out: 'Who has been watering this plant?' And a little further on, 'Someone has forgotten to water this shrub!' But 'they' understand perfectly!

THE EASY WAY IS BEST

It's a thrilling experience to own a big heap of interesting-looking stones and a place where one may build them up into a garden wall. Once when the building of some stone pillars for a pergola had just been completed we found ourselves possessed of a large heap of leftovers, and were a little appalled at the prospect, not only of wheeling them away, but of finding a spot where to dump them—always a burning question, this storing of surplus materials. However, we held a consultation and unanimously decided that what we really wanted was a low double wall a mere yard or two away from where the stones were lying!

Everyone was much more interested in applying themselves to this task than to the dull and laborious one of trundling endless barrowfuls to some distant spot, and so three pairs of hands swiftly got to work (for there was to be a garden party next day), and soon a broad low wall, some 20 inches in breadth, and about 22 inches high, enclosed the paved area between the pergola and the garden cabin. The best stones were used for the two faces, and all the rubble was packed into the centre of the wall. Some of the stones extended well across the centre of the wall to tie it together, and although the main part of the wall was dry-built, a mixture of sand and cement was poured into the centre when the top had been levelled and roughly trowelled off to give a comfortable surface on which to sit.

The mixture was a very lean one, perhaps one bucket of cement to seven or eight of sand, and this for two reasons: so violent was the disapproval when I said, 'And now I am going to top it off with some cement', that I promised the effect should not be of hard grey cement, most carefully trowelled to a respectable neatness that can be so stifling I agreed, but would, in a very short time, resemble sandstone, and would weather quickly and soon become mossy, because of the rough careless finish.

There is no earth whatsoever in this wall, and what a lusty plant of Italian lavender is living upon is more than I can tell. A little dirt and a lavender seed must have decided to occupy the same crevice—that it should have sprouted is not so surprising—but that it went on assuming larger and larger proportions is a mystery indeed. A wall with little odds and ends of plants growing out therefrom can be a delightful thing, but sometimes it is a little artificially assumed, don't you think? But more of this next month.

Yours, still hoping.

Edna Walling

APRIL 1, 1939

Dear Gardeners,
I'm sending you a picture of 'Winty' grown up this month. At least, the tiny little cottage that it was has matured into a two-storeyed house, and even since this picture was taken the garden is growing around it, making it look a little more friendly every day. That mass of nubbly ground in the foreground will be an outcrop of rock one day, in which will grow the little lowly treasures so dear to the heart of the owner.

Hidden by the blackwood tree in the foreground on the right of the picture there is a low stone wall which encloses a gravelled area, where chairs and tables are pushed out when the days are suitable for out-of-door eating.

That wispy-looking plant on the corner of the porch is a flowering apple, *Malus sonningensis*, which has now grown sufficiently to be trained against the wall around the window. The effect of this deep rose-coloured apple in spring against the white walls of the house certainly gives one the idea that it is one of the most delightful ways to display these blossoms, and the training is not difficult; to leave all the pruning until winter is not advisable, in fact, after flowering and through the summer is the best time to do any necessary cutting back so that the least amount of the flower buds are removed. At present the berries are almost as attractive as the spring blooms, and the summer foliage, like all the dark-flowered apples, is a rich bronze-green with a reddish reverse to the leaves. And so we find that of all the blossom trees, flowering apples seem to give us the longest period of beauty.

Sydney's Rock Gardens

Always one returns from Sydney green with the jealousy. Oh! Those natural rock gardens; their 'difficulties' are so attractive, so often there is nothing to do but to preserve carefully what already exists—what we in Melbourne would pay hundreds of pounds to create, and yet so often they spend large sums of money in blowing it up, and carting it away, endeavouring to produce the better horticultural conditions found in Victoria!

What horticultural splendours could possibly compare with the native evergreens and the picturesque outcrops of weathered sandstone so prevalent around Sydney? And the outlooks! One walks into a garden and is struck speechless with the view! Yes, it's a bit hard on the garden owners, but one could wish that sometimes they would cease struggling with the conditions and subjugate their gardens to the grandeur of the prospect. All one asks is a peaceful place in which to sit and enjoy the scene ahead, with flower growing chiefly left for the nether regions.

WHITE FLOWERS THAT WEAR

Always with the greatest pleasure I look upon a sheet of *Alyssum procumbens*, 'Carpet of Snow'; one sows a few seeds and the next season it appears in all sorts of unexpected places, carpeting inhospitable pieces of ground with its snowy whiteness. I am rather glad that this was a popular little fellow before the present vogue for white flowers came into fashion, and sincerely one hopes that this craze for white flowers will not pass, as others have done, for never have our gardens been so lovely and so restful! *Gardenia radicans* really is one of the most desirable little rock garden shrubs; it is worth growing for the evergreen foliage alone, and it has found its way into this dissertation because of its white flowers I suppose.

For a ground cover *Vinca minor flore pleana alba* is delightful; it does not ramp, as does the old *Vinca major*, and will be found to be invaluable under trees and other places where bare ground is so often the problem. *Rhyncospernum repems variegata* also promises to be most useful in this respect.

And then jumping up to the towering heights of 'Australia's most beautiful tree,' as it has been so fittingly called in a recent publication, one meditates upon the beauties and the possibilities of *Callitris columellaris*. It was an apt description: 'It appears as a spire composed of innumerable eruptions of green smoke', and to my joy I found myself unexpectedly driving past the very institution at Gladesville, NSW., where a grove of the finest specimens of this tree is thriving. Again on the way back from Leura I spied a specimen in a State school garden. It is being propagated by means of grafting in New South Wales now; whether because it is not easy to raise from seed or whether the seed is sparse, I know not, but we can only hope that these grafted specimens will produce quite satisfactory trees, for this unsung beauty should certainly soon become one of the most useful and decorative of landscape plants for Australian gardens. There is not the slightest doubt that overseas visitors will be far more impressed with it than they will be with a planting of *Torulosa cupdessus*, which shows so little imagination, and which they can behold in so many other parts of the world.

And this is only one instance of the superiority of native planting over exotic in prominent positions where those who visit Australia hope to find something different from that which they have left behind.

Yours,

Edna Walling

MAY 1, 1939

Dear Gardeners,

When these letters to you first started I said to myself, 'Now we'll talk about the construction of gardens because everyone writes about what to plant, and what they have in their gardens that is looking simply marvellous at the moment', and yet almost without exception have these letters been all about plants!

Well, it's not entirely my fault; just as I am about to tell you what a wonderful effect you could get with a colonnade in such and such a position the 'head gardener' pops her head in the window to say 'Do tell them about that adorable little perennial aster, *Aster compacta ramsayii*,' and encouraged by the extra speed of the typewriter whilst I 'get it over' so that I can get back to my colonnade, she literally yells from the rock garden—because it is not really within normal ear shot—I say! *Cyclamen africanum* is in flower!!!' I have tried to convey the degree of excitement by using three notes of exclamation ... it's not enough!

As a matter of fact I had intended mentioning this little foot-high aster, but could not find it anywhere in any of my reference books, and have no idea where I got it, so thought it best not to irritate you with an enthusiastic description of a plant that was more than probably wrongly named. However if, in your peregrinations, you come across a plant under this name it may be worth the gamble.

Retaining Wall or Rock Garden

Of all the easy and most fascinating planting spots in a garden there is surely nothing more delightful than the top of a stone retaining wall. It is most important that the soil should come right to the top of the wall, and when it has been recently filled in it should be higher to allow for sinking. Here so many rock plants show to such excellent advantage and revel in the perfect drainage. Such positions, and the edges of paved pathways, afford all the opportunities necessary for the growing of all the rock plants one wants without a rock garden, if such a feature is not appropriate or possible, and yet quite often one sees someone busily constructing a rock garden in a corner of a garden that looks so much nicer without it. When you have plucked up enough courage to ask why they are doing it, they, of course, make the obvious retort 'to grow some rock plants in it'. Poor little plants; what sins are committed in their name. It is of no use forcing a rock garden, and no need either when so often a stone retaining wall would be so much more fitting, and just as comfortable for the plants.

The wall in the picture I am sending you faces north, and it is pretty hot I can tell you! And so good old 'toughs' were used to assure the owner of successful growth, without tears. *Eriocephalus africanus* delights in the position and has been in flower continuously for months. Next to it is *Rosmarinus prostrata*. If you say this backwards you will know it is prostrate rosemary: that's an easy one. And on the corner there is that old trusty *Convolvulus mauritanicus* with its delicious little blue flowers. Whilst one would never use this in a rock garden in close proximity to smaller treasures, it is not really a nuisance in these hot positions where one must select plants that are willing to ramp a little under the trying conditions ... it is not nearly so bad as *Felecia petiolaris*!

The stone one uses for these walls is of course a matter of taste. For myself I do lean towards quite inexpensive material, that will not compete with the plants, and a stone that is rather soft in texture rather than that flint-like quality that gives such a hard angular look to a wall. Of the 'brawn' walls spattered around Melbourne sufficient has already been said, and of those with patterns of ferns (I should be, but am not, ashamed of not knowing the specific name for these markings) appearing on the stone ... well, I prefer these finger-prints of Father Time in a museum.

THE ABBREVIATED COLONNADE

What I wanted to say about colonnades was this: if you have a small garden

you may make it appear much more extensive by building a colonnade. In my dictionary a colonnade is described as 'a series of columns with entablature'. Now, the architecture of the average house of today would hardly stand the entablature, which includes an architrave, frieze and cornice. So we simplify the scheme by having just the columns supporting either a single or two beams, and this forms one of the most satisfactory supports for climbing plants, enabling you to display them in a manner unsurpassed by all other methods.

With this piece of construction you may divide one part of the garden from another without completely cutting it off, and it is looking through the columns that creates the impression of distance! It also frames little pictures of what lies beyond.

What you use for the columns depends largely upon the type of house. Sometimes just stout saplings would serve the purpose, and at others graceful and well-proportioned pillars finished with a capital would be necessary. Running parallel with a boundary 10 or more feet away from it, and with a low wall at the foot the effect is sometimes most satisfactory. I must go now. Goodbye for the present.

Edna Walling

JUNE 1, 1939

Dear Gardeners,

What magic there is in these words, 'A cottage in the country!' Instantly they conjure up something which is lovable, restful and utterly different from the houses we leave behind in the city but too often we are whisked off, full of expectation into the country and on arrival at the 'cottage' we feel slightly deflated, and with some difficulty suppress the longing to say, 'but it isn't a cottage, it's just a house; why didn't they use less money and more restraint?'

WANTED—SWEET SIMPLICITY

That the country or seaside cottage should be inexpensive seems to be an intelligent stipulation, and that it is invariably more pleasing and restful when it is inexpensive is encouragement indeed. To achieve the accommodation required at a minimum cost of construction is the desire of everyone about to build and yet it is amazing how much is often wasted in the choice of building materials, and in the intricacy of the design, resulting in a building that could never be called a cottage, and would be much more suited to the suburbs.

Here am I talking about cottages again instead of gardens! Perhaps it is the picture that is going forth with this that started me off. It seemed a good one to illustrate some ideas on country gardens. The making of country gardens seems naturally to call for the exercise of restraint, and what we should do without weathered stones, sometimes, I do not know.

One of the most encouraging things about the country is that often there are native grasses present that make the most excellent lawns, and it nearly breaks one's heart to see some people ploughing them up and spending vast sums of money in grass seed and labour, only to produce something much inferior to the lawn the native bents would have given them, and probably landing them with the labour and cost of watering that could have been avoided. By cutting, fertilising, and top-dressing many a natural sward will far surpass one that has been sown at much cost of seed and labour.

COUNTRY GARDENS

Somehow when we go to the country we do not want gardens so much as landscape. I believe in preserving as much as possible of that which is growing naturally. Hardly dare I to go to town when I have a new man in the garden for fear he 'cleans up' the bracken as a pleasant surprise for my return! Of course, it *is* difficult for them to realise that the bracken *is* as precious, nay more perhaps, than the rhododendrons of which I have so few—they are so demanding, much as I love some of the species. They don't particularly like us here, and we must needs have mountain loam conveyed to the spot, and regularly mulch them with oak leaves, and joyous as the resultant blooms may be *do* they give more pleasure than the glistening fronds of the bracken these crisp autumn mornings? I wonder. And then the frosts; who would forgo the exquisite designs of the bracken sparkling on a winter's morning? And again, there is the tea-tree. Many a clump of *Leptospermum scoparium* is doing most valuable work in my garden; here it is creating a glade; there it forms a background, and with what shall we replace it? Could we ever achieve so natural an effect again? Down in the lower regions where it is moister, *Leptospermum lanigerum*—known as the woolly tea-tree because of the soft hairs at the base of the flowers—groups itself magnificently amongst the swamp gums, and one looks down towards the meadow with a comfortable feeling of satisfaction towards Nature for making such a nice job of the planting for us. LEAVE WELL ALONE is a slogan not to be sneezed at by those with broad acres in the country, and it is amazing how much may be achieved if full advantage is taken of what grows naturally upon the property.

When we come closer to the house it is reasonable that some exotic trees and shrubs may be desired, and if the selection is careful they should harmonise with the natural landscape quite pleasingly. In the picture the little tree with some weathered stones placed about the base is a flowering apple. There is no doubt about it that these apples are better landscape blossom trees than some—the peaches, for instance. There is something about them that is more picturesque. Another tree that is simply lovely in the country garden is *Crataegus tanacetifolia*, the tansy-leaved hawthorn; the grey-green foliage and the dusky red fruits have a picturesqueness that almost leaves one breathless with delight. One or two large flat lichen-covered boulders somewhere near the foot of this little tree will make a picture that is a joy to behold the whole year around.

Beyond the flowering apple is a planting of shrubs and small trees that serve the dual purpose of providing autumn and spring colour, and of breaking the wind that sweeps towards the house from the north. spireas and viburnums that give spring bloom and autumn colour, grow in with Indian currant (*Sympthoricarpus vulgaris*), and chokeberry snuggles up against the shad bush. *Spirea multiflora arguta* should be there somewhere if I remember rightly. Do you know it? It is one of the most fascinating of the spireas, wreathed all the way down the stems in spring with its tiny flowers. Really it's a fairy shrub!

Until next month.

Edna Walling

JULY 1, 1939

Dear Gardeners,
You all know the little Japanese flowering crab apple no doubt, but some of you may not be familiar with the large fruited form of this variety, which, by the way, is botanically known as *Malus floribunda*. I happen to have a photograph of a small tree of this large fruited variety, and so will enclose it with this. By comparing the size of the fruit with the leaves you can easily

see how much bigger the berries are than those of the ordinary *floribunda*. The colour of the fruit is a beautifully clear yellow. It is worth growing for the fruit alone, but the spring picture when it is in bloom is simply exquisite! Small wonder that these dual-purpose apple trees are ousting some of those species whose short season of bloom is the one bright spot in their year. The Japanese crab is a small-growing tree that fits charmingly into the landscape towards the front of the border; it is fairyland beneath this little tree when the red buds all along the branches begin to pop open, showing their white petals in spring.

A Question about Garden Design

Once again the controversial question of formal versus informal design in gardens crops up. Someone writes me today to say, 'I don't agree with you when you say, "there is nothing more permanently satisfying than a garden designed on formal lines".' It is understandable that there is so much abhorrence of the formal garden for so exquisite in proportion and line must the design be that we very rarely see an example that is likely to move one to admiration. Then again, the planting of a formal garden can utterly ruin it. I do think this is one of the most difficult tasks of the garden designer; for to be a success the planting should be mostly informal, so that it becomes the softening influence that is so vitally necessary to the formal design.

Here and there clipped specimens will accentuate the design of course, but with great restraint must these be introduced. That the planting of a formal garden should almost entirely conceal the formality in construction in the height of the growing season, and that in winter there should still be the softening growth of evergreens to break up some of the constructional lines of walls and pergolas would seem the important points. I should say that the average formal garden is usually very much under-planted, and that when winter comes with the resultant clearance of spent annuals and the heads of the herbaceous perennials, there is a 'coldness' about the formal garden of which so many quite naturally complain. With the liberal use of trees, shrubs, and climbers this condition need never exist, and I have said that there was nothing more permanently satisfying than a garden of formal design for the reason that, however charming may be the landscape garden at the outset it is so much dependent upon those who come after one in the maintenance. We have all too many instances of how much of Guilfoyle's work in the Melbourne Botanic Gardens has been cramped, instead of being developed, through the slaughtering of the material with which he built up his pictures; some, of course, he would have granted, but for some ... ah, well!

WHERE DO THE LAURELS GO?

I believe the nurserymen sell lots and lots of kalmias every year, but where on earth do they go? It is almost impossible to imagine a more delightful evergreen of medium height than *Kalmia latifolia* for a southern aspect, and ordinary rhododendron conditions are all that it demands. What a marvellous sight it must be to see great masses of these mountain laurels lining the highways of America where they are indigenous. The glossy evergreen foliage of this four-to-five feet-high shrub makes it a comely plant the whole year round, and when the clusters of little pale pink chalices

come into bloom in spring, you wonder why in the world every garden with a suitable position for it has not several specimens of this gorgeous little plant. *Kalmia augustifolia* I found a little disappointing, but no doubt we could have placed it to much better advantage. In any case it would never do as a substitute for *latifolia*, so be warned!

A CLEMATIS TO CHERISH

If you are lucky enough to get hold of one don't neglect to find a position for *Clematis jackmanii* this planting season. It is not by any means a newcomer, but there are all too few of them about, and yet is there a summer-blooming climber that is more beautiful? Fences that have a trellis fixed to them or thick sticks of tea-tree form excellent support for these climbing plants, and when it is regularly pruned, so that it does not become an unsightly tangle, that dark-leaved honeysuckle, *Lonicera japonica*, can look simply delightful growing up the weathered grey sticks of the tea-tree.

I have just remembered that once I saw the common rosemary trained on the side of an old shed; it had reached to a height of five feet and looked perfectly sweet. This treatment seemed to display its grey-blue flowers to much better advantage than usual, moreover, it seemed to be flowering more luxuriantly.

This training of plants to walls and fences is a fascinating form of gardening, and it is very appropriate to smaller and smaller. It is amazing to find just how much one can cram into a small garden by taking advantage of every available fence and corner.

Yours, till next month,

Edna Walling

SEPTEMBER 1, 1939

Dear Gardeners,

Great activity and excitement at Sonning prevail at the moment. It is having a redwood shingle roof, the dream of many years, I don't think anything surpasses these shingles for roofing the country house. Yes, there is a certain amount of danger as regards fire, but not half as much as many suppose, for it is not nearly so inflammable as hardwood, and a fire very rarely starts in the roof. In heavily timbered country one would not use them perhaps, but having gathered up the scraps to use them in the fireplace I now know that it is not a very good burning wood! I've gone redwood mad! I would like to build a whole house of it. Imagine those delightful wide clap boards for the walls, and the nice comfortable feeling one has that it does not deteriorate, nor is it very palatable to the termite.

CULTIVATING OUR NATIVES

During a recent visit to New South Wales I met Thistle Y. Harris, the author of the recently published book, *Wild Flowers of Australia*. It was a delight to go through the bush with her, and I came back feeling more than ever that every child, and grown up, too, of course, should have this book. At all events one can easily imagine that many an overseas visitor will leave these shores armed with a copy. We do seem to have rather an unfortunate genius for propagating the least attractive of the native plants, and of allowing hundreds of treasures to go unseen in the wilds. Of course, all that can be done to protect and help their increase in the bush must be done, but one would also like to see some of the best of them more frequently propagated by enterprising nurserymen. Again and again one hears, 'I did try a few natives, but they were left on my hands', and yet I am willing to aver that the public never leaves *Prostanthera ovalifolia* (mint bush), *Eriostemon obovalis, Eriostemon myoporoides, Boronia megastigma, Baurea rubioides* (native dog rose), *Ceratopetalum gummiferum* (NSW Christmas bush), *Eugenia Luehmannii* (small-leaved lilly pilly), *Chamaelaucium uncinatum* (Geraldton wax plant), *Leptospermum rotundifolium,* and *Hardenbergia lindleyana* (Sarsaparilla) to become dead stock in the nursery.

THE OVERWHELMING DIANTHUS

What a diversity of effects one may get with the different varieties of dianthus. *Dianthus alpina,* with its bright green leaves and short-stemmed, large, pink flowers, makes a charming carpet to lay before some taller plants. Then there are those tight little grey foliaged hummocks which are types of *Dianthus arvernensis.* Idly one takes down Reginald Farrer's book, *The English Rock Garden,* and turns to dianthus, only to close it up hurriedly after one glance at their enormous numbers, and after reading again that 'it is a very confused race'. At the moment I do not feel able to cope with dianthus!

The white daphne, *D. odora alba,* which has cream rather than white flowers, fills me with immeasurable satisfaction; the substance of the blooms reminds one of the blossom of lemon trees, and how exquisitely beautiful lemon blossom can be when used for indoor decoration. We brought in a bunch the other day, cut off most of the leaves and placed it in an off-white jar, and never have we had a more satisfying picture *Viburnum tinus* (*Lauristinus*) treated similarly is extremely useful in the winter, too.

I could wish that winter sweet (*Calycanthus praecox*) would not be quite so shy with us; with most covetous eyes I look upon the sprays of butter-coloured flowers, which deck the plants in other people's gardens. So that one may cut lavish branches for the house it is wise to have several plants of this most fragrant of winter shrubs. And so that indispensable blossom tree, the flowering almond, *Prunus communis pollardii*, is of Australian origin. It needs no paean of praise from me, so well is it known, but perhaps some of you did not know that this almond-peach hybrid was raised within these shores.

Beautiful as are the hybrid crab apples I must confess to a deep regard for the common hedgerow apple, *Malus sylvestris*, for the exquisite loveliness of the blossom. How picturesque are the crab apples. It is no earthly use trying to prune them into shape, for it is characteristic for them to crisscross their branches, and except for the removal of any that are rubbing badly it is best to leave them alone.

THE NEGLECTED MAGNOLIA

Berberis rubrostilla has certainly justified its position in the garden. The leaves have coloured magnificently, and the berries are considerably larger than most of the other berberis. There are lots more than most of the other berberis. There are lots more new barberries, but this seems to be the most outstanding amongst those that we have tried here, and I do want to leave a little space to say why so few magnolias? When in bloom *Magnolia soulangiana* never fails to make one halt before the breathtaking beauty of its blooms; the single fair and mighty blossoms against the background of bare and stark grey stalks is a never-to-be-forgotten sight. They are so easily grown, demanding nothing more than a good loam and plenty of leaf mould. There are too many other varieties available to talk about them just now, but never fear, you can't go wrong with *Magnolia soulangiana*.

Yours, till next month,

Edna Walling

NOVEMBER 1, 1939

Dear Gardeners,

I'm the luckiest person in the world! I have just been asked to design a garden where lovely birches and other treasures already exist! A long time ago I planted this piece of ground when it was the lower part of a large garden, and now a house has been built upon this block, and, as luck would have it, the trees are in the happiest positions possible, and it is only a matter of a restraining hand and the most careful introduction of some very large weathered boulders, and we shall have a piece of restful landscape that should prove of much joy to the owner and those who will share it with her.

THE WELCOME DRIVE

The drive will be of limestone toppings, which is more appropriate to this informal type of design, and much more pleasing than most gravels, which are often too meticulous in texture, and too bright in colour. Little thymes and other creeping plants love wandering into this material and if they are allowed to do so the drive soon becomes a delightful piece of country roadway, contributing to the scene that will bring the country to your doorstep and make you feel at peace immediately you enter the gate.

'Coming home' is such a wonderful experience. I never cease to be thrilled when entering my own gateway (although I have done so for 20 years!) and always feel that entrance gardens should give the first sensation of rest to those returning home. There's nothing very restful about masses of annuals, conjuring up, as they do, hours of labour, and much expenditure of hard-earned cash on seed, fertilisers and water.

I do always feel that the more brilliant garden displays should, whenever possible, be kept for the rear of the house. There are, of course, those who prefer to display their horticultural powers and wares for all who pass to see; and there are those who have not thought that there are better and more interesting ways of dealing with the area between street and house than with standard roses and annuals; and to the latter may I suggest lots and lots of trees and lawn and evergreen shrubs to conceal the boundaries?

I'm rather hoping that the picture of the three birches, taken in this new garden, will break down the prejudice of some who think that trees must never be planted closely together. I have forgotten to mention this new garden is that of my sister; that is one of the reasons why I am so lucky— she couldn't very well have given the job to anyone but her own kith and kin! And yet I almost hear her say, 'Couldn't I?'

HAPPY ASSOCIATIONS

Magnolia soulangiana is looking very lovely with *Rhododendron racemosum* at its feet. I wrote to you about this magnolia quite recently; it is one of the most popular of all, and grouped with *Rhododendron racemosum* makes a charming picture, the one with its huge single blossoms on the bare stalks, half hiding the other smaller and more delicate blooms. This rhododendron is a native of north China and is one of the most distinctive of the dwarf Chinese rhododendrons. Just near this group there is a *Viburnum tinus*, one of the delightful old-fashioned English shrubs that is very much in favour for its winter blooms. Another viburnum which is particularly attractive just now is the *V. burkwoodii*, which is a hybrid; one might almost say 'by *V. carlesii* out of *V. utile*!'

The flowering fruit trees will be nearly past their prime when you read this, and their beauties are too well known to you to need much description, but I must tell you of the picture the bright crimson peach makes together with the *Prunus spinosa purpurea*. This crimson peach certainly needs toning down with something and I had to stop and admire the picture it made with a background of the delicate white flowers of *Prunus spinosa purpurea*. You may have seen the common variety of the *Prunus spinosa* in England, where it is generally known as the sloe, or as the blackthorn. Those charming hedges which so greatly enhance the beauty of the English countryside are very frequently composed of this hardy shrub.

A third attractive group is the *Forsythia aurea*, growing up behind a pear tree in full bloom. The glorious golden flowers of the forsythia with the white of the blossom are particularly lovely together. This forsythia is generally planted because of its golden foliage, but it is the particularly good deep golden flowers that justifies its planting in any garden, more than the 'golden' foliage which is really not a sufficiently clear gold to attract those who lean towards variegated and golden foliaged plants.

Yours till next month,

Edna Walling

Dear Gardeners,

It seems to be the exception rather than the rule to see flowering climbing plants that are really well managed, and this, apparently, for the reason that quite often the owners are puzzled as to the manner in which they should be pruned, and trained. Well, it is all very simple, the general rule being the same as for flowering shrubs: prune immediately after flowering. The canes to be removed are those which have just flowered; this makes room for the succeeding year's growth and prevents the plants from becoming the terrifying spectacle which results from the neglect of regular pruning. So often there is only one course to adopt after such neglect, that is to start all over again by cutting the plants almost level with the ground and dealing regularly and intelligently with the rapid growth that will spring up after this drastic treatment. You would then take each sprig which grows up from the butt and train it into the position you wish it to occupy, curtailing or removing those which prove too numerous or precocious. Of all plants that need constant and persistent damping of their ardour, climbing plants are perhaps the most demanding upon one's attention.

A CHINESE CLEMATIS

We have to thank Lady Amherst for introducing *Clematis montana* in the year 1838, for it never ceases being an ever-welcome picture in spring; the pink form, *Clematis montana rubens*, is exquisitely beautiful, but it is a pity to allow it to oust the old *montana* where space permits the planting of both.

The picture chosen for illustrating *Clematis montana* on a pergola pillar is interesting as an example of the treatment of garden steps. In this case the steps have an overhang of approximately one inch, which is appropriate to the formality of the design, but it is important to remember that this overhang is not always desirable. Sometimes when the steps are informal, such an overhang may appear quite incongruous and absurd, and it is the observance of these small matters of construction that is so important to the finished design. I have observed with much interest how steps have so frequently proved the downfall and confusion of those who build gardens. They are more important than may at first be supposed. They should not merely be treated as a means of connecting one grade with another, but should also be considered as an aesthetic feature of no mean importance. For example, I recently saw a small set of semi-circular steps that had been built with an overhang, which gave them a ridiculous degree of importance; a great measure of improvement was effected by rebuilding them without the overhang. As a guide it may be taken that small steps are generally best built as simply as possible, preserving any extra formality produced by the overhang for the more magnificent and dignified designs.

What a romantic life is that of the plant hunter, even if his work so often goes unsung. With what infinite satisfaction must he sit back in old age and see the plants which he has introduced become more and more important to the making of present day gardens. There is much that a plant hunter could do in Australia, in the popularising of many of the treasures that abound on these shores. *Eriostemon lanceolata* with its huge fresh pink buds and star-shaped flowers on the Hume Highway made us quite forget that we were bound for Melbourne in one day when returning from Sydney in early October. What a plant for roadside planting! In America it would be grown by the million for such a purpose. I wonder, are we someday likely to awake to the possibilities of such wonderful plant material in this country? It is to be hoped that the very practical fact that all forms of ground cover are the most economical means of the prevention of erosion will soon be universally recognised by those who are responsible for dealing with this very important subject.

THE FREEDOM OF THE GARDEN

Hound's tongue (*Cynoglossum amabile*) came and went somewhat rapidly, surely. It sprang into popularity with its exquisite blue flowers, but because of the rate with which it grew and its capacity for sowing itself in unexpected places it seems to have become less desired.

Strange isn't it, this objection to plants that readily sow themselves about the garden? One hears so many say, 'Foxgloves are such a nuisance; they come up all over the garden', and they do in mine, but never yet have there been too many; never yet enough! And with foxgloves it is much fun:

they are sticklers about the 'Rotation of crops!' If you have had a marvellous show in one corner of the garden one year, you need not imagine a similar display there the following year; for they will most probably have marched off to another part, and where you had never thought of planting them they will quietly send up their little spires and say, 'Here we are! How do we look in this setting?' Of course, you cannot expect to have all these delightful surprises in a garden that is regularly spaded over the minute some crop is past its best. A garden should, I always feel, be just a little too big to keep the whole cultivated, then it gives it a chance to go a little wild in spots, and make some pictures for you. Hand weeding is the only safe way to deal with these wild bits, carefully removing weeds only, and allowing the self-sown foxgloves, cynoglossums, columbines, sweet williams, and forget-me-nots to fight it out among themselves. Try it!

Edna Walling

FEBRUARY 1, 1940

Dear Gardeners,
You will think I am always harping on the subject of steps in the garden: well, this time the 'come back' is due to a photograph I secured in a garden the other day which will serve as an illustration of how a picture may be made if a little imagination is exercised when planning the ascent from one level to another. You can't have a picture of the flight of brick steps that nearly took the place of the ones illustrated, for the obvious reason that the plan for them faded into the limbo of the forgotten, never—let us hope—to be resuscitated, and put into action anywhere else!

Really, some of the steps appearing in gardens are only fit for the backest of backyards. I can hear you ask, 'Why even there?', and am adding hastily, 'Behind factories', only to hear you repeat, 'And why even there?' You are quite right, boiled down it would almost seem that money, the thought that must go into its expenditure, the materials, and the labour for construction, should never be expended in any way that does not produce something good to look upon— wherever that is humanly possible.

THOSE 'ADJECTIVE' ANDROMEDAS

Afraid I'm getting the collecting habit: I find myself collecting andromedas. This morning I noticed *A. speciosa* in flower. What darling little waxen white bells! But it was for the autumn foliage that it was chiefly acquired, for it is so lovely then. Were you to come and ask me, 'Where is your collection of andromedas?' humbly would I take you round to a sheltered corner by the wood shed, where we have found suitable homes for *A. speciosa*, *A. catesbaei*, and *A. formosa*. Then to the nursery where the remainder still grow patiently in pots. *A. polifolia* is down in the rock garden hanging on to life. I must remember to put some peat moss round it to give it a cooler root run. (How we are going to miss peat moss!)

But don't collect andromedas: you will go crazy never knowing whether you are possessing andromedas, cassandra, cassiope, lyonia, leucothoe, zenobia, *Oxydendron pieris* or enkianthus. Yes, they are all synonymous; isn't it infuriating?

PRUNING WISTERIA

The pruning of wisteria is a mystery to many and yet it is very simple and very important if you would avoid the terrifying spectacle a really lusty wisteria can become. In a few words, this is the procedure which will make your wisteria flower more freely and keep it within bounds. Shorten the side shoots in summer to six inches; in winter cut them back to two or three buds. This practice helps the development of spurs—the short shoots which bear blossom buds. The leading shoots are only pruned in summer when the wisteria has filled the space allotted to it.

SUBSTITUTE FOR GRAVEL

Some of you may have discovered what a marvellous substitute for gravel may be found in limestone toppings, but it is much more than a substitute for by its use you may have a satisfactory driveway without any foundation material at all. When the driveway is newly laid the car will probably make indentations, but all that is necessary is to have some extra toppings on hand with which to fill in the holes, and in time it will become perfectly firm and level. I surfaced a drive with limestone toppings at Heidelberg about four years ago, where the house was quite 50 or 60 feet from the road, and the slope down to the garage was three to four feet in the 50, and other than one long one at the garage entrance, no catchpits have been necessary.

We were just about to put one in on either side, midway between the house and the gateway, but as funds were so limited we decided to try it out without the catchpits first, and these still stand, with only the long pit at the garage, and the driveway is in perfect condition!

SIEVING NOW UNNECESSARY

It is very interesting to learn that the practice of working all loam, for potting purposes, through a sieve, discarding the rough stuff has been given up by many who now cut up the rough fibres with a pair of scissors, replacing them in the potting soil. (Ye Gods!) Close packing caused by frequent watering prevents quick drainage, and a ready influx of fresh air, therefore mortar rubble, crushed bricks, stones of various sizes and coarse quartz sand have proved of benefit in pots. It seems that sieving, therefore, has become an unnecessary labor where potting soil is concerned.

Nierembergia hippomanica will be in full flower by the time you receive this. This little gem of blue loveliness is remarkably slow in becoming more familiar in gardens. Time and again *N. azurea* is sent out for *N. hippomanica* and it is worse than useless as a substitute; for the former grows to a thin uninteresting bush of three feet or more with washed-out mauve flowers, whereas *N. hippomanica* is a round, compact, little plant of 12 inches, smothered with little, clear, blue cup-shaped flowers. Do try and get it—it will make your mouth water.

Yours,

Edna Walling

MARCH 1, 1940

Dear Gardeners,
There is no doubt about the bad effect of petrol fumes upon plant life, as I have just learned to my sorrow. I planted an *Oxydendron arborea* in the most desirable place in the whole of Sonning's six acres, only to discover that it was within smelling distance of the electric light engine and it is showing its resentment in no uncertain manner! Really it is very trying.

Is anything more exasperating and more utterly stupid than to walk around a property with a pot plant in one hand and a spade in the other? You feel such an ass, because you know you should not have brought the jolly thing without first thinking out its possible location. It's of no use persuading yourself that 'There must be room, why we have six acres', for in all that six acres there may not be a square yard left that is suitable for that particular plant.

An Arboreal Error

Sometimes it's a positive blessing when a plant dies, and here's an instance. Algeranoff of the Russian Ballet (you may remember him as one of the sisters in *Cendrillon*) arrived at Sonning some time ago and tripped lightly up to the house. On the spur of the moment we decided, 'He must plant a tree', Hurriedly we looked around for something suitable and found a *Magnolia grandiflora* in a pot. Equally hurriedly (and here lies the tragedy) we looked about for a spot to plant it. I bow my head in shame when I admit that we found 'an open space' and planted it there. That little plant lived long enough to be a constant reproach to me and every time I saw it, it seemed to say 'You call yourself a landscape designer and you stick me out here in the middle of what should always have been an open grassy glade!' Well, we faithfully watered it through that devastating drought, but it needed more than moisture on its roots, and in the end the hot searing winds mercifully drew a curtain over this arboreal error, and the gods have indeed been kind, for Algeranoff is here again and this time there shall be no mistake.

On Buying a Country Property

It's not exactly gardening talk but I feel I must tell you something that may one day be of value to those of you who may not already know it. When you are looking at a country property, with a view to purchasing it, remember that when the light is behind—that is when the sun is in your eyes—it gives a much more attractive appearance to the prospect. MORAL: if you visit a place in the morning and are very attracted to it, go back again and see how you like it in the afternoon light. We walked over a beautiful hill overlooking Mooroolbark the other evening and it was so lovely I wished I were a millionaire. 'And if I were', I thought, 'I'd probably come and see it again in the morning. Millionaires always seem to be more wary than the impecunious!'

CUT FLOWERS FOR THE HOUSE

When I do the flowers a most annoying little 'titter' goes round, but I don't care. I'm rather pleased with the bowl on the cedar table today. And at last this brings me to gardening (I've probably brought myself to the Editor's W.P.B. long before this!) Now for the contents of the bowl. There's a shaggy-petalled shasta daisy or two, some pink milfoil; a few pieces of *Trachelium*, (Mary d-e-a-r, will you please look up the common name for *Trachelium*? I think it's liverwort, or bladderwort—oh no, that's that lovely little bog *Utricularia-dichotoma* we found in the Strathbogie ranges. I always add dear when I want something done that I know I should get up and do myself!); a sprig of aster 'King George', that most delightful of all dwarf perennial asters; three heads of different coloured perennial asters; and three heads of different coloured perennial phlox, one of which is the soft mauve celeste, another a mauve pink, and the other cherry pink (sorry I haven't the names of the last two). There's a little scrap of a soft biscuit hollyhock, and another piece of the deepest cherry red, which was stuck in as an afterthought and which has enriched the bowl immeasurably. In addition to the penstemons, the pale pink spikes of a *Primulinum gladioli*, the perennial asters, and the yellow milfoil, there are one or two lesser-known flowers which are invaluable for such collections: *Campanula latifolia*, for instance. What a delight this pale blue perennial can be: and *Achillea grandiflora*. I doubt if this is its correct name for I have never been able to trace it since it was sent to me from New Zealand under that name some years ago. The individual flowers of this lovely white milfoil are much longer than any other variety known to me, and the large flat heads of this variety are simply perfect for these mixed bowls. Outside the back door there is a group of *Trachelium* and *Achillea grandiflora* with a few self-sown pale blue lobelias at their feet. A plant of *Penstemon hirsutus* is throwing up its flowers and spikes and promises to be in bloom in time to group itself with the others. There is a tall blue *scuttelaria* which is useful for cutting too; but there, I must leave this question of cut flowers to someone who knows more about it.

BIRDS' BATHS

I thought you would like this little picture of two mushrooms: one of which forms a bird's bath. Where there are cats it is safer to have the bath off the ground, and these mushrooms certainly have proved very satisfactory. They are so easy to place in either formal or informal gardens. The birds like it best when there is only a little water in the top and then they can bathe delightedly without fear of getting out of their depth. I've noticed there is always more excitement round the bath when there is only a little water than when the bath has just been filled. I'll have to stop now, I seem to have been writing for a long time, so until next month—Good gardening,

Edna Walling

PS—It's throatwort!

APRIL 1, 1940

Dear Gardeners,
I've been sent up to my attic to work! It's no hardship—I found my camera up here and so I've been shooting pictures from the windows. If they're any good I'll send you them one day. It's such a wonderful place from which to view the effects—and the defects—of one's landscape.

SHADE TREES FOR LAWNS

The objection of plane trees as shade trees in gardens on the score of their being used so extensively for street planting can be ruled out by the fact that they are so mutilated on streets that they become recognisable only by their bark and leaves! Allowed to grow in their natural form there are few trees more delightful under which to sit. The plant has all the points a lawn tree should have; an interesting bole; foliage which is not too dense, and which will let a little sunlight through; quick growth, in spite of the competition of the grass roots right up to the bole of the tree, and an immunity to disease. As a courtyard tree the plane is superb, but never, never, never, should it be hand-pruned. If you do it you will lose the delicacy of the smaller branchlets, and do dreadful things to the winter effect of its natural form.

With astonishing frequency one hears the remark, 'Do you think it ought to be pruned?' (they even say 'topped' sometimes!) And on receiving an emphatic denial they will say, 'But the ones in the streets are.' 'Ah, that's because there are wires to be cleared.' 'But there aren't any wires in this street!' And so you see what an insidious habit this disfigurement of trees can become and what a sad example it sets to others.

Welcome Plants

Last night I had dinner with a charming person who shared with me the secret delight of growing creeping rampageous plants! And we fell to talking of all those plants of which earnest gardeners will adjure one 'not to have them on the place!' But think what we'd miss! Not to have that darling old pink milfoil (*Achillea millefolium roseum*) or bugle flower (*Ajuga reptans atropurpurea*) or penny royal (*Mentha pulegium*) or Michaelmas daisies (perennial asters)! Why, they are all indispensable in a mixed bowl for indoor decoration, not to mention their value in the garden. I can't quite see the objection there is to digging them up each winter and planting just a little bit back. The only difference I can see is that you get next year's picture for nothing! If you drag out annuals and replace them with some more annuals there is always some expenditure attached, even if you save the seed and raise them yourself. These perennials are so extremely easy to manage, really. In the case of milfoil (that is, *Achillea millefolium*), even the smallest piece will grow into a lusty plant the first season, and freely produce its flat heads of tiny cerise and white eye flowers. When winter comes all that is necessary is to take a heavy garden fork and loosen the ground around the plant (taking care not to break off any more shoots than possible) then thrust the fork into the centre of the plant and lift it out holus-bolus—in light soil it will come out in one entire mat! Destroy all but a few of the outside shoots, cutting these off the parent plant in lengths of six to nine inches. Two or three shoots together in the hole when planting back is a wise measure, and next summer you will have joy again from this old-fashioned herb.

Other achilleas are quite unlike *A. millefolium* in their habit of growth and if lifting and dividing is neglected they will not invade the garden as *A. millefolium* will do. *A. Eupatorium* grows into a compact clump, with rapidity certainly, but never does it wander. It has large flat heads of yellow flowers and grows to three or four feet in height in good soil. It is an excellent perennial, not grown as often as one would expect. In winter lift the clump and chop it up into pieces of about three or four inches square and discard all but a few pieces, for the average garden is not extensive enough for too many of those strong-coloured and lusty-growing perennials. You can, with perfect safety, pass this plant on to your most sceptical gardening friend. *A. tomentose* is the dearest little low-growing, yellow flowered, grey-leaved perennial, and the white form of *millefolium* is rather charming, too, and it doesn't seem to ramp as much as its pink cousin.

An Obliging Campanula

Looking out of my window I can see a clump of the loveliest blue spikes. It's a self-sown plant of *Campanula celtidifolia.* Yesterday I noticed that a few plants had also sprung up in the pathway in the semi-shade, hard against the potting shed wall. Every year this campanula delights us by appearing in odd and unexpected places. I do hope we never get the garden so tidy that it doesn't get a chance to go on putting on the little 'turn' for us. I believe it is closely allied to *C. lactiflora,* which is a treasure of a perennial. *Celtidifolia* is taller, with larger individual flowers, and coarser and rougher leaves. It really won't ever be a nuisance, so don't be afraid to plant it just because I've been talking about rampageous plants. You will be able to gather lots of seed from this campanula, and it would make delightful small Christmas presents.

Yours till next month,

Edna Walling

M A Y ,   1 9 4 0

Dear Gardeners,

Here's some really good news for you, particularly those of you who live in
the country. We seem to have struck the ideal grass for country lawns; when
it is watered through the summer it produces the most delightfully soft
velvety sward, but when water is not available it will withstand the most
severe drying off through the summer and spring into life again
immediately the autumn rains appear.

I think you will agree that the last two seasons have been the most severe
test any lawns could possibly have: even where turf is watered the lawns have
suffered severely, and yet this grass has survived with no artificial watering at
all! It is an agrostis with underground stems and has been named *Agrostis
palustris* and also alseabra, 'neither of which it is', quoth a Melbourne
seedsman. Anyone who has had anything to do with grasses knows how
difficult it is to determine some of them, and so we have got into the habit of
assuming the first name this bent was given by local authority (Melbourne
Botanic Gardens), namely *A. palustris*, though anything less marsh-like than
the conditions under which it seems to thrive one could hardly imagine!

All I can say is that if you want a lovely even sward of velvety grass, either
in the suburbs or in the country, and are fortunate enough to get hold of the
roots of this bent it would be worth about a pound a sack. You see you have

no bother with birds eating the seed, no worry that the sun is too hot for the newly germinated seed; you just chop it into the ground and give it a thorough soaking and nothing will hold it back.

SAND FOR TOP DRESSING

Some of you may not know that pure, washed sand is one of the best top dressings for lawns. It encourages quick growth of new roots just in the same manner as it does when striking cuttings of trees and shrubs; it trickles down to the roots of the grass more readily than loam and does not consolidate or cake. Having no fertilising qualities, however, it is necessary, or wise, at least to follow the sand with a dressing of blood and bone manure to feed the newly formed roots, even though the sand does produce a wonderful color in the turf, which sometimes deceives one into believing that no further treatment is necessary.

Anyway, enough of lawns, although I have forgotten to tell you that it was on a poor shallow soil, not a deep rich loam, that the agrostis has proved such a success; I feel that half my troubles as a designer of some country gardens are now over!

THE BEAUTIFUL BIRCH

The photograph I am sending to you with this letter is a corner of the Methodist Ladies' College, Kew. I selected it to show you what a delightful effect a two-stemmed birch can give. When such a young tree is developing I am always terrified someone will come along and cut off one of the leaders. Luckily, this one escaped.

If the nurseryman did not go along his rows of trees trimming off such growths he might find himself possessed of a stock that would not be at all appealing to the average purchaser of trees, but when you do find a birch with two or three stems, and you have a suitable position for it, guard it zealously and let no assiduous gardener 'trim it up a bit' for you.

The purple-leaved form of the silver birch has not gained much popularity, which is understandable, for it is inclined to be rather thin in habit, but it is to be hoped that it will not altogether fade out of existence here, for there are positions where it is the ideal tree. It is one that I would always use on the sheltered side of the house wherever possible. In such a position it will develop its foliage more freely, and its thin habit is rather desirable on the shady side of a building, where trees are needed more for softening walls than to provide shade; the sparse foliage will let in more light than many other species do. The branches of this birch are particularly black, though the trunk itself takes on the same silvery tones of the silver birch as the tree matures. The tracery of these black branches against a white plastered wall in winter is picture enough to warrant the planting of this purple-leaved birch. That was an excellently written article on topiary in the March number. Those of you who did not get the March *Home Beautiful* should certainly try to get one at once.

BUILDING SMALL GARDENS

I've come to the conclusion that very small gardens have to be *constructed*, that is, the need for constructional features such as low walls, wall fountains, steps and pools is more vitally important than in an expansive garden where long vistas, variety in foliage texture, wide sweeps of lawn and grassy glades are more easily achieved. A small area simply *must* be more elaborated—not elaborate individual features, but designed to produce a variety of pictures that costly town properties should provide. It's all very well to lay out a simple rustic little garden that is a delight while it is young and fresh, but the time comes when such a garden 'goes off' and it is then that one looks around for another scheme that will never let you down. After the architect and the interior decorator have finished with the client, the garden designer starts the battle of trying to achieve a fitting garden for the existing exterior and interior with what is left of the funds—and the client! The client is still there, but the funds, alas!

Yours till next month.

Edna Walling

JUNE 1, 1940

Dear Gardeners,

If a census of plants of that glorious climber, *Ampelopsis henryana*, planted in the newer gardens of today were taken, I believe it would reveal surprisingly low figures. Of course, at this time of the year it catches the eye most perhaps, and yet the beauty of its leaf form and the strange greyish-green streaks on the soft green foliage in summer, make it well worth growing even if it did not colour so marvellously at the fall of the year. I know no climber that will grace a piece of architecture more beautifully; it has characteristics that make it peculiarly appropriate on either formal or informal stonework. You know, of course, that ampelopsis is the botanic name for a Virginia creeper; however, *A. henryana* is unlike *A. veitchii* (the better-known species) in the form of the leaf, which is bolder, and in the colour of the foliage which is a darker green with the greyish splashes I have already mentioned.

POT-BOUND BEAUTY

The oak-leaved hydrangea, *Hydrangea quercifolia*, has put on the most wonderful 'turn' for us this autumn; it is still in a pot, which is a fact to be wary of, for some plants do that! The restricted area of the pot seems to

encourage autumn leaf colouring; in fact, so often has it happened here, and so often have we been able to bring glorious pieces of leaf colour into the house, or on to the porches, from amongst the plants in the nursery waiting to be planted out into the garden, that I'm inclined to think it an idea to be considered. In future, when I see something that takes my eye in a nursery I shan't look at it in a deedy fashion, calculating where on earth it could be planted and snugly muttering, 'It's only because it's in a pot that it's colouring so exquisitely'. No, I shall snatch it up before the nurseryman has a chance to say, 'Sorry, that is our only stock plant', or some other thing that always sends one down to the depths of despair.

Apart from the possibility of achieving more brilliant colouring by keeping the plants in pots, and the joy of being able to move them about where they may be most enjoyed at the moment, I'm of the opinion that a lot of horticultural breach-of-promise cases could be avoided if other treasures were kept in pots. Instead of planting out a particular pet, pot it on into a slightly larger pot where it will be safer than out in the open garden where there are so many things abroad capable of violating its virgin beauty! In this way you soon find yourself in possession of a most enchanting family. Yes, it's a sign of old age ... pot plants and such like! Well, it's very nice this business of growing old, full of delightful discoveries. But what a long way I have wandered from the oak-leaved hydrangea!

GROUNDLINGS

We have been potting on the *Leptospermum rupestre*. Strange that all native plants seem to resent being pot-bound more than exotic plants, which will remain in pots too small for them for an amazing length of time without becoming sickly specimens. This little creeping tea-tree is certainly running true to form; the opinion was expressed that it might not remain procumbent when it came down from the mountain tops, but it couldn't hug the ground more tightly! I leapt upon a little matt-like plant in the bush the other day (metaphorically speaking) in the vicinity of Lower Plenty, and to my joy discovered that it was rooting down wherever the slender branches extended and touched the ground. I have since been told it is *Pultenaea pendunculata* or matted bush pea. These native ground covers should prove of great importance one day when an appreciation of their inestimable value in the prevention of erosion and in the intelligent improvement of the barren roadside of our highways is more generally apparent.

A NATIVE GARDEN

We have just made a remarkable discovery, and it is one that might easily happen to anyone of you who have a few broad acres somewhere around Melbourne. Down in the northwest corner of the Bickleigh Bale Village there are three blocks that have been left because they are lower-lying than the rest of the land; life is so full of a number of things that I had not given the matter any thought until one of the Village folk remarked, 'I love that corner, why don't you clear it so that we can enjoy the grassy slope'. Always eager for any excuse to escape from the office on the plea of 'going to see how they are getting on', I took the advice and, lo and behold, a careful survey revealed a delightful natural landscape garden made up of woolly grey tea-tree, white swamp gums, blackwoods, and the black tea-tree. Glades have been cut through where the tea-tree was excessive; picturesque old clumps of both the woolly and the prickly tea-tree have been left and brought into view by clearing away the spindly young brush around them, and now, with not one penny spent on plants and very little on labour, we have opened up one of the most restful landscape gardens anyone could wish for the setting of a country home; grass could roll right up to the very doors and windows. This I always feel is the ideal setting for the people who come to the country to rest, not to garden; it can be so distressing to sit on the porch and look out upon ground covered with jobs you should be doing instead of reading that book, or dreaming those dreams!

Yours, etc.,

Edna Walling

D E C E M B E R ,   1 9 4 0

Dear Gardeners,
If my letters have been missed one half as much as I have missed writing them to you I shall be more than satisfied! All the work that has interrupted the regularity of these effusions is now completed, and I am very glad for I've been literally aching to get back to the typewriter; every day something crops up that makes one murmur, 'I must remember to tell them about that'.

An Unplanned Border

For instance, into quite a small new border made at Sonning last winter I crammed a miscellaneous collection of plants with little or no thought for picture-making. It was just a convenient place to plant a lot of things that had been in pots quite long enough; and if someone brought me a plant that went in, too! It was like some people's curries, and it has turned out just as well!

I think the loveliest little bit is the piece that is in the semi-shade; here is a saxifrage of the London Pride type covered with soft sprays of tiny pink-tinged white flowers, thrown up on nine-inch stems from amongst the glossy deep green rosettes of foliage.

Next to it is a plant of auricula of the most exquisite shade of faded mauve or amethyst. There is nothing more like old faded velvet than these auriculas, is there? They come forth in such glorious colours. I don't know why I added a *Penstemon heterophyllus* in this shady spot. Anyway, it was an extremely lucky shot for it has bloomed more prolifically, and more vividly than it ever has before at Sonning (moral: plant in semi-shade). As most of you will probably know it is one of the best low-growing blue perennials, with a tinge of pink on the back of the petals that is very pleasing. There is another blue penstemon in this border which is much taller—about two to two-and-a-half feet—namely, *P. hirsutis*. I nearly went crazy with delight on first seeing it in Hobart, and with difficulty refrained from hugging the rather austere gardener who gave me some seed! A herbaceous border without it is like a garden without a tree to me now. The blue is soft and ethereal, and it is a sturdy, upright-growing plant that seems to have no particular whims.

As a ground cover in front of the saxifrage and auricula, *Veronica bidwillii* is ramping away happily. You know that you must watch this little fellow, don't you? No, it doesn't become a nuisance; on the contrary it is liable to disappear, so it is wise to be sure to have at least two plants always in the garden, and frequently to propagate it by planting out rooted pieces in the autumn, or early spring. An equally satisfactory little ground cover with similar characteristics is *Raoulia tenuicaulis*, but whereas *V. bidwillii* has tiny rich and shiny green foliage, raoulia has silvery-grey foliage, and is even more likely to flee your garden. You'll miss it when once you have enjoyed this little carpeter, so when it has spread sufficiently get to work with your pointed trowel, and plant two or three small clumps about the garden, to insure against its loss.

THE FOXY FOXGLOVE

Iris germanica, variety *Alta californica*, was stuffed into the warmer part of this border and its towering spikes of yellow blooms have been simply glorious, with a creamy white foxglove which came uninvited. Really, for gatecrashing commend me to foxgloves! They do amuse me. They just make up their minds and off they go to some spot in the garden, perhaps to some corner you have not had time to think about (and how one loves them for that alone), or perhaps into a border where you had quite different ideas. You can imagine them forming fours and marching off to some fairy parade ground they have planned to invade. They did that to a patch of ground below the attic window that I had tightly packed with all sorts of little rock treasures. Four sturdy fellows came and took up their quarters there, and every time I weeded that patch they were all but pulled up, but they wheedled and wheedled, and so they remained. I explained that I'd have to remove their lower leaves if they started to smother the little plants, to which they had no objection. Now they are saying, 'You see what a lovely picture we are giving you whilst you are having your shower in the bathroom, you can't see the littler plant you made such a fuss about—except from upstairs'. 'Yes, but,' I pleaded, 'they look exquisite from up there—you look a bit funny seen from above!' I've taken a picture of this invasion, but it's not ready yet. Watch for it!

ALONG THE ROADSIDE

My friends are apt to say, 'Let's have a little harping', when I start off on the subject of roadside planting. Well, it does make one sick to see some highway planting schemes when you think of the beautiful native trees we have, and the glorious samples of natural grouping that exist for us to copy. I don't think anyone can deny that the keynote to the successful planting of Australian highways is to recreate the best of what already exists. I could scream when I see one golden poplar, one grevillea, one golden poplar, one grevillea for miles over hill and dale. What is the alternative you may ask? Well, in the first place between townships informal grouping is more restful and more appropriate than specimen trees planted at regular intervals. Secondly, blackwoods in the hollows, and native cypress (*Callitris*) and other natives that thrive on the more arid high places, will provide a more satisfying picture to overseas visitors and Australians alike, than will the unimaginative planting of exotic trees mixed up with a few natives, for all the world as though we were almost ashamed of our native plants! But there I am giving you the very meat of an article yet to be written on this most important subject of Highway Planting. Never mind, you will all be good champions of the cause one day, I'm quite sure. And who knows, one day we may hear that the authorities that be have decided to go into the subject thoroughly, taking a leaf out of the Americans' book, developing a Highway Planting scheme that will not be the haphazard thing it is today, but a comprehensive and well thought-out scheme calculated to be beyond the reproach of anyone. It will be music indeed ... it would be like listening to a glorious symphony to hear of the unfoldment of a beautiful roadside planting scheme. What a task—what a glorious task! Advance Australia, and all that sort of thing!

One thing we gardeners must always remember is that the secret in all landscape work, whether it be the tiniest plot or the open highway is to conceal one's hand. Success is only ours when the finished job looked as though it had 'just growed'.

Yours until next month without fail!

Edna Walling

PS—There you are, I knew I'd do it! I've over-shot my space by a full page—however, perhaps the Editor will spare the space since it's a sort of 'reunion' letter.

(If Garden Lovers will turn over the leaf they will find that he has spared the space—Ed., *H.B.*)

JANUARY, 1941

Dear Gardeners,

Really, the Editor is very trying! I was just about to tell you such a lot of things I'd thought of since last writing when the telephone rang ...! 'I want you to tell them something about some stone work this month', came the request in dulcet tones. Me, very meekly, (I always console myself with that promise that we shall inherit the earth): 'Very well, Mr Editor'. But I'm going to tell you this first in case the type won't stop when it smells the stones.

FIRST AID IN THE HERBACEOUS BORDER

When I first set forth on this career of being a maker of gardens I put in two years of maintenance work (ugh!), and amongst the many ways in which I irritated those who employed me, the one thing that made them positively claw the air was the convenient blindness with which I approached all plants that needed staking. One of my 'dear' clients just couldn't recommend me to an inquiring friend because of this little peccadillo which I have carried with me all down the years.

... But is my own herbaceous border beraggled because of plants that sprawl? No, on the contrary, if a spray so much as leans one degree further over than I think fit and proper in perennial plants, back it goes without the slightest delay in action. None of your 'I must do that tomorrow' methods persist in this particular spot, and now I'll tell you how this marvellous reform came about. Being unable to withstand any longer the accusing fingers that pointed at me every time I walked down the herbaceous borders, I called up what inventive powers I had and set my man to work one wet day cutting No. 8 fencing wire into 20-inch and 30-inch lengths. The top of these we turned over and twisted round, allowing just sufficient gap for the stalk of a perennial aster, phlox, or penstemon to pass by. It was then only necessary to push one of these stakes in alongside any stalk that needed the support. This proved only about 50 per cent efficient; the wind would sometimes blow some of the stems out of the slot, and I still found it necessary to do some tying, and there was the rub. But wait, what should I behold on one shopping expedition but a packet marked 'plant supports'. This contained some rings made of fine wire, and cut so that they could be opened. When it comes to plant supports I'll try anything once, and so I took the plunge. When you walk into my herbaceous borders now you will see a bundle of the aforementioned wire stakes under the rosemary hedge, and you will also see one of them stuck in the ground with a supply of wire rings hanging on the top. Isn't that service for you? All I have to do is to place a stake in the position the wayward stalk is to assume in future, wrap the little ring around it and push the ends together, lapping them over a little of course. The leaves on the stalk prevent the ring from slipping down.

I'm not so sure that I agree with that maxim that 'the secret of life is not to do what one likes, but to try and like what one has to do'. I'm going on hating some of the things I have to do and see what else happens!

WHAT NOT TO DO WITH ROCKS

Now stones ... what on earth shall I say about stones? Well, first I will enclose a picture of a rock garden which was built by a man called Stones. You can say what you like about it, he won't hear you, but I think it is rather lovely and hope you will too.

Ah! It's just occurred to me what a lot could be said about what *not* to do with stones. Here are a few don'ts for instance. Don't put stones all round your garden beds if it can possibly be avoided. In exceptional cases stones set in the ground so that the top of them runs along level with, but not higher than, the bed which they retain will not look amiss if you are satisfied that it is the best solution of the problem. But remember, many a paved pathway has been ruined in effect by edging it with stones. The fact that the earth will trickle on to the paving for a little while until the edging plants have grown together, is insufficient reason for a piece of construction that destroys the quietness of the garden design.

ROCKERIES AND ROCK GARDENS

You will have read in every modern book on rock gardens of any worth that the use of lots of smallish stones piled together is certainly a 'rockery,' but will never be a Rock Garden. That the stones must be boulders that have lain on the surface and became weathered is obvious to all who appreciate the difference. The possibilities in any ordinary suburban backyard are simply immense when you begin to consider the idea of creating a bit of natural landscape therein.

But what has this to do with stones, you may be asking? Quite a lot, really, for I have found that in landscape gardening a few weathered boulders, especially those that are large and somewhat flat, will give stability to a design that might otherwise be rather dull. That sounds rather technical, it would have been better had I said 'naturalness' instead of 'stability', perhaps. In front of a tree and shrub group there will often be a bare patch of ground that somehow spoils the picture. Instead of looking round for some plant that will successfully clothe the earth, try using a large stone. Perhaps even two stones may be used without fear of a messy effect. Of course, if this is done all over the garden, it—the garden—will look as though it is suffering from an attack of hives! Like most other things, it is all a matter of knowing when to stop. Stones in some people's hands would be like a pot of paint in a woman's. So don't ever be tempted to 'use the stones up'. It is much better to store any surplus ones in some corner for future use should occasion arise, as it is almost sure to sooner or later.

Do you know I am thinking of doing my future garden-building with a blackboard and a projector! Yes, the more I think of it the more fascinating the idea becomes. 'Short Cuts for Garden Makers' sort of thing. When you've been doing a job for 20 years, it's time one got to work with a piece of chalk and some film methinks. So perhaps, in the near future there may be a little knot of people gathered together somewhere in the city o' afternoons and evenings, thrashing out the various aspects of garden-building, or perhaps E.W. will be sitting in a solitary state because no-one else has thought it a good idea! Oh! dash, I'd forgotten all about those beastly stones again, and there is one thing about stone walls that I must mention. It's about the joints. You know its not *always* best to rake out the joints. A very soft and pleasing effect is given when the mortar is brought out flush with the face of the stone. This tends to reduce the proportion of stone and, incidentally, the severity; it is in fact like a cross between a stone wall and a plastered wall, I think you'd like it. When the mortar is partly dry it is rubbed over with a piece of sacking to remove any trowel marks. If the joints are 'tuck pointed' you will cruel the whole thing of course.

And so goodbye,

Edna Walling

FEBRUARY, 1941

Dear Gardeners,
Yes, *Hesperis matronalis*! I've just been reading about it in an English magazine ... had forgotten all about it. In the most mysterious way a plant of it bloomed in one of the funny little bits of garden I seem to have acquired all around this domicile. This glorious head of soft mauve flowers on a stalk about three feet-six high just appeared; it looked somewhat like

a perennial phlox, but I was told it was 'sweet rocket', or hesperis, etc., etc. Seed is available here, I believe, but I hope you have better luck than mine, for although I have managed to raise the plants all right, we just never seemed to get the plants up to the flowering stage, or if we did, they were such a poor representation of the former beauty that walked in uninvited that we gave it up in despair. However, I am going to try again and I do hope some of you will as well! Perhaps we shall be more successful now that I have made a discovery! Really, gardening is thrilling. There's not one moment of boredom for those who love their gardens, only never, never enough time to do all the exciting things there are to do.

I really think that all gardeners should drive utility trucks instead of sedans! Then we would always be ready for any emergency. We wouldn't have to come home without that load of cow manure a friendly farmer would be only too pleased to let us have; we wouldn't have to turn a reluctant back upon that marvellous river sand; we wouldn't have to leave those plants to the tender (?) mercies of the railways and the carriers. (No, I shouldn't have put that interrogation mark in, for I never cease to marvel at the little damage that plants do suffer at their hands, but it is the occasional delay that irritates.)

And after all this preliminary canter, let's have the discovery. Well, here it is—GRIT. 'Thou shalt not covet', I know, but when you see plants growing at the rate they grow in the garden of one of my friends, it does make you want to back your truck in and cart some of the soil home. It doesn't look anything marvellous, but there is coarse grit or sand running all through it and that is the secret of the growth, I believe. It means that the roots have a free root run. The soil is similar in texture to that in which cuttings readily strike, and you all know that that must be the very reverse to a sticky, close soil. And so when there is a plant that is a little difficult in future it shall be treated to a few handfuls of very coarse-washed sand mixed with the soil in which it is to be planted. I've been using this sand to top-dress any special rock plant in pots, too, and they seem to love it. It prevents the ground from becoming caked on the top, acts as a safe mulch (that is one that will not retain too much moisture around the necks of the plants) and retards the growth of weeds also. Finally, it certainly sets the little plants off rather well. I do think most of the rock plants that we like to have in pots, so that we can move them around and enjoy them at close quarters, need to have the soil covered with either limestone screenings or coarse sand; somehow bare earth is never very pleasing. A hint ... but not necessarily a good one!

Quite by accident the other day we discovered an excellent idea. When laying out a garden contrive to have a very large and very deep hole in the centre of the unfinished plot! Into this all the flotsam and jetsam that accumulates around you as you are creating your garden may be pitched instead of wheeling it out and waiting for some unwilling truck driver to come and collect it. You'll find it a glorious receptacle for old bits of broken china, large lumps of clay, broken flowerpots and all the odds and ends that come to the surface in the trenching of the average piece of ground. There is one disadvantage in the idea in the shape of the sinking that will sure transpire after the first heavy rain or hosing, but this is not insurmountable in some positions where the depression can easily be filled in.

What actually happened was this: we were laying out a small back garden in the natural landscape manner, with a few weathered boulders, when someone walked across the area where the lawn was to be and almost disappeared from sight! The ground had become perfectly firm on top but underneath there was a great chasm where they had excavated for the sewer. We hauled out the victim and replaced him with all the unwanted articles that everyone working on the job immediately came to light with! It IS an idea.

I've no doubt that many of you might have better success with *Erica vulgaris minima* than I have had. Anyway, do try it as a ground cover. It's delightful! I can imagine few things more thrilling than owning a sheet of it.

Those who can succeed with rhododendrons should find it an invaluable foreground both from the point of view of effect and of keeping the roots of the rhododendrons cool; and in the proximity of a large weathered boulder it is simply lovely.

AN INTERESTING LITTLE NATIVE

Once when we were wandering over the cliffs at Peterborough we noticed a little mauve and pink daisy growing in the turf. It was as short as the closely nibbled turf itself and we knelt down and dug up a small patch of it and brought it home. This we learnt was *Brachycome graminea*, and have since found it to be a treasure I would never like to be without. A fair percentage will strike from cuttings, and as with all plants that you would not like to lose it is wise to have some young ones coming on in case any fate befalls the parent plant.

And so goodbye until next month,

Edna Walling

APRIL, 1941

Dear Gardeners,

The Editor has just sent me a handsome apology for not posting my last letter to you per medium of his pages, and has also added a postscript to say that government restrictions on paper are so severe that in future everything has to fit into smaller spaces.

Well that appears to be the order of the day.

Gardens certainly seem to be getting smaller and smaller as the new buildings crowd in upon the available land, so that any form of construction that will provide a garden feature as well as conceal some part of the boundary fence is of considerable value. The picture shows a circular pool with a high semi-circular wall to provide a permanent background. *Clematis montana rubens*, that small-flowered, pale pink clematis, is ideal. It finds this wall a most satisfactory place on which to display its charms. That's one very good thing about any high pieces of construction in gardens, they do provide adequate and attractive supports for climbing plants. I don't suppose any of us would like to go back to those arches which used to spasmodically span the garden pathways, but their elimination has left us without sensible supports for our climbers.

The small gardens of today needs these climbing plants to get as much effect as possible in the limited growing areas.

Two foliage plants which you don't often see, and yet which are very lovely, are the purple-leaved vine *Vitis vinifera purpurea* with its deeply lobed leaves, and the evergreen virginian creeper *Ampelopsis sempervirens*. My purple vine has never yet borne fruit, but a friend has one that was a picture this summer. Muttering in my beard, 'It's water that's done it'. I came straight home and let the hose drip on mine all day! 'I know what terrors those people are for watering'; of course they got no credit at all for any other loving attention probably given it!

Did you hear that bang? That was me shutting Bailey's *Encyclopedia*. First I turned to Rehder's manual of cultivated plants to find out where this evergreen *Ampelopsis sempervirens* comes from, and found that Mr Rehder evidently doesn't agree with me! According to him, 'there ain't no such a person'; most irritating. I swung around and grabbed the aforementioned tome, and felt weaker and weaker as I read on and on, with no sign of *sempervirens* in sight. Was just beginning to compose a little note to the man who called it '*sempervirens*' when there, right at the very end of the dissertation upon ampelopsis in very small print was a whole list of lots more ampelopsis with funny little signs beloved of the botanist but double-dutch to the average man in the street, and here was *sempervirens*. And with a 'how extremely helpful!' I shut the book.

Aster 'King George' has done itself proud in the herbaceous borders this summer. It is one of the best of the low-growing perennials without a doubt. There is a little risk in dividing it up too early. It is safer to wait until winter is almost over, or if the clumps must be lifted, split and plant out when they begin to grow.

If you use artificial fertiliser when you are sowing field peas you'll get twice as much green manure and will catch the maximum in nitrogen if you turn them in just as the peas are in flower.

Till next month.

Edna Walling

JUNE, 1941

Dear Gardeners,

Out in the garden early this morning, when the dew was heavily upon everything, I found myself thinking: 'If I could write a poem like Rupert Brooke's "The Great Lover" I would add woodend bent to my list of the "things I have loved".' When the dew is on the narrow blades of this most pleasing of all lawn grasses it takes on a greyish-green which looks crisp and beautiful as the sun comes up, and all the aliens in the lawn look so rusty and coarse beside it. It takes a considerable amount of restraint not to fall upon these usurpers and remove them forthwith—especially that heathen

Sporobolus capensis, the rat tail grass—but one is always hot-foot to another job. People who come in to talk when I am in the garden find a much more willing listener if at the end of the session there is a little pile of *sporobolus* on top of the lawn instead of in it.

Magnolias! Isn't it rather strange how rarely we see these glorious plants in gardens? They're breathtaking in their loveliness, and though they are not as foolproof as some shrubs they are not difficult to establish if leaf mould is incorporated into the soil in which they are to grow. In districts where frosts are prevalent there is sometimes a risk of the flowers being injured by excessively heavy frost. Shelter from wind is, of course, desirable or the petals would soon be torn from the branches, and some form of mulch, such as decayed leaves or cow manure or well-rotted stable manure is necessary to prevent the rapid drying out of the surface soil. But there, these little attentions are appreciated by most plants. It is just that some are more tolerant of our neglect to provide them. It is risky to even mention varieties, because one

might go on for pages and pages. I will, therefore, content myself with the mention of *Magnolia conspicua*, a most exquisite thing; it is almost too much to see it in full bloom against a blue sky! These white varieties which bear their flowers on the leafless and softly grey-brown branches in spring do go to one's head.

Crataegus smithiana is simply glorious with me this autumn, the fruits are large and a bright orange-red colour. Whether it is that the birds do not like it or that it is not yet ripe enough for their taste I do not know. The tansy-leaved hawthorn, *Crataegus tanacetifoli*, is a delight with its soft grey foliage and those rose red little apple shaped fruits. I'm just longing to get to work with some of these tansy-leaved hawthorns and some huge weathered boulders, on some country property one day with prostrate junipers sprawling at their feet and amongst the boulders just those three things, boulders, grey-leaved hawthorns and junipers and what a picture one would have. Moreover, you would never have to do anything about it. That's the sort of gardening I like! I think the amount of patience, perseverance, and hard work some people put into the growing of annuals is nothing short of amazing, and yet how adorable some of the annuals are! There is one with the loveliest blue daisy-shaped flowers called *Felecia bergeriana*, or kingfisher daisy because of its kingfisher-blue flowers. It seeds quite freely and will often come up of its own accord in gardens that are not too strenuously 'tidied'. And I like that little dwarf cornflower jubilee gem, and *Linaria* 'Fairy Bouquet', and *Anchusa* 'Blue Bird', and the very dwarf *Phlox drummondii nana compacta* ... not in a straight row though!

Till next month, goodbye,

Edna Walling

A U G U S T, 1 9 4 1

Dear Gardeners,

WINTER FRAGRANCE

What delights await those gardeners who plant trees and shrubs freely about their grounds, and for a June delight I know no greater than the winter sweet, *Calycanthus praecox*, or (according to Rehder's manual of cultivated plants) *Merathia praecos*, after Francois Victor Meratia, French physician and botanist; yet again it is sometimes called *Chimonanthus fragrans*! It's very trying, isn't it? However, try the first name when ordering; it is the most likely one to be recognised.

Get a fairly large plant if possible, for it is slow. With me it just doesn't do any good at all. Never yet have I been able to secure anything more than the tiniest sprig to bring proudly into the house. I suspect it is just grit it wants, so many things resent the absence of it in my soil that I am acquiring the habit of taking a bucket of it out with me every time I go forth with a new plant to place. Winter sweet is deciduous and bears its primrose-coloured, stiff little blooms on the silvery-grey leafless branches. It fills the air with a heavenly fragrance as if to vie with the daphnes that put on their act at the same time. It is a shrub of six or eight feet, which apparently has no special preference as to its situation and soil, providing the latter is a normally good garden loam. If you like plenty of show avoid it, but if you love fragrance try it.

Mrs Sinkins! Wonder what on earth made me suddenly think of her. This old-fashioned pink is one of the garden's indispensables for the habit is good, it is a good clear white, and the fragrance! We take so many of these old plants for granted until they disappear and then look feverishly around until we find them again after much exhaustive hunting.

Autumn Beauty

Oh! I say, don't forget to plant the Manchurian pear if you like autumn foliage. *Pyrus ussurensis*, the botanists call the poor thing; it's a picturesque and noble tree. Don't ask me if it bears fruit for I don't know! Mine is about 20 feet high and it hasn't, to date, if that's any help.

Opening an English garden magazine the other day I was overjoyed to see a paragraph about the whortleberry, *Vaccinium corymbosum*. My goodness! What brilliance of autumn colour this shrub produces. I think it likes plenty of leaf mould—rhododendron conditions, in fact, but you will not grudge it that when you see it in autumn. It eventually attains about 12 feet in height, but not by any means rapidly.

Gardens for Flat Dwellers

You know I'm not so sure that those living in flats with only a courtyard or roof garden to play with are so badly off after all in these days when so many enthralling things may be grown in pots. Why, it's the only safe way to grow some things. Directly you put them out in the garden some fell disease befalls them, a cat scratches them up, or the one slug that has escaped the Metabait attacks them. Take for instance that charming little rock plant *Aethionema* 'Warley Rose', I've just planted one out today but I'm sure its safer in a pot. Think, too, of the darling little miniature bulbs.

There's that little dwarf snowdrop ... in my opinion much superior to the ordinary variety and the hoop petticoat daffodils, and all the rest of them. *Campanula isophylla* and its white variety the slugs adore. If you can bear a hanging basket you will find this campanula at its best grown thus, and can't you imagine it cocking its snook at the slugs grovelling about the ground beneath?

For a light sunscreen for rhododendrons the shad bush, *Amelanchier canadensis* is one of the best tall shrubs or small trees. It has a good landscape effect, flowering very early in spring as it does before the rhododendrons are at their best. The greyish-white flowers wreathe the bare branches and make a glorious picture against the deep grey storm clouds of early spring, and the handsome foliage of the rhododendrons certainly makes an excellent foil for this dainty tree; and how lovely birches are with rhododendrons, too! Have you ever noticed how unutterably dull a mass of rhododendrons can be if there are no trees to accompany them? It seems that these glorious shrubs should always be part of a picture—the chorus, perhaps, but not without the scenery. So often you will be asked, 'Have you ever seen the rhododendrons at so-and-so?' and after a description of the scene you are tempted to reply, 'No, and I hope I never do, until they have softened them down with trees'. And why so many rhododendron collectors plant so sparingly of white varieties I can't imagine. It makes me so mad I feel I'd like to plant nothing but white varieties, because they are so lovely. Don't forget the oak leaves on these shrubs every year; it's the secret of success.

Yours till next month,

Edna Walling

S E P T E M B E R ,   1 9 4 1

Dear Gardeners,

There is one thing that distresses me about that delightful small-leaved and tiny-flowered plant, *Rhododendron racemosum*, and that is that it 'ultimately reaches six feet in height!' Crash went my joy in believing that I had found another low-growing evergreen shrub. It is so difficult, this matter of low-growing evergreens. 'But there are tons of them,' said a helpful little sunbeam the other day, proceeding to reel off a list of plants that were certainly dwarf, but so repulsive that I clapped my hands to my ears and cried out for mercy.

About Rhododendrons

However, that it ultimately reaches six feet sounds more hopeful than 'soon reaches six feet', and perhaps with judicious pinching back it would refrain from being so inconsiderate. The tiny pink flowers of this species are produced in the leaf axils along almost the entire length of the previous year's growth, as well in a terminal cluster. Sometimes 12 inches of growth may be packed with blossom. It is native of western China and was introduced into England by W.J. Bean (you know his enthralling volume, *Trees and Shrubs Hardy in the British Isles*). The foliage measures from three-quarters of an inch to an inch-and-a-half long and half as wide, and in colour is a glaucous green.

The foliage of my *Rhododendron aureum*, which I have growing in a tub, has turned the most exquisite shades of dusky pink this winter. It seems perfectly healthy, and it is probably the confined root run which has encouraged this colouration. A pot of *Leptospermum keatleyii* in full flower was accidentally placed in the vicinity of this rhododendron and has for a month made a picture with its large pink flowers against the pink-toned foliage, and it is still a delight. What pictures shrubs in pots are capable of producing when they are in flower! Even if there is no room for them in the garden, it is quite sensible to buy any things which attract you and keep them in pots for a year or so if you are prepared to water them consistently.

TREE PLANTING

There should yet be time to plant evergreen trees, and this year tree planting should take a much more serious trend than the mere planting of trees for ornament. Much has been said deploring the cutting down of trees for fuel. Well, I suppose we must have fuel. The point is we should be planting and preserving young forests just a little faster than we cut them down. Quite a lot could be done by individual gardeners, since numbers of people have blocks of land on which timber trees could quite easily be planted. It is a very simple thing to plant pines eight feet apart each way, and amazing the number that will go onto quite a small plot of ground.

IT IS A PITY

What is urgently needed is some publicity on the matter to inspire people to do it! It's of little help merely to say what we should be doing. What we want is some good, sound advice and practical hints on how to go to work. There is no doubt at all about the wisdom of growing timber, I don't mean only the government growing it, but the individual. Just about 20 years ago I was supervising the construction and the planting of the entrance driveway into Toorak College at Frankston. To the south of the school building there was a large tract of land belonging to the school that was to be reserved for future buildings. This came under discussion, and upon learning that it was not likely to be utilised for 15 or 20 years I suggested that it should be made an asset instead of a liability by planting it with pine trees in forest formation. Visiting the college recently I observed that there were no new buildings ... and no pines! It's a pity about those 20 years, but it can serve as a lesson.

A barberry that has attracted much attention in my garden from time to time is *Berberis pruinosa*; it is very well-named for the fruits are exactly like miniature prunes of the most lovely shade of powder-blue ... and I don't suppose it was called *pruinosa* for that reason at all! My! What thorns it has! And what a decorative barrage against marauders it would make. The foliage is a glaucous green (occasional leaves turning bright red), but its chief beauty is the fruit which is at its best in late April and May. It comes from southwest China and was introduced in 1894, if that is of any interest to you. You will be anxious to know the height it grows, well, it's approximately eight feet.

THOSE PROSAIC GARDENERS!

The photograph I am enclosing this month is of the entrance to a house in Toorak. The step makes an interesting incident ... and a trip-up for the unwary! These little informal woodland tracks can be very charming and refreshing. Of course they wouldn't last a minute if the owners could afford a 'good' gardener, he'd have it trimmed up to a perfect curve and he would rush every leaf off to the compost heap immediately it had made a safe landing, and away would go the picture! Happily the owner has little time for gardening and no money for assistance; result, a garden full of pictures! Life is funny, isn't it? There are lots of things that need attention in this garden, but also lots of things that have just happened, that it would be sacrilege to interfere with. How desperately we need gardeners trained in an appreciation of landscape effects: trained to know when to leave well alone. Do you know that some of them actually move shrubs that have been most carefully grouped to form a certain permanent picture? Yes, they will dig a young shrub up and move it back a bit to make room for a patch of *Phlox drummondii* or something equally futile. Of course the whole picture is ruined and as the years go on the plant that has been moved has to be taken out because it is too close to those with which it had originally been grouped. It's just like daubing some masterpiece or rubbing off some of the paint in one spot.

Goodbye—before I become too abusive!

Edna Walling

OCTOBER, 1941

Dear Gardeners,
What a lot some people miss that they need not, through living in rented houses. Perhaps they know that at most they will not be there for more than five years, and so they suffer a treeless garden and have nowhere to sit out of the scorching sun on a summer's day. The fences remain stark and unclothed because it is not thought worthwhile planting anything but annuals.

QUICK COVERING
Personally I would cut the labor and expense of these, and the minute possession was taken, go buy me a ceanothus or two for the fences, a

Virgilia capensis for a shade tree and a 'Souvenir de Leonnie Vionnot' climbing rose, Oh! And a 'Lorraine Lee', of course, for cutting. (Put a little cow manure in the bottom of the holes when you plant all these and just watch them romp away.) I'd even buy a *Buddleia veitchiana* (no rude remarks!). Well cared for, this can be a jolly useful cover for boundary fences or a screen for ugly vistas, when time is the essence of the contract. The not so well-known *Buddleia salvifolia*, which has the loveliest soft mauve flowers in late winter, is really a beautiful evergreen shrub of the most extraordinary rapid growth, and it doesn't need half the pruning *B. veitchiana* should have. If you can get one, the bee balm (*Echium candicans*) will help to cover the ground and produce enormous spikes of violet-coloured flowers held well above the decorative grey-green foliage. It will cover a space of six feet in about two years if it likes the spot, and since it thrives in not dry and rather hungry ground it will often be most applicable to the rented garden.

It's strange how inhospitable the soil of the rented garden can be. Perhaps it knows nobody loves it and it gets embittered!

When I look upon this white daphne in the full bloom of all its loveliness, Walter De la Mare's words go singing through my brain: 'Look thy last on all things lovely every hour', for we must part, this beautiful thing and I. In one of my gardens there is a white magnolia (*Magnolia denudata*) and beneath it this daphne must go! I'm consoled with the thought that it will be duly appreciated, and that there could surely be no more lovely foreground for this most exquisite of all magnolias. It is *conspicua*, of course, but apparently we have to get used to calling it *denudata*.

THE ASPEN'S RUDDY BLUSH

The silken buds of the aspen trees 'breathe gently of spring', according to the poets. I can't help it, but to me they always seem to bring it in (the spring) with a ruddy blush! They make such leaps and bounds as if to say, 'Well, we may have small leaves on stems so genteel that all we can do is quiver for six months of the year, but you just watch us in spring! First we have silvery-grey buds that get bigger and bigger until we can't hold back the next act any longer and down come the ruddy-coloured catkins which we hang out all over the tree as thickly as we can.' So you see I wasn't swearing, they are ruddy and they do come quickly. Ho! Heavens! No!! I mean they do blush ... Oh let's talk about things to eat!

SPRING'S ROLL CALL

Am not quite sure if there is anything lovelier in the garden at the moment than the cherry plum trees. One thing is certain, plum blossom is exquisite against the faded blue walls of the room in which I write to you at present. I'm glad so many more people are planting them in their gardens for the sheer joy of their blossom. Sometimes I fancy I hear the Headmaster calling the roll and feel quite sad at the too frequent piping up of 'Absent' in plaintive tones in this and other gardens. Here we are in the first week of September and the Headmaster is calling: 'Cherry plums? ... Hoop petticoat daffodils? ... Primroses? ... Kurume azaleas? ... thryptomene? ... Rosemary? ... Daphne? ... spirea? ... Magnolias? ... Snowdrops? ... japonica? ... Violets?

Two of the most beautiful plants in the world are not only made available to us by two nurserymen (blessings upon their heads!)—one in New South Wales and one in Kew, Victoria—but the plants are natives of our own country. One is the most lofty and beautiful evergreen tree one could wish to see, and the other a small shrub with the most exquisite double pale pink flowers on slender branches clothed with softly grey-green foliage. Their names? Well the first is *Callitris columellaris*. It's commonly called Australian cypress, and many a thorough-paced Australian citizen gets a shock when told it is a native of this country. I must admit it doesn't look native. At a distance it has something of the appearance of a particularly fine Roman cypress. The little slender pale pink shrub is *Eriostemon obovalis flore plena*. Don't take a fit; we have a more merciful name for it, 'fairy wax flower.' I believe this double form was found somewhere in the vicinity of Bendigo; anyway, wherever it was, the main thing is that it was discovered, not artificially produced by cross-pollination. I have a very strong preference for plants that are not manhandled. Oh yes, I use them, frequently, and know what a loss it would be if all such plants were purged from the world. If gardening does not teach one to be flexible, would anything?

Goodbye till November,

Edna Walling

N O V E M B E R ,   1 9 4 1

Dear Gardeners,
Forsythia intermedia spectabilis is in full bloom as I write, and there is no doubt that it is far superior to *intermedia*. The branches of this variety of the

'golden bells' of the American woods are packed with the large clear yellow bells that almost weigh them down. One of the sweetest shrubs to plant about four feet away, and a little to the front of the forsythia, is *Spirea multiflora arguta*. This spirea flowers later than *S. thunbergia*, which it resembles a little, but if they both flowered at the same time and I had to make a choice it would certainly be *arguta*, much as I love *thunbergii*, because *arguta* is really exquisite when it is laden with its tiny white flowers.

This is October 4th, and we have *Olearia dentata* in full flower in odd corners and borders all over the garden ... I can never get enough of this native shrub. The flowers are very like a perennial aster (Michaelmas daisy) with a little more substance perhaps, and of the loveliest clear mauve in colour. It needs regular pruning in the manner that the prostantheras also require, that is a liberal, and yet not too heavy, cutting back immediately after flowering; otherwise it grows rather spindly and top heavy.

At the foot of this olearia we have Westmoreland thyme flowering madly. It's glorious! I've never enjoyed anything more. I hope I have the right name for this olearia. In a frenzied search for a title for it, I found it in Thistle Harris' book, *Wild Flowers of Australia*, but can't quite make up my mind if it is *dentata* or *asterotricha*. It's simply lovely with *Viburnum carlesii* and flowering cherries.

Dianthus freynii is a most exciting little fellow with its clear pink flowers on inch-high stems all over the little mat of grey-green foliage; so small is it that one is reminded of Reginald Arkell's poem upon someone's rock garden. Do you remember? The owner was expatiating about some treasure and the visitor asked 'Where is this lovely thing', he cried; 'You're standing on it!' she replied.

The grey foliage and the small white flowers of *Anthemis aeizoon* thrill me. I bought it under the name of *Achillea ageratifolia* many years ago now, and am always terrified of losing it. Of course, the only thing to do with a treasure when you have only one is to hurry and propagate it by some means and have several in various parts of the garden. I planted one of these anthemis in a blue cement pot yesterday with most satisfying results. These little rocks certainly make the most delightful pot plants; it's so nice to be able to enjoy them in different parts of the house and on the piazza. I've not yet found any plant that revels in the north wind so we always rush out and grab our pets and put them in some sheltered spot when that wind is tearing around the country, and back they go again when the bluster is over.

I'm afraid I haven't appreciated *Silene maritima* to the full until the other day. We were placing a soft grey lichen-covered boulder in a spot needing a little stability and were carrying a spade around the nursery in search of a plant to make a picture, when we came upon this little fellow in full bloom. Out of the funny little grey balloon-shaped calyx came the soft white flowers, and the pale greyish-green foliage looked as if it would be just the perfect foil for the stone. With infinite care the whole clump was lifted and at once there was a picture. This gave me an idea. 'We must plant out a lot of rock plants in the nursery so that we can make these immediate pictures', and away went a whole barrowful.

The flowers of *Vaccinium corymbosa* are really the sweetest little waxy lanterns. I secured the plants for their exquisite autumn foliage, and it's a pleasant surprise to find it a dual-purpose plant. I don't know much about its requirements but imagine from the little I've read about it that it favours rhododendron conditions; poor things, they won't get them in my garden.

Had a letter from a friend the other day who addressed me 'Dear Anti-annual!' Oooooh, what have I said? Something rude about Iceland poppies or asters? How narrow-minded of me. 'If you can't grow them yourself you needn't be so snippy about them', she thinks.

The Wayward Ones. Yes, that's what they are—wayward! I decided this morning that forget-me-nots are in league with foxgloves. That new little track through the viburnum border was to have been a primrose path. 'We'll have primroses here', we said brightly, surveying the freshly turned-up earth, and if only our hearing had been more acute we would probably have heard those forget-me-nots chipping in with their, 'No, you won't. WE'RE going to be here'; for last night as we sat in the car on the drive waiting for that burst of energy necessary to dive into the back for the parcels, the lights shone right across the lawn down to that little track. 'What's that patch of blue?' said the Littlest one. 'Forget-me-nots!' said the Biggest one. 'But where are the primroses?' asked the Littlest one. 'Underneath!' admitted the Biggest one. Anyway, I'm going right out this very minute to move those foxgloves, which have found the leaf mould heap.

Cheek!—Yours,

Edna Walling

DECEMBER, 1941

Dear Gardeners,
Do you know I've just remembered that we must have lost our plant of *Azalea occidentalis*, well it serves me right, fancy having only one instead of a drift of at least half-a-dozen! It's a plant that always makes me long to throw a toothbrush and a clean shirt into a bag and board the first ship for America. How glorious the roadsides must be when this small-flowered, biscuit-coloured rhododendron is in full bloom. It's hard to understand why so great a number of the large fat, hybrid rhododendrons are planted to the exclusion

of so many other species that are so fascinating. Of course, 'for them that like SHOW' the smaller-flowered and softer-toned species may appear insignificant—a term most inappropriate to them to my mind.

Voice from the depths of the potting shed ... Don't forget to tell them about that prostrate broom growing alongside the *Veronica hulkiana* (sometimes called New Zealand lilac). I can't help chuckling at the effect the first few taps of this little typewriter has upon those I have been around the garden with that morning. They always guess I'm writing to you and they are very often right. This prostrate broom certainly is most satisfactory. I don't know where we got it, or where, and if, it can be obtained; we'll put in a few cuttings so that we can pass it on some day. I have one plant growing on top of the drive wall, right under a gum tree; you couldn't imagine worse conditions, and it's looking simply marvellous at the moment. It is more suitable for the wilder parts of the garden, and simply lovely for country gardens. If you have a hot dry bank of pure clay which has been the despair of your life, it will do things to it of which you had never hoped even in your wildest dreams, and, heaven knows, gardeners are given to wild dreams. It's an incurable disease; even ninety-nine failures out of a hundred tries won't cure it! Let's hope they'll never find a cure.

Ajuga reptans is so tough and so obliging that one is inclined to treat it somewhat casually, but really it is indispensable; it's not a plant to use in those parts of the garden where the soil is so good that more exacting plants will thrive, for there it will ramp away at such a rate that it is hard to keep pace with it in these days of limited time, but it is a plant that leaves us with no excuse for bare and unattractive ground on the plea that nothing will grow in it.

I think that's the wonderful part about gardening, the fact that there are so many plants that will grow in the most impossible places. I don't mean impossible plants either, but really attractive ones. Take baby's tears for instance (*Erigeron mucronatus*). Yes, it certainly takes possession ... one man said that he bought a plant for a shilling and now he has a thousand pounds worth! But that's what we want it to do in some spots. It's better than dust, at any rate.

To return to the ajuga, I saw a very charming picture composed of ajuga, phlox, 'G.F Wilson' (or it may have been the variety named 'Lisbeth') and *Anthemis aeizoon*. The soft blue of the phlox, the deeper blue of ajuga, and the grey and white of the anthemis is very soothing in combination with a large weathered boulder or two.

We have an improved form of *Veronica hulkiana* which has flowers with a little more substance than the old form; we must do something about getting that distributed, for it is a very useful low-growing evergreen. *Cytisus purpurea*, that quite low-growing mauve-flowered broom, already mentioned several times, is no trouble to us at Sonning, though we still do not succeed with *C. Kewensis*, woo it as we may; it's knocked all the conceit out of me!

Another plant that literally appreciates poor hungry ground is the Egyptian daisy, *Dimorpotheca eclonis*. It has the most fascinating white flowers with a blue centre and is an excellent bushy perennial. We have this growing in a bed under a gum tree with *Veronica hulkiana* (improved variety) and the pale mauve and white makes a cool and satisfying picture on the landscape.

Marguerite daisies are the loveliest ground covers for hard dry conditions, too; the old single white is simply lovely with Roman cypress and the bee balm (*Echium candicans*).

We were working in what we call the big nursery this morning and I noticed that the air was filled with a most exquisite fragrance which puzzled me for a moment until I looked around and discovered that it was that glorious late-flowering apple called *Malus ioensis* (syn. *Malus augustifolia*). The plants have been in full bloom for two or three weeks and seem to have a substance about the flowers that will stand a great deal more adverse weather conditions than will the earlier-flowering apples.

Edna Walling

JANUARY, 1942

Dear Gardeners,

I've just returned from visiting an old friend in the Village*. Her garden was looking so marvellous that I told her a story of a friend of mine who, in a weak moment, invited two small girls to spend the weekend with her. An outing was arranged and the two repaired to their boudoirs to adorn themselves for the occasion. One was quite a nice little girl but the other was a perfect terror. The quite nice little girl came down first and a little later the terror; she took one look at the nice little girl and said: 'Darn it, you look nicern I do!'

FOXGLOVES AND DIANTHUS

The place was a mass of foxgloves! And I'm far more moved by such a sight than by an expensive array of rhododendrons. Don't ask me why. I could never explain. It's a true cottage garden, that is, flowers everywhere, the sort of flowers you see in the cottages of Cornwall and Devonshire. I came away with a deep feeling of satisfaction, murmuring, 'I'm glad I started this village scheme.'

Dianthus are in full bloom in all their great variety. Could there possibly be a race of more charming variety and fragrance? Roysii is smothered with its cheeky little blooms of brightish pink on stems under three inches in height, and amongst the rest the old clove pink known as 'Mrs Sinkins' is the same joy as it always is at this time of the year. Whenever a visitor exclaims, 'What is that lovely fragrance?' I'm always terrified they may detect the touch of smugness that accompanies the reply, 'That's 'Mrs Sinkins', haven't you got it in your garden?' You see I feel that no garden is complete without it.

THE LURE OF THE POTTING SHED

I don't remember whether it was to you or to someone else that I once wrote at much length expounding the wisdom of owning a potting shed. Now that was the most dangerous thing one could possibly have suggested. Why a potting shed is the most insidious, the most time absorbing, the most bewitching spot on the property!

There was a note on my desk reminding me to make cuttings of the 'Mrs Sinkins' pink. 'Yes, I'll do it now', I said, and dashed over to the potting shed. That was at 10.30 a.m. At 4 p.m. I was still there! 'I'll just pot on this *Azalea narcissaflora*, it's such a sweet, small-flowered, pale yellow little shrub, I couldn't risk putting it out until I'm quite sure of a position for it, and it's a little pot-bound. Um! Yes, those cuttings of *Campanula isophylla* have struck nicely; it wouldn't take a minute to pot them up. Oh, heavens! Here's that plant of *Genista pilosa* I've been looking for everywhere. Cuss! Also blow! The slugs have been at it. Better go round with the Metabait (half an hour). Wonder where I'd better put the *G. pilosa* to trick the slugs (ten minutes or more gyrating with pot in hand). Here's a good spot, but perhaps it's not quite sunny enough; perhaps over there, no, that's too sunny. Oh, dash you! You'll have to take your chance here. I'm getting dizzy, and I'm sure you are—you look it, anyway. What I've kept you for all these years, heaven only knows, for you're no oil painting at present. I've changed the potting mixture. I've top-dressed you with limestone chips. I've moved you from hot to cold, and cold to hot, and still you've never flowered. Suppose I've done everything but the one thing in life that you really enjoy, fling you out on to the most unpromising spot in the garden and forget all about you ... I haven't the pluck!'

ROADSIDE PLANTING AGAIN

It's not a figure of speech, it's an absolute fact that I went weak in the knees, and only with great restraint prevented myself from 'clutching my heart' when confronted with that glorious plant *Boronia pinnata* in full bloom yesterday (November 23), all sorts of mixed thoughts went teeming through one's mind. First and foremost, as ever, came the thought of drifts of this exquisite thing for roadside planting in Australia, followed by the fury that always springs up at the sight of poplars, planes and golden cypress on roadsides where existing gums and blackwoods are all-sufficient. If the inhabitants of country places, or the councillors they elect, feel they must do something about roadside planting, why oh! why don't they buy a hundred boronias and select a spot that's not attractive and show our overseas visitors that we have plants as lovely as the American laurel

(*Kalmia latifolia*) with which the roadside planters in America clothe the highways in places. Could anyone with the slightest imagination at all believe that overseas visitors or Australians either, want to go up to Olinda to see poplars dotted amongst the blackwoods and the gums along the lovely country roadways. It's crazy, it's barbarous! 'That's enough', comes a voice from the kitchen (they had evidently detected violence, which was being taken out on the typewriter).

One day recently I found myself at a loose end and went a-wandering amongst the trees and shrubs that had grown too big to be lifted and utilised in the making of gardens. The thing that particularly struck me was the happy appearance of the plants. 'This is the way they like to grow, apparently', I thought, 'protecting each other'. Amongst the trees that lovely pink-flowering American dogwood, *Cornus florida rubra*, looked more contented than usual and it was covered with bloom. It has an architectural beauty about its flowers that makes it unlike most other shrubs and all the more desirable. Yes, there's certainly wisdom in having thickets of trees and shrubs, and it is ever so much more exciting than a collection of widely-spaced specimens.

We were potting up little plants of *Hypericum reptans* today, and I came inside to make sure it was *reptans* and not *repens*, and am so tempted to quote Reginald Farrer in full on *reptans*. What a delightful person he must have been! However, it will have to wait until next time, the Editor had to do some pruning last month, and he would have to use the saw if I started on Farrer!

Yours,

Edna Walling
* The Village is Bickleigh Vale, which has grown up around the writer's home, Sonning, and was inspired by her. (Ed. *H.B.*)

FEBRUARY, 1942

Dear Gardeners,

I don't know whether it could be relied upon to perform in the same manner every year, but I feel I must tell you of a picture I have in the garden this morning (November 26). It's that lovely yellow Germanica iris 'Chasseur' with *Hypericum repens* in full bloom at its feet. I'm inclined to think that if you set out to make such a picture the iris may be too far gone before the hypericum came into full bloom, but it's worth trying in a part of the garden that you can spare for such an experiment. An addition I shall make when recreating it somewhere else will be *Achillea grandiflora*, that lovely white milfoil which has larger flowers than any other of the species; and don't be frightened of it if you're ever lucky enough to secure it because it doesn't creep all through the soil as *A. millifolium* will do. It just makes clumps which you divide like any other perennial, and a word of warning here: it does not like being split up too drastically, so don't be tempted to get too many plants from one clump.

Campanula muralis is a sheet of bloom. The bright blue bells on three-inch stems are a wonderful sight at this time of the year. You will notice that I am writing this almost on top of my last letter to you. It will be months before you get it, but it doesn't really matter; the main thing is to get it down so to speak.

Boxing Day! You see, it is as I feared; many weeks have elapsed since starting this letter and now *Campanula garganica* is in flower. It is one of the star-shaped campanulas and very, very charming as most of the campanulas are, of course. Very soon now *Campanula pusilla* 'Miss Wilmot' will be abloom. This is 'fairies' thimbles.' It's adorable! I shall never forget it in Tasmania, where it spreads so wonderfully. It looks like a pale blue lawn. Although some gardeners place all things that increase readily amongst the 'nuisances', I've never yet heard fairies' thimbles maligned, and I should think not! If anyone could stoop so low as to criticise that little plant they deserve to be hamstrung!

There is a very old-fashioned plant that you will sometimes see in old gardens, but rarely if ever in modern gardens, yet one of the most useful permanent ground covers that grow. You might know it as 'Rose of Sharon'. Botanically it is *Hypericum calycinum*. It has been a lovely sight this summer, with its clear yellow flowers with the fascinating fluffy mass of stamens, which are characteristic of the blooms. This particular variety grows but 12 inches high, and covers the ground beneath trees where few other plants will thrive. It spreads by means of underground stems and that is just what you need in a ground cover that is to furnish inhospitable earth. For heaven's sake be sure to get the right variety: for although the more commonly stocked *Hypericum moserianum* and *H. patulum henryii* will thrive under trees, they grow much taller and do not spread over the ground and cover the earth.

Today I am hoping to find time to make a little picture under the *Clematis jackmanii*. It is in full bloom and has been for the last month or six weeks; a really magnificent sight with its rich purple flowers. There are one or two mossy stones already in position but a scrubby lot of plants clothe the ground between them, except for the white form of that dear little rock geranium, *Geranium sanguinium album*, that, of course will be allowed to remain. When the undesirables have been removed some leaf mould will be spread over the ground, and some gritty river sand, and then I'll plant frankenia near one of the boulders and fairies' thimbles (*Campanula* 'Miss Wilmot') and *Nierembergia hippomanica*.

When I was watering this morning it suddenly occurred to me that this little plant would make a delightful ground cover for *Clematis jackmanii* and so it shall be done. Actually the frankenia will be the ground cover with its minute grey-green foliage and tiny pink flowers, for *hippomanica*, though but nine inches in height, does not creep along the ground but ends up little wiry stems with little saucer-shaped mauve flowers on top.

It gave me so much satisfaction to see people sitting about under the trees at Sonning when we opened the garden for the H.M.A.S. *Sydney* fund that I decided to give lessons in landscape gardening at Sonning. I'm always having 'ideas', but this one really is going to be carried out, because it will bring the experience of more years than I would like to tell you within the reach of many with garden-making problems to be solved. When it is wet we can repair to the cabin which has the right atmosphere for informal lectures. I'm not worried about transport, for people are regaining the use of their legs amazingly, and nobody even faints if it's hot!

My little tree of the English sloe, *Prunus spinosa*, is covered with tiny grey-blue 'plums', and I'm dying to have a sloe pie! It really was not planted for the fruit, but for the tiny white blossoms in spring, which are so exquisitely sweet.

Edna Walling

MARCH, 1942

Dear Gardeners,

As we are all getting more and more interested in growing things to eat, you will be interested to know that the weeping variety of 'flowering' apple called 'Eliza Rahke' produces apples that are full size and excellent both for cooking and eating raw. It needs to be grown on a standard at least six to seven feet high to allow room for the branches to hang down naturally. I never do a thing to mine in the way of pruning and we always get plenty of quite good fruit.

SOMETHING NOT TO DO

This month I am sending you a photograph of the driveway at Sonning because it is a very good illustration of what to avoid in landscape gardening! You will notice that the stones on the right-hand side look very like a row of not very inspiring teeth, and the effect is not at all pleasing. One day an improvement will be made ... I'm waiting for the mood, the time, the energy and the boulders.

It isn't easy to break away from the retaining wall which copes with the higher level of the shrub border as the drive approaches the house, nevertheless, this row of stones is no way to do it, and the alternative is one or two larger weathered boulders so placed as to give the appearance of always having been there. The other day I saw an attempt that had been made at such an informal edging to a driveway, and it wasn't exactly impressive; in fact, it was nothing but a mess. It would have been better to stick to a row of stones.

Plants take an extremely important part in such a problem and when I say plants I mean such things as Westmoreland thyme, Mother of thyme (*Thymus serpylum*), prostrate rosemary, and similar low-growing evergreens. These cover the ground between the boulders and make it unnecessary to use so many boulders, which is a mistake often made. For example, in the section shown in the picture not more than three or, at the very most, four boulders would be used. They would be large, of course, and partly submerged. Perhaps two would come to the edge of the drive, and the others would be back in the border a little, and plants would take the place of stones where it was necessary to separate the earth from the driveway.

HEDGE OR SHRUBS

Not many people will face the upkeep of a hedge when they know that they can secure the same degree of privacy by the planting of informal shrubs which need nothing more than a yearly pruning to present a well-groomed appearance to the boundary planting. This pruning is work that may be undertaken by the owner who might fight shy of tackling the trimming of a hedge to a perfect line and there's nothing more exhausting than snipping away at a 60- or 70-foot wall of verdure. Flowers, berries, and autumn foliage may all be had in the mixed planting of shrubs which replaces the hedge; cotoneasters, pyracanthas and barberries for the berries; weigelias, lilacs, prostantheras and spireas for the flowers; and viburnums (Guelder Rose, for instance), barberries and vacciniums for the autumn foliage, to mention only a few.

TWO GOOD ROCK PLANTS

By the way, I don't think I have ever told you about two of the best little rock plants that grow, and they are perfectly good Australians. My goodness! I'd like to get to work on a national rock garden one day which would be a revelation of the marvellous diversity of native plants that are never utilised as they should be ... Anyway, I had better not start ranting. The two plants I'm thinking of at the moment are *Brachycome graminae* and *Brachycome multifida*. The first-named clings tightly to the ground and has little mauve daisy-shaped flowers on stems an inch high, and the second one is a mass of fine dark green foliage growing about three inches high, with pale mauve daisies all over the plant for many months of the year. It spreads by means of underground stems and forms a very charming ground cover for the pathways' edge or in the foreground of low-growing shrubs. *B. graminae* is really a choice (hideous word!) little rock plant and is a splendid little fellow for pot culture.

WHY NOT A VOYAGE OF DISCOVERY?

Samolus is another charming little native ground cover with small white flowers. I don't know enough about it to say anything more at present, but you'll not be spared when I do. Meanwhile, you might collect a specimen from somewhere (Oh! no, not a nursery; it would have to be somewhere in the bush), and find out for yourself what a treasure it is. Of course, quite a number of people do go forth on voyages of plant discovery, but it is amazing how few do in Australia. It's my idea of heaven to find myself on such an expedition in a future not too far distant to find me with no longer the health and strength to carry it out.

Do you know that tiny-leaved ficus, *Ficus minima*? It's the sweetest little creeper and quite safe where *Ficus stipulata* may be too rampant. In places where the house's petticoat shows in a rather ungainly fashion it is a help for covering the brickwork and it doesn't require the clipping that must be given to *stipulata*. The evergreen Virginian creeper is another lovely thing (*Ampelopsis sempervirens*), but I think I have already mentioned that in a previous letter. It's not easy to come by, but well worth a search. I'm off before the scissors arrive!

Edna Walling

A P R I L ,   1 9 4 2

Dear Gardeners,

There has been an arboreal tragedy at Sonning, all the more tragic because it could have been averted. Half the Manchurian pear tree blew down yesterday. I didn't know just how deep was my love for trees until this happened. I could hardly choke the tears back at the sight of so lovely a thing lying on the ground just as it was coming into all its autumn glory, and this year it promised to be more beautiful than it had even been before.

What should have been done is this: a hole bored in each of the two leaders which were gradually growing apart, and a bolt with an eyelet instead of a head pushed through each hole. Broad washers prevent the nuts from being drawn into the wood when the strain is placed on the cable that joins the eyelets and prevents the tree from splitting in two. It doesn't hurt the tree a bit to bore holes through the trunk, but it can do a lot of damage to tie

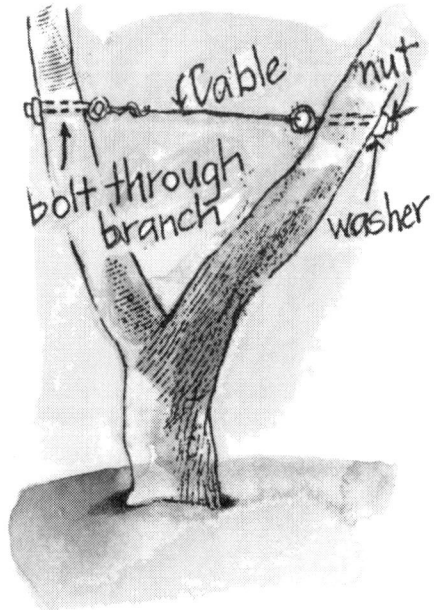

things around it even if the greatest care is taken to prevent the cable from cutting into the bark. It amounts to this: the bolt method is permanent and demands no regular inspection, whereas the other method must be constantly watched owing to the natural expansion of the tree.

I suppose you have been saying rude things about the matches these days, too. After a series of flying heads and broken shafts I stopped to look closely at one. The head seemed all right and the striking part was almost new. 'But the wood looks different; hah! I wonder if they have run out of *Populus tremula* (the aspen tree)', I observed. Ages ago when I was told that the aspen was the tree used for making matches I felt we should be putting in acres of them or some substitute. We've evidently found the substitute, but the only trouble about it is it isn't a good one apparently. Let's plant some aspens as well to be on the safe side. (Of course, I should have gone off to interview the head of the match-making industry to enquire upon these things before holding forth ... they're probably still using aspen wood ... if they ever did!)

With the terrific increase in the consumption of timber brought about by the production of charcoal, I do think we should all take tree planting more seriously next winter. Perhaps the Forest Commission will publish regular short articles in the press giving those with suitable ground to spare some simple directions as to how they can perform this national service and at the same time improve their properties, reduce erosion and improve the water catchments.

I can't help thinking that the native cypress *Callitris cupressiformis* and other varieties of the callitris should be cultivated. Heaven knows it's easy enough. A few years ago I saw this tree for the first time and was thrilled with its beauty, and to my joy there was seed on it. This we sowed and now have some very vigorous specimens of this compact-growing softwood. Recently at the side of the road I saw masses of seedlings of this tree coming up under the litter which had formed a naturally shaded seed bed for them, and so you see the re-afforestation should be quite simple where this species is concerned.

Another timber tree that I'd like to see in hundreds of acres, ready for future use, is the tallow-wood, *Eucalyptus microcorys*. It makes the most beautiful floors which need no waxing, merely rubbing up the natural tallow that exists in the wood, and it shows no marks of the heels of boots as other hardwood floors will do. It is thinking of these timbers which makes me hate the sight and sound of *'Pinus insignis'*, which are planted in such millions, and rightly so, no doubt; but surely not to the exclusion of the native timbers? A lot of people have moved and will be moving into the country with their children, and on some of the properties they have acquired there will be a lot more ground than they require for vegetables and grazing. With the spare ground you can do no better national service than plant every square foot of it with native timber trees. It is not a big job of work; for the seedling trees are quite small, about six to nine inches. More harm than good is done by laboriously preparing deep holes for them. They will thrive much better if a few thrusts with a pick or mattock are made to loosen the ground where the seedlings are to be planted. The reason is that the deeply-dug holes become waterlogged in winter, which the roots of the little trees just will not stand; they'd much rather have to fight their way in a bit of rough ground than be asked to live in rich soil that is wet and soggy.

There is one thing of which you may be assured: if you teach your children how to plant trees for timber and tell them all about the trees that make the houses in this country, and do so many things besides, they will bless you forever for protecting them against this form of ignorance which must make us appear such fools in the eyes of those who think so much more of the timber than we do. It simply amazes me that the average public school girl and boy knows so little about trees and the wood they produce; that there is so little encouragement given to boys to become foresters, and that parents hardly ever use trees as a subject of conversation with their children. Few subjects could be more delightful and instructive, and some delightful fairy tales could and have been woven around them for the tiny ones.

What has all this to do with gardening, you may be saying? Well, I think timber and vegetables are more important just now, and the vegetable question is being marvellously handled by the press. Talking of vegetables, I've decided that it requires a special sort of brain to grow them successfully. You have to be very methodical, for instance, or you'll have masses sometimes and nothing at others. There are lots of other reasons why I'm not much good at it but that one will do for the present! Anyway I can dig like fury, and a farmer only has to give the word and off we go with sugar bags and shovel and return with bulging bags of cow manure. I was once caught taking it from a paddock where I hadn't secured permission. I'd adore to tell you the story, it was so funny, but even now this is too long, so goodbye, and good hunting (cow manure, of course!).

Edna Walling

MAY, 1942

Dear Gardeners,
Well, I'm very sorry to have to be faithless to the Honourable Edith Gibbs, but I can't help it, and the old girl will just have to take it because 'Silver Spray' IS ever so much better. This year the perennial borders had to be sacrificed, for the time and water spent on them previously had to go on to the 'Truck Garden', as we call the vegetable garden with deference to the good old Stars and Stripes. I felt so sad about it that I studiously avoided

going into that particular part of the garden during the summer, but in the rain this morning I decided to inspect the ruins and was amazed to find that very little had actually died and there was a plant of Silver Spray flowering away as if it had received all the attention in the world! Well, if I could only have one variety of perennial aster, it would certainly be that one, I thought. The Hon. Edith Gibbs was growing alongside, coming a rather bad second. Both these asters are of the *Ericoides* type, that is, the very small-flowered species. They are really very charming. They are pale mauve in colour, and Silver Spray is so stiff in the stem it rarely needs staking, greatly in its favour in my opinion!

SONNING DOES ITS BIT

To my great joy I am finding that 'Sonning' is a wartime garden par excellence. Its appearance is really not at all bad, in spite of the fact that it receives little more than a tremendous spurt of the combined efforts of two women on Saturday mornings from 9.30 a.m. to noon! I'm a great believer in teamwork, and am quite sure two people get through more than double the work of one. It is impossible to keep all the shrub borders dug and hoed, so we have concentrated upon keeping the grass down and using the clippings and leaves as a perpetual mulch on all parts of the garden that are not lawn. Of course this is the best thing to do, war or no war, but it takes a war to make us realise it.

I look at the trees and say, 'Bless you for giving us such beauty and making so little demand upon our time and expenditure. By the time you receive this, the autumn foliage should be a dream! It has been such a wonderful year of generous rains, and the trees have responded wonderfully to them. Two of the trees I am eagerly looking forward to are the English maple, *Acer campestris*, which, as its name implies, grows in the fields in England, and the white mulberry, *Morus alba*. Both are fairly quick-growing, the latter more so than the former, and both turn a beautiful clear yellow, which throws a golden light about them and into the rooms through the windows which look out upon them.

The American blueberry, *Vaccinium corymbosum* has coloured brilliantly enough to satisfy even our American visitors, I should think, and it's just another thing that makes one long to visit America in the fall; it must be very heady. Someone returning from Washington said, 'It's heart-breakingly cold; flowers just won't grow there'. 'But what about these glorious trees?' I asked. I couldn't believe that one would ever notice the absence of flowers with such arboreal beauty everywhere about.

The claret-leaved ash is coming right up to expectations. It's a tree that colours best in rather poor ground, where it doesn't get too much water—the ideal tree for Sonning! The manna ash (*Fraximus ornus*) is also promising well. The reddish bronze of its foliage is very distinctive.

Oh, how dull that sounds for such a glorious tree! What I'm trying to convey is that it IS distinctive; it's not vivid or spectacular, but a soft, dusky bronze-red; I don't suppose it would suit the person who likes his colours bright.

Oh, I must tell you a little story. I was called in the other day by a very expensive-looking person. 'Hollywood', I found myself thinking. 'Goodness, he'd never like my "simple" scenes of sylvan beauty, and I'm no earthly good at those "See what we've done" kind of gardens.' So convinced was I of the correctness of my first impression that the poor man hardly had time to open his mouth before I said, 'I'm afraid I won't be capable of giving you the garden you would like; my knowledge of floral displays and the culture of specimen plants is extremely limited'. 'I don't want floral displays and specimen plants', he fired back. 'I want woodland glades, shady places to sit, thickets of trees; I want it to look more like a little forest than a suburban garden.' How I had maligned him!

Do you know I have been thinking that instead of using fertiliser in the crowbar holes one makes around a full-grown tree in order to fertilise it when it is growing on a lawn (which makes it impossible to feed it in any other way), it would be possibly better to use fowl manure and liquid cow manure. After all, there is nothing better than the latter, and fowl manure is marvellous. So make your holes from a foot to 18 inches apart all around the tree from the butt out to the spread of the branches and fill them up several times with liquid cow manure or ram them tight with dry fowl manure; the rain will do the rest.

AUSTRALIA'S FOOD SUPPLY

And now food! And isn't it just too pathetic that nothing has yet been done to safeguard Australia against a food shortage. 'It can't happen here', seems to have been the swan song of some who have been asked to express their views. When I say nothing, I mean nothing by the government, which will no doubt eventually start a women's land army. The Y.W.C.A Garden Army will help the vegetable shortage very considerably, but they can't introduce cows and pigs into their scheme.

Editor: 'But, my dear girl (yes, he's frightfully tactful), what on earth has this to do with gardening?'

E.W.—Nothing, and everything. Don't you realise we've got to be cow-minded and pig-minded as well as vegetable-minded these days? Where's that morsel of pork in the pork and beans tin coming from if they don't get busy on a land army? Heavens, they'll recruit the women when the shortage is really acute and then expect old Dame Nature to perform a miracle with her raw recruits.

What I was really going to say about food, when my indignation got the better of me, was this. Have you ever used the tops of red beet for spinach instead of throwing it away? When you bring these straight out of the garden it is positively criminal to throw away the tops. I'd rather throw away the roots, fond and all as I am of them.

It's amazing what can be grown by the most ignorant person. I had a job not to get so puffed up that my most carefully preserved waistline nearly disappeared when I surveyed my plot after an absence of ten days.

Edna Walling

J U N E ,   1 9 4 2

Dear Gardeners,

A feeling of frustration came over me when it became clear that the shortage of labour would mean that the planting of trees would be very reduced, in fact well nigh impossible this winter. Then suddenly out of the blue came the idea that much could be done with no labour at all. I had been looking out of my office window straight at a lovely specimen of that beautiful American tree, the red oak, *Quercus rubra.* 'Hem' ... (that's that thinking sound we make preliminary to the exposition of some great theory) ... 'that was an acorn picked up from the lawn in the Botanic Gardens, I raced a squirrel to it.' Well that's proof, if we need it, that we can all do some sort of tree planting this year. What is more, it will be planting oaks the only way they should be planted, i.e., burying the acorn where you want the tree.

Oaks have tap roots, and unless it is a very small tree you are transplanting it is impossible to avoid cutting this tap root. They simply hate that; just as birch trees hate to have the tips of their root systems cut off with the spade when they are being transplanted. There are lots of trees that don't mind it a bit, but with birches one should carefully remove all the soil around and on top of the roots (with a fork, not a spade) until the whole of the root system is exposed, and the tree can be lifted out (in winter, and without any earth, and on a calm, dull day, I need hardly add). The fibrous roots may be yards long sometimes, but never mind, trace them out until you come to the end and when the tree is in its new position spread them so that they go straight out from the hole of the tree. Don't, for heaven's sake, twist them around in a small hole or you will become an unwitting member of a suicide pact. No, make the hole a large shallow one and square, not round, so that any extra-long roots may be pulled out into the corners, and so that the roots will be encouraged to spread out into the new ground, not go around in circles when they strike the sides of the hole, as they sometimes will when the hole has been made circular.

OAKS FOR ME

But it is of oaks that we were speaking because the acorns may be planted even by the weak and infirm. Lovely and all as the English oak can be it is not as suitable for this country as the American varieties. Oh! But I must tell you about the upright form of the English oak which grows like a Lombardy poplar, that is, with a narrow columnar head. Its botanic name is *Quercus pedunculata fastigiata* (poor thing) and it certainly makes a very interesting specimen ... that's the second time that word has appeared and as you

must know by now I don't believe in encouraging the specimen habit, it should be the exception rather than the rule in landscape gardening, then the specimen tree becomes more valuable and the effect less monotonous.

Certainly I would count the upright oak amongst those trees that are best as specimens, and now having said that, I suppose it will be my lot to come upon a group of them looking simply magnificent one day! Ah well, that's nothing new, no sooner one expounds a theory when something pops up to make the author look ridiculous, and if you'd escape that you might as well content yourself to be nothing, do nothing, say nothing. No thanks, I'd rather look silly.

Oh, I've just remembered, one of the most magnificent specimen trees that I know is the Australian cypress, *Callitris columellaris*. On the lawn which rolls down to the lake in the Botanic Gardens, it is a glorious column of billowing, dark green velvet, and if I hadn't been gadding about the outskirts of that alluring city Sydney one day I should never have known how lovely it can look in a group. We were scooting along through Gladesville when my eye was attracted by an old stone wall and there, within the garden it enclosed soared heavenwards five at least of these beauties. There are moments when I wish 'Little Willie' really was human instead of being only nearly so, and merely an Austin, at this particular moment I wanted someone to pinch me.

Food and Yet More Food

How feverishly we shall all be scratching up every available bit of humus making debris to dig into the ground that is going to be planted with potatoes; they so love loose ground in which to develop their tubers and with the shortage of fertilisers we shall be forced to provide every other form of encouragement for their healthy growth. I'm going to rake over a grass paddock and gather up all the odd bits of hay and leaves from it and spread it over the ground that is to be ploughed for potatoes so that the plough will turn it under ... it's very good for the waistline, this raking!

Life is full to the brim when you own land in normal times, but in wartime it's rammed down and brimming over. Do you know, there are some people who own land and have never yet experienced the thrill of it? You suggest that such and such a thing could be done with it, to which they reply that they cannot get anyone to do it, by which time you're screaming 'Get to, and do it yourself' (and nobly refrain from adding 'you cripple').

It's time I stopped, but when I think of one friend of mine who is so stiff with rheumatism or something, that she can hardly get out of bed sometimes, and of what she has done without any help at all in developing and maintaining a landscape garden of over an acre I get mad with the flabby ones.

And so the cabbage moth attacks the leaves of swedes, too! Huh, off comes swedes from the menu. That's my system with the moth ... starvation.

Yours till next month,

Edna Walling

PS—Isn't it curious how things turn up? After the letter was written this paragraph from the Editorial Gossip Page of *House and Garden* turned up:

Sometimes, in an unthinking moment, we are apt to picture our Colonial forefathers as hacking down trees willy-nilly and having no great regard for arboreal beauty. Well, maybe we're right. For in February, 1657, the town-fathers of Weymouth, Mass., were moved to pass the following regulation: 'Whoever shall presume to fell, kill or top any tree or trees which grow before his own or his neighbors Dore or that stand in any place upon the common or highway which may be for the shade of either

man or beast, or shelter of any house or otherwise for public use, every
person so offending shall be liable to pay for every such tree so felled,
topped or killed 20 shillings for the Town's cause ...'

J U L Y ,   1 9 4 2

Dear Gardeners,

I've just come in from the garden purring contentedly over the sight of a patch
of *Cytisus kewensis* cuttings planted last winter. It was a remarkably good
strike ... hardly a miss, and there stand a score or so of this little treasure
ready to be distributed about the garden and amongst one's friends. How easy
it will be to repay a kindness until these give out! And *Cytisus purpurea*, that
has done well, too, but that usually does, it's *kewensis* we hold our breath over
and say 'abracadabra' as we gently insert the cuttings in the soil.

The mail was there when I came in and no time was lost in seizing the
latest copy of *My Garden* from London, and on opening the little book at
random what should I behold but an article entitled, 'A Trailing Rock
Broom,' and it was all about *kewensis*! So now I can tell you that this little
fellow is an offspring of two such diverse parents as the tall *C. albus* (which
we see far too little of) and the small and almost prostrate *C. ardoinii*. The
tough and wiry almost leafless twigs are grey-green and these bear in spring
crowds of blossoms in a soft ivory-yellow. It is a free grower in any light soil,
indifferent to drought and is usually a long-lived shrub. It seldom rises
much above a foot, but sends out trailing branches of several feet in length.
There! There's a whole article in a nutshell for you, much better than I
could describe the plant, so wasn't it lucky I opened the book?

Cytisus purpurea I love! It's such a sweet Old World mauve in it's colouring,
and I love the way it bends over when it is about 18 inches high as much as

to say, 'There, we've gone high enough, now, we must go back'. It's a nice compact little shrublet, not tightly compact, but shapely without any pruning.

[Later—I've been digging the potato crop, not from choice (though there are many less enjoyable tasks), but from shortage of labour and lightness of crop—not an unusual occurrence in these parts. Some patches were extremely dull, the tubers just like any normal potato and a sufficient number under each vine to make digging very monotonous, but in other patches (the most numerous) there was excitement galore. Down would go the fork and up would come the most amazing roots of the most astonishing shapes, sometimes one large potato with ten or twelve corners to it and lots and lots of tiny ones which they rudely term 'pig feed'; sometimes a large number of these potato-cum-artichokes, sufficient in quantity (if not quality) to satisfy the most blasé grower of the *Solanum*. Is it *Solanum officinalis*? I feel it should be, but don't expect it is—the botanist always seems to do the unexpected just to make it a little harder to guess. Anyway, what I'm so pleased about is that when 'they' (those who cook) ask, 'Are there any artichokes?' I shall now be able to conceal the fact that none were planted, and reply, 'Why, of course', and trot along the 'best' of the potato-cum-artichokes and bolt for my life.]

ANOTHER PICTURE

Oh dear, oh dear, oh dear! This is too 'buch for be', Over at Lynton Lee this morning I stood entranced at the sight of *Jasminium nudiflorum* in full bloom with a carpet of that little mauve rock plant *Brachycome multifida* (native) still in flower, oh, and a clump of prostrate rosemary covered with its grey-blue flowers. *Jasminium nudiflorum* is the winter jasmine, of course, which covers itself with pale yellow flowers in early winter when it has shed most of its foliage, as the term '*nudiflorum*' implies.

The mistress of Lynton Lee sent me back to my own garden posthaste the other day with the remark, 'I think my garden is better than yours now'. Well, of course, there is only one way to respond to such a challenge, and I chuckled with somewhat unseeming delight at the fact that in the nursery were plants by the score that could be moved into positions that were undeniably weak. Several days later I looked out of my attic window to behold about ten women escorted, Cook's tourist fashion, by the said mistress of Lynton Lee. I poked my head out of the window, all the better to be heard, and said, 'I thought your garden was better than mine!'

I don't know what has set the pace, but there is no doubt about these villagers, and if I'm not very careful Sonning will come a very bad last. I'm going for my life, but there doesn't seem much time between digging and sowing in the truck garden, building chimneys and making shower recesses (to make the barn habitable), and helping people with new houses to gloss over their surrounding earth for the duration. After all, we must stop erosion, and newly broken-up ground will erode if it isn't planted. That's the one thing that appeases my mind when planting pleasure gardens of late. It seems so wrong to be doing anything but digging potatoes or preparing some ground for another crop. 'You could plant the pleasure gardens with potatoes', you may say. Well, no, I don't hold with that. I do think that everyone should grow some of their fresh foods, but I do think that we should try and keep the properties looking as presentable as possible, so much of the ground that has been torn up for vegetables is not sufficiently fertile and friable to warrant the destruction of flowering shrubs and lawns, when we have run out of all that ground which is still available without starting on the front gardens will be time enough for such activities.

Edna Walling

AUGUST, 1942

Dear Gardeners,

I started to write this on May 18 when *Viburnum fragrans* was abloom! There's nothing spectacular about this shrub but it is as exquisitely dainty and fragrant as its name implies. At this time of year I always carry a pair of secateurs in my pocket (baby ones, of course) so that wood for cuttings may be gathered as one happens upon some treasure that must be propagated. There are many reasons why all true gardeners should do some propagating every autumn and winter. (a) You may loose the original plant and then where would you be if you had neglected to effect its increase? (b) You'll want to give some away to friends. (c) And (in my particular case) I feel in duty bound to distribute any plant, that will strike in the open ground, to all those who have come to live at Bickleigh Vale. (d) Once you have known the excitement of having a little nursery, you'll never let it go; however it may have to be curtailed in wartime.

THAT DESIGNING LANDSCAPIST!

This morning I decided it is extremely useful to have a landscape designer living on the spot, so that you may call upon them at a moment's notice, for criticism and ideas, instead of having to make an appointment, on a day that turns out to be one on which you are not at all in the mood for the garden or worse, a day when you feel that your garden is really rather beautiful, which means that if the designer dares to do anything but praise, you all but rush at her throat. Yes I am lucky to have mine laid on, so to speak. Of course we have heated arguments on various points at times, whether that tree really should come out; if that new border should be a spring effect or a picture at some other season, and so on. You can just imagine how endless the arguments *could* be in a garden, especially when both people are as keen as mustard.

This morning in the walk around the garden I was subjected to the severest criticism, 'You have the garden looking too 'oney',' she said with vehemence.

'What in the world do you mean?' I asked.

'Well, one of this and one of that—why didn't you put six of that low-growing plant in instead of one, for instance?'

'But I only had one', I replied meekly. That winded her a bit, but she gathered up her forces again and shot 'This looks a bit messy here, a *Viburnum sargentii* right up against *Cotoneaster buxifolia*. Why, they're only a foot apart.'

'Yes, I brought them home one day and rowed them out for the time being.'

'But that was two years ago! Well, aren't you going to do something about it, it wouldn't take five minutes.'

Here all meekness left me (it never does last very long) for there's nothing that makes me see red so much as that 'It wouldn't take five minutes' remark unless it's 'In your spare time',—such a little observation would reveal that there is no such a thing on this property. I picked up my spade and stumped off in the direction of the *Viburnum sargentii*, 'Yes, I AM going to do something about it,' was shot back. What a glorious escape!

A WONDERFUL HAWTHORN

You know that marvellous hawthorn called *Crataegus smithiana*? I'm sure you must, for I answered the query 'What's the name of that lovely tree at your back door?' at least 365 times one day on behalf of the Red Cross. Well, I took some cuttings in late autumn when the leaves had hardly fallen, and heeled them into sand to callous. In about four weeks I lifted them to see if anything had happened, and nearly did Catherine wheels at the sight of the callous that had formed on most of them. 'This means roots will follow', I explained to Freddie, who stood by appearing to require an explanation for the demonstration of joy. 'Let's have a look at those *Viburnum carlesii* whilst we are at it.' She took them up tenderly (plants are always safer in her hands than mine) and reported, 'Yes they have calloused, too'. 'Oh! that's marvellous, we will go and row them out in that extra special bed of nice deep loam in the vegetable patch right now.' 'What about the peas you were going to sow in that patch in spring?' There was no answer to that so we just put them in!

A LITTLE P.O.W. WOW

Just to make this time of the year a little more overwhelming than usual, there is a new scheme afoot. Sonning is to be held responsible for the upkeep of at least one prisoner of war, and to raise the wind, so to speak, plants from the garden will be sold to all those who come to buy for this purpose. You will have to write or ring up to say that you are coming, for without making an appointment I can't be sure of being at home, or being available at any odd time. We have already raised many pounds by means of a tour around the garden with me leading the way with a spade. We even sold some cutting of something there were no small plants of the other day, three for threepence! And the purchaser was thrilled to bits. Haven't you often longed to ask a nurseryman for a cutting if he has no propagated plants of something you desire with a mad pash? Well you needn't have any scruples about asking for cuttings here. Just pipe up and we'll collect the cash. In fact we will sell anything within the bounds of reason for the P.O.W. fund. It's going to cost a terrific amount to keep our prisoners, and here's a chance for gardeners to go on indulging themselves without a pang! I'm going to extend the idea to other districts by getting someone to carry on the idea in each country town. However, more about this later.—Yours,

Edna Walling

S E P T E M B E R ,   1 9 4 2

My Dear Gardeners,

(I feel we have known each other long enough to be a little more familiar, so I've added the 'My').

I wish I didn't get so excited. I just went over to the potting shed to take some seeds over or something and now I'm all of a heap. All I want to do is rush and put on some Chopin, some Tchaikovsky, ballet music ... anything that fits this mood, or do handsprings on the lawn, turn Catherine wheels off the piazza (that would make the natives sit up and take notice), or tear over and tell the Mistress of Lynton Lee that the white daphne is out. As if that were not enough, the white Kurume azalea, which I love so much, is out too. Ernest Wilson said that these little fellows were the sweetest of all the azaleas (I don't suppose he said 'sweet'—men don't, or shouldn't; but that's what he meant, and, of course, they are).

I intended putting in masses of cuttings of them in the autumn, but of course only a few were achieved, as it was, it's a miracle *they* went in, for as soon as the autumn leaves begin to fall, the owner of an anything over a two by twice-sized garden must hang onto their wits for fear of going batty with all there is to do in the short time Nature allows us to do it all.

All too soon the increasing heat begins to knock back all hope of planting just one more tree, or taking cuttings of one more treasure, and we must content ourselves to wait another nine months until the favourable conditions return again. Of course I know that lots of people don't indulge in much of that form of gardening that simply must be done just at the right moment, and I can't help thinking what a frightful lot they miss; it must be awful not to have a garden that is so big that it nearly drives you mad!

A very good gardener (at least she was my idea of a good gardener—she made some lovely pictures) once said: 'I think a garden should be just a little bigger than one that can be cultivated in its entirety, then Nature can take a hand in some corners.' ... I've got one of those, and the corners are nearly meeting in the middle!

Anyway I've an implement that is being of great assistance to me now that labour is scarce. It's a short-handled shovel that is nice and broad. It turns over half as much again as an ordinary digging spade, though it is not so heavy an implement. It is thin and sharp with use (and a file of course) and it's grand for skimming weeds from the paths as the digging progresses. I don't like making another job of the paths, and find it much simpler to turn under the weeds from them as I go. It all means more humus for the soil, too.

'But don't you get frightfully tired lifting such heavy masses of earth?'

'Yes, of course I do, but no more tired than lifting a heavy spade, and I find that the thought of the reduced time per square yard of digging is a mental cocktail of no mean potency! If only Hitler had been a gardener, I'm sure there'd never have been a war. He wouldn't have had time! But no, we will have to make everyone gardeners before we cure war. There are lots of other people responsible for this one besides Hitler. Make them grow their own food, that's what I would do with guilty men; it's strange, isn't it how rarely we set the guilty to dig? It would be such a humane way of dealing with them, and if some really couldn't dig they could sow or save seed or do any of the other lighter jobs that go to make up this most humbling of all and yet most dignified of all work. (I'd better be careful. I can see the Editor getting a sort of horticultural expression. 'Now get on with some gardening advice, my girl, your 'ideas' grow a little wearisome.')

I hope that some of you will have planted the American hornbeam this year. It's a mistake, I feel, to run a thing to death, and much as I love and appreciate liquidambars we are perhaps inclined to plant them to the exclusion of other trees of equal beauty and attraction.

The American hornbeam (*Carpinus americana* or *C. carolina*) is a small-growing tree which colours well in autumn, and equally appropriate to the small suburban garden as the liquidambar. There is quite an interesting variation in the way the leaves turn colour; some will be bright red and others clear yellow. The form of this little tree is spreading and quite picturesque.

Do you know I am beginning to think that one of the best ground covers may be *Erica darleyiensis*? By Jove! It's a hardy little fellow, and what I like about it is the way it clings to the ground and smothers itself with its little tiny bells of bright pinky-mauve for literally months in the year; and most of all I like it for liking us! By that I mean so many plants don't! This seems to be one of the ericas that is more indifferent to soil and situation than others, and that it strikes readily from cuttings is a characteristic to be considered in the matter of *ground cover*, for one must propagate one's own for the

ground-covering jobs or be broke in no time at the rate ground cover plants must be acquired. It's a habit we haven't yet properly achieved, this matter of ground cover, and it's the secret of success in landscape gardening. So let's get onto it without further delay. Let's drop this 'one of this and of that' habit, and get into the way of planting in drifts instead of ones.

The accompanying picture has nothing to offer in the way of suggestions to you, but isn't it interesting as regards pattern? It's where we partake of many a meal in summertime at Sonning. And what an excellent foil for those summer days these crisp winter mornings can be!

Edna Walling

OCTOBER, 1942

Hello Gardeners!

'How about a little harping?' they said, looking at the head, supported in two rather earthy hands, drooping over the typewriter, waiting for the muse to strike up the band.

'What do you mean?' I snapped aggressively, suspecting they were merely rude.

'Westmoreland thyme, of course!'

'Oh! Marvellous. You're not rude, you're wonderful!'

Their acknowledgment was almost drowned in the rattle of the typie; for off we went at a canter.

You see, it is said that I am always harping upon Westmoreland thyme. Well, it's worth harping on, and if I find myself with some ugly, bare earth when summer comes, I shall bow my head in shame; for with so good-tempered a plant to cover it up there'll be no excuse.

WINTER MEMORIES

One of the plants that brightens the winter days with its soft yellow blooms is the winter-flowering jasmine (*Jasminium nudiflorum*). I think this is one of the most delightful flowering shrubs we have. I'm not so keen upon *J. primulinum*, which flowers later in spring, it's so rampageous. Not that this characteristic would put me off if I were sufficiently interested in it otherwise, but the heavy mass of foliage rather spoils it for me. In contrast to this, *J. nudiflorum* flowers before the foliage develops, which, as you can imagine, greatly adds to the effect.

I only wish we could succeed as well with winter sweet (*Calycanthus praecox*) at Sonning; then we could have a group composed of these two winter delights. The flowers of winter sweet are much paler in hue, and have a fragrance for which one could almost leave home! I believe I gave you a picture of it last year sometime. It grows about six or eight feet high and seems to have no special preference as regards position. Its soil, it is evidently particular about, and I can't find information that gives the infallible recipe. Of course, one could experiment ... How I envy those with the methodical minds, the patience, the scientific brains, the capacity for keeping records ... (and not losing them!); also the perseverance to start all over again when the first batch of experiments fails to uncover the secret. By that time I'm always on to a dozen other things that have flashed into the mind and seem too good to miss. I wonder who achieves most in the end. I fear 'tis the ordered mind.

PERKS FOR THE PRIMROSES

'How you spoil those primroses; anyone would think they were de facto widows!' They were just receiving a little encouragement in the form of liquid manure, which seemed the least one could do for them. Only in hungry ground do they need this little attention. In ground with plenty of humus to keep it moist they flower more prolifically without any extras in the way of food; in fact, they are inclined to look a little bloated after stimulants at times, and that's intolerable with primroses. I always hope that one day I'll have the perfect position for primroses—the shady side of an earth and stone wall. When you stop to think how marvellous a setting this is for so many shelter-loving plants it is rather strange that this feature is so rarely seen in Australian gardens. You tuck your primroses and ferns and other treasures in as the building of the wall progresses, always making sure that there is plenty of good earth in the centre. Yes, I feel distinctly ashamed to think that after all these years there still is no earth and stone wall at Sonning, except the little bit which runs away from each stone pier at the front gate. The shady side of this wall is on the road side, and I have never yet had sufficient primroses to hand out to souvenir hunters!

THE AFRICAN CYPRESS

A cypress which I'm afraid has rather been taken for granted at Sonning until recently is the African cypress—really a lovely specimen, making a perfect pyramid of verdure. It's like a cross between *Cupressus torulosa* and *Cupressus sempervirens stricta*, which is the one we generally know as the Roman cypress.

Torulosa is the variety often recommended for a narrow hedge, and very excellent for the purpose too, but for those who lean towards specimen trees, and conifers in particular, this cypress should certainly be in their collection. Heaven alone knows where this particular specimen came from.

I have a hazy idea someone gave me some seed way back in the dim recesses of the past; at all events this one is covered with seed at the moment, and as their propagation holds no terrors, those who would like seed could write to me, and don't forget to enclose sixpence for the Prisoners of War Fund (plus a penny-halfpenny stamp) or you may be wasting your twopenny half-penny stamp; we're willing enough to send the seed for nothing, but time is the essence of life at the moment, and someone must reap the benefit of any extra effort we are called upon to make, and so let it be our prisoners of war.

Any plants that you are having difficulty in securing you'd better write to us about, because if we have it at Sonning it will soon go along to you if there is any hope of reaping a little for the P.O.W.'s. By the time you receive this it will probably be a little too late for lifting plants from the open ground, but don't let that deter you; we can stick a label on a plant and let you have it as soon as it can be lifted safely. Meanwhile, you will have the satisfaction of knowing your money is speeding to one of our men in the form of all those things the Red Cross Society thinks best to send them.

Yours till next month,

Edna Walling

NOVEMBER, 1942

Dear Gardeners,
Having fortified myself with honey ...
  'Honey! Why honey?' you ask.
  Well, yesterday a friend called whilst breakfast was in progress. She's one

of those nice people who always has some pleasant remedy for the particular ailment of the moment … mine was increasing weight (surely there is nothing worse!). We both agreed that we must keep up our health and strength and she gladdened my heart by saying 'Honey is not fattening and is similar to barley sugar in its benefits'.

Then I remembered the story of the old lady who, when asked to what she attributed her great age, simply replied, 'Honey!'

The fortifying referred to was preparatory to going forth with a pick and a basketful of wattles and gums to that piece of bush where we one day plan to have all the lovely native plants that one longs to see massed and grouped instead of as lone and rather depressed-looking specimens.

Acacia prominens, that glorious wattle which grows into such billowing masses of small textured greyish-green verdure; *Eucalyptus maculata*, the spotted gum which has a trunk so like and even more spectacular than a plane tree and *Acacia baileyiana*, the Cootamundra wattle, were in the basket. The latter is to be used as a quick-growing screen to conceal an ugly vista, and the golden rain wattle, *Acacia prominens*, will act as a background to the spotted gums.

Into this landscape garden of native plants will later go groups of the cypress pine, *Callitris cupresiformis*, masses of *Boronia pinnata* (syn. *B. muellerii*) if we can get it, drifts of *Baeckia plicata*

(we're not worried about this because I put in pots of cuttings last year and they all struck splendidly) and lots and lots of *Eriostemon obovalis*, the Bendigo wax flower. I've lost many of these in the garden but hope still runs high, for in masses I feel we might be more successful. Moreover, as they will be in wilder parts of the garden, consequently less disturbed by the tidying-up operations that are so often resented by native plants, they may favour us with their faintly pink flowers more consistently than of yore!

'How often shall I water it?' is a question which always fills me with the utmost despair. How absurd it would be to say briskly 'Once a week!'... just like that. Why, it may rain for three weeks on end; it has been known to. A much safer reply would be 'Never!' and if the tree was well-mulched immediately after planting it probably would survive quite happily without artificial watering. Of course, plants in pots and tubs must receive careful watering, and when they do need it the pot or tub should be given so thorough a soaking as to insure that the soil is moist right to the bottom of the container. Over-watering is almost as great a fault as under-watering, the only difference being that the over-watered plant usually dies more slowly! And so when the earth is moist it is better to refrain from watering.—Yours,

Edna Walling

Dear Gardeners,

Thank goodness for lawn clippings! What on earth I'd do without the sackfuls that come off my grassed areas, I don't like to imagine.

You see, one simply doesn't have to worry about noxious things like sorrel if there's a supply of grass clippings. Just dump a layer of six inches on the infested patch and forget about it for a few months, and you will return to a piece of ground that is entirely weed free. It makes my heart ache when I see anyone laboriously spending precious hours removing every vestige of sorrel or couch roots when they could be doing something else. Of course, you have to do this if you want to use the ground right away, but so often the patch could be spared for a little while and it gives it a rest, anyway, and by the end of the summer the mulch of grass may be turned under and the surface left rough to sweeten the ground ready for spring planting.

Summer hoeing will eradicate these pests, but I for one haven't the time for this method, and a better use for my energy, so on to the lusty heads of plantains, dandelions, sorrel and couch go great masses of clippings and in place of neglected and weed-ridden borders we have comfortably mulched ground, with nothing but the trees and shrubs that should be in them surviving, and not only surviving but thriving!

A Climbing Rose

Yesterday (Nov. 14) that exquisitely white, cream-budded climbing rose, 'Silver Moon,' which has large single blooms, looked marvellous close to a group of Roman cypress. White flowers do look very lovely against these dark blackish-green conifers; think of the Yulan, for instance, that loveliest of all magnolias—*Magnolia denudata*, which used to be called *M. conspicua*, and still is by some nurserymen because it is the more familiar if incorrect appellation.

What extremely satisfactory little fellows the dianthus are in open situations free of tree and shrub roots. Of course the lover of 'two shows a year' will probably prefer to go on fertilising and cultivating for a blaze of spring-flowering annuals which are quickly ripped out to make way for the next batch of seedlings; but some may not have thought of having several varieties of these drought-loving and heat-loving perennials.

Yes, Annuals Have Their Uses

Seeing me surrounded with all the paraphernalia which suggested that a book was in progress—masses of photographs, a pot of paste, a more than usual quantity of typewriting paper, and a more than usual (if possible) mess, a friend enigmatically remarked, 'What are you going to call it?' '*Gardens in Australia*,' I replied. 'Or ... "Down with the Annuals",' she added!

That's not really fair—I adore stocks and nemesias, and, er, quite a lot of the others, but I don't like to see them grown to the exclusion of so many other lovely things, and so I always seem to be slating them instead of being more subtle about it. Perhaps it is because one's store of tact gets all used up in the process of earning a living, and you can't expect to earn one without it, and there's no place on earth where it is needed more than in other people's gardens!

For instance, it was most tactless of me to have raved about that little plant of *Primula winterii* that had wandered unnoticed into that awe-inspiring orchid house (I was certainly awed—but not inspired!). It was on a conducted tour through the orchid houses, oh, yes, they had LOTS of them—which were set in the midst of a large garden to which I had been called to do some landscaping; my expletives (except for the primula) were so unsatisfactory that my prowess in that particular garden was damned at the outset, I'm afraid. In fact, I almost ran when I reached the front gate again, for fear of choking before I got outside. I longed for the breath of honeysuckle, for the sight of foxgloves, and for the feel of grass under my feet that hadn't been rolled and clipped until all the spring had gone out of it.

Oh! I'm sorry. I'm not really telling you anything about plants, am I? Well, I must tell about that lovely group that was at the height of its beauty about two weeks ago. It was in close proximity to kalkwitzia (sometimes called the Chinese beauty bush), which, as you probably know, has arching sprays of the softest shell pink flowers. *Azalea rosetta* and *Azalea occidentale* were in full bloom. *Rosetta* is a double Ghent with rose, white-tinted flowers, and *occidentale* is completely covered with cream and biscuit flowers. These are in an easterly aspect, with conifers sheltering them from the hot afternoon sun and providing a background for their beauty. The azaleas are about three feet-six to four feet away from the beauty bush, and a little to the fore.

Moss Roses

I think they need a country garden atmosphere for their right setting because they have a rather wild look about them and that's just one more reason I'm glad I live in the country, where there is plenty of room for moss roses. At the moment we have a tight bunch of them in a glass bowl of venetian blue; the old rose colouring of these quaint flowers against the dusky blue walls is very satisfying.

I am enclosing a picture which shows what depth and breadth can be achieved on a 50-foot block of land by adopting a landscape treatment. The garden is very young yet and will look better when there is a little more shadow on the lawn.

And so goodbye for another month.

Edna Walling

FEBRUARY, 1943

Dear Gardeners,

I seem to have a positive genius for doing the wrong thing when it comes to vegetable production.

Long have I known that the only things I should touch are potatoes, peas and white stone turnips (the only 'spinach' I dare attempt!), but these spasms of enthusiasm won't be denied, and with never-to-be-daunted optimism I loudly declare, 'I must get in some so-and-sos', and along we go to some seedsman, who must be awfully glad to see the likes of me, and home we bowl with this and that. The local storekeeper is a very astute man. I always tell him what I intend to do and he nearly always says, 'Too late!' or 'Too early!' or 'It's no good your doing that!' and it generally is or isn't, respectively; he's taught me such a lot in these staccato answers to my tentative queries, and what seems most apparent is that I should stick to peas and potatoes—they appear to be foolproof!

I simply love hoeing up potatoes. I view with delight a weedless patch of the gentle *Solanum*. Sometimes I think I should study potatoes and become a potato expert. When I told the local storekeeper this he said, 'Don't. You wouldn't!' Just like that. At least he doesn't mince matters.

Do you know (I know you won't believe this, but it's perfectly true) that since I started writing this letter several days ago—a little habit of mine with correspondence—something else has gone wrong in the vegetable garden. My brain was never so fertile as on the day I planted a bed of onions. It produced a new invective for every onion plant; it became quite fun after a while. Well, yesterday we (the friend was one whom I judged would be so winded at the vast area of digging that she wouldn't notice the almost total absence of edible vegetation) were wandering casually through the 'truck' garden when she remarked (to display her knowledge, no doubt), 'Isn't it rather soon to be bending those onions down?' and following her eyes I beheld a sickening sight. About three of my onions still assumed the vertical, the rest were definitely prostrate and the ground unnaturally smooth, and yet undulating so extraordinarily that I clapped my hand to head and said, 'Is it the sherry? Where did you get it?' 'No, it's the horse, I think. Look'. And sure enough there was his card. In taking his dust bath he evidently likes onions for bath salts. It is disheartening, isn't it?

A Summer-Flowering Ground Cover

Now don't swoon when you hear that it is called *Campanula poscharskyana*; take it syllable by syllable and you'll find it's quite easy. I always think of char and sky, and stick the pos in the front and the ana on the end—then it's simple. This is the most adaptable and easily propagated of all the rock campanulas. It resembles *Campanula garganica* but is much more vigorous and for long periods is smothered with larger lilac-blue flowers than *garganica*. I'm putting it everywhere to keep down the weeds, a sort of living mulch, and flowering too, which is a distinct advantage, of course. A little rock hypericum, *H. reptens*, is also proving a good helpmate in this respect.

Rhododendron imbricatum is in flower, and I was just about to go into raptures about this mauve-flowered, small-foliaged miniature when I thought 'better look it up first'; and nowhere can I find *imbricatum;* *intricatum* is there, but that is blue, and this is decidedly mauve. Anyway, it's a lovely little evergreen and you might come across it some day. Several enterprising nurserymen have seen the value of these rock rhododendrons and have imported them from time to time. Fortunately they nearly all grow readily from cuttings and so there is no reason why the stocks should not continue now that the importing of such luxuries is out of the question. I can't tell you how high this one grows, but am just about to plant it out in a position where it simply must not grow higher than three feet-six. It doesn't look as though it will, but plants can bluff one so.

One of the sweetest rock plants flowering in a blue cement pot at the moment (Dec.12) is *Androsace lanuginosa*. *Androsace* is a huge clan, but I content myself with *lanuginosa* and *A. sarmentosa chumbyi*, an adorable little thing more compact than *lanuginosa*. The flowers are a little like miniature candytufts and are flushed white with a brownish-red centre. The foliage is silvery.

Farrer says that 'it is beautifully adapted for contrast with the violet and lavender autumn crocuses upspringing through the slack tissue of its gleaming sprays'. What words that man finds for describing plants!

Yours till next month,

Edna Walling

MARCH, 1943

Dear Gardeners,

Well, I give it up. I was about to tell you all about that glorious little perennial from Argentina which started off in my acquaintance with the name *Tweediana coeruleum* but is, evidently, more correctly *Oxypetalum coeruleum* (yes, it's very trying, isn't it?) You succeed in mastering the botanic name of an attractive plant only to be rudely awakened by some deedy tome which bluntly says: 'See *Oxypetalum*.' Turning to it for assistance in the matter of colour description, I saw *Oxypetalum*, and there got: 'Flowers, pale blue.'

IN SEARCH OF A BLUE

'I could have done better than that myself', I said, closing the book with a bang in protest. For the last week all have been asked, 'How would you describe that blue?' either bringing in a specimen to those who languished in deck chairs, or leading the more energetic ones to the spot where it grows. Energetic, or languishing, the answers were much the same. In short, they were floored, but would one of them admit it? Not a bit of it. One and all gave it a fly.

'Dawn blue,' said one. To me that sounded most inadequate. 'Why not?' she asked in hurt tones. 'Well, er—so much might depend on where you dined the night before, don't you think?'

'Celestial blue,' came another, but no one seemed to know what celestial blue really was, and probably more in the spirit of argument than anything else it was ruled out.

'Provence blue,' said another. 'That sounds nice, what does it mean?' Here followed a hail of explanations which subsided into a sort of chorus of: 'Well—er—Provence blue, of course', 'Why, of course, I understand perfectly. I only hope THEY will!'

I think it's powder blue, but there, everything that isn't some other sort of blue is powder blue to me; all I can say is that it is unlike any other blue I have ever seen, except in the little white kitten I saw yesterday. It has one blue eye and one that is brown, and I couldn't help saying, 'You'll call it *Tweedia coerulea* of course?' Whereupon the little girl who owned it looked a little blank, so I suggested 'Tweedie'—for short.

Grow this charmer from seed if you can get it, or better still, get plants— I know at least one nurseryman who stocks it—and you will not be disappointed. The foliage is a soft greyish-green and the whole effect is very lovely; I have it near some weathered boulders with thymes and various other rock plants of a similar nature beneath it, and from the bathroom window it gives me a picture that has been enjoyed for weeks past.

THE CUT-LEAF BIRCH

I really think that the most fairy-like tree in my garden is the cut-leaf birch, *Betula urticifolia*. It is growing amongst a lot of other trees, adoring the shelter and protection they provide for it, no doubt, but giving me quite a headache because two trees at least must be slaughtered otherwise they will swamp the birch completely in time.

I don't want to make a 'specimen' of it because its chief charm lies in the fact that it is tucked away in a seclusion all its own at the moment. The trunk is the loveliest chalky white I have ever seen on a birch, and I was relieved that the person I took to see it yesterday pulled back only the tiniest bit of the paper bark to peep at the extra whiteness of the bark beneath. It's always very tempting to peel off quite a lot of it, but one always wishes they wouldn't.

You'll simply love this tree, and if you content yourself with a young one that is not more than five or six feet in height, it will start growing into a dream tree much more quickly and happily than a large specimen that feels the wrench of being transplanted so much that it just remains alive for a year or two before it starts to thrive once again.

The very next word that must be tapped out upon this old warrior of a typewriter is one of thanks to that kind person who has anonymously sent donations to my Prisoners of War Fund. I do think it is a particularly nice thing to do, and take this opportunity of acknowledgment. Oh, and I must tell you that on April 10 Sonning is to be open to the public to assist the Red Cross funds and I do hope lots of you will be able to come because the wonderful summer rains we have enjoyed should mean good autumn foliage this year.

Thyme for Summer Flowering

Savory is a herb that has little culinary use, I am told by those who should know, but this small-leaved, stiffly, upright-growing little bush which is crowded with white blossoms in summer, when lavender is also in bloom, is a very charming little plant to grow in places where the soil is poor and the sun is hot. It is an ideal summer-flowering plant for rock gardens. It has proved invaluable in positions where I have been in despair for ground cover, and I can see that next winter it will be running Westmoreland thyme a very close second when we go forth on our planting expeditions.

It depends, of course, upon the picture one aims to get. For a spring effect it would always be the Westmoreland thyme. Do you know it has just

occurred to me that this seems to be the only thyme that does flower so early in the spring, and as it begins to fade the common thyme, which we all know, comes into bloom? The very low-growing ones, called 'Shepherd's thyme' or 'Mother of thyme', do not flower until summer.

It's a pity we have no simpler name for *Thymus nummularius*; it holds its rosy-lilac (that sounds silly but it's the best I can do!) flowers higher than the Shepherd's thyme, and is a mass of bloom as I write (January 20). It is really quite a valuable little plant for summer effect. Well, I must be off before I am cut off!

Yours till April,

Edna Walling

A P R I L ,   1 9 4 3

Dear Gardeners,

Making the garden over, so that its upkeep will balance with the total lack of manpower, has proved such an absorbing task, and one that has taught me so much, that I feel I must tell you about it.

At present I'm working on the herbaceous borders. During the previous summer these were allowed to run wild; it did not seem right to give time and water to such a luxury when that same expenditure of labour and water would produce food. So with a slightly heavy heart I turned my back on this part of the garden which I have loved so much and bent it (my back!) over the digging in the vegetable plot to the refrain of 'Dig for Victory'.

WORKING TO MUSIC

I wish someone *would* write a song on that theme with a sufficiently vigorous tune to put speed and strength into one's digging! It would be such a help to those who are not enthralled with the growing of vegetables; I certainly need some encouragement and why not music? It always helps tremendously with garden plans that are not materialising as quickly as they might. Often after staring at a blank piece of paper for what seems to be hours someone will suggest Beethoven's *Concerto in C Minor* or something as stimulating, and the result is magical! Won't somebody compose a *Digging Matilda*, please?

The herbaceous borders were surrounded by a rosemary hedge that it was necessary to clip twice a year. In addition to this the roots grew into the borders so vigorously that there was never any escape from the yearly trenching of the borders, however one may have tried to persuade oneself that 'They will do this year; I'll just fork them over and divide up the lustiest of the occupants'. THAT year always proved to be a failure in that particular part of the garden. So out came the rosemary hedge.

'Oh, how could you!' one darling old sentimental friend exclaimed.

'Quite easily,' I replied. 'Look at the pictures it has revealed.' And she had to admit that those Kurume azaleas were not visible before, and that the trunk of that Mexican hawthorn is very beautiful. 'Well, we didn't see it before, did we? Be adult!' I added, and we both laughed because it recalled the remark of someone, not long out of their teens, who once addressed me thus in answer to my outburst upon caged birds. It was not considered 'adult' to object to birds in cages.

One of the things I shall strive to eliminate in this transformation of the herbaceous borders is the staking. It's no use trying to sidetrack the staking of most of the tall, herbaceous perennials and it's not merely a matter of bunching them up to a stake and saying, 'There, that's done'. Oh, no, it's a tedious business supporting the spraying branches of perennial asters, and such things, so that the supports won't show when the job is done. I'd almost rather see the things lying flat on the ground than bundled together like a faggot of sticks. And so only a very few of the tall varieties will be included this year and the rest will be low-growing perennials and even some shrublets such as *Erica darleyiensis*, an erica (and one of the few) which does very well with us. Of course, it is not a summer bloomer and one generally treats the herbaceous border as a summer-flowering feature, I know; but I can see that this is now going to be an interesting part of the garden the whole year around, and the erica will be part of the winter picture which will also have *Rosmarinus prostrata* (prostrate rosemary) giving forth its exquisite grey-blue flowers at the same time. Kurume azaleas are also going to spill into the borders—not many, just an extension of the group that already exists beyond the previous boundary of these beds.

PENSTEMONS AND FOXGLOVES

A patch of that low-growing and blue-flowered penstemon, *P. heterophyllus*, will be in a spot where they will not get the full belt of the hot afternoon sun. It is, I find, so much happier in semi-shade, though it thrives well enough right out in the open.

Penstemon hirsutus is already in; it is tall, but rarely requires staking, and I love its soft blue flowers. *Aster* 'Silver Spray' is there, of course, for it sends up its stiff, stiff stems to a height of four feet and is most independent about support; and *Aster tartaraca* is there for its contracting form. It is also stiff and upright, but the leaves are very much larger and the flowers too.

'Silver Spray' is one of the most charming of all the asters, with its tiny mauve flowers smothering the branches in autumn. It is extremely useful for cutting, of course, but don't cut it from your garden picture. Grow another plant of it in the background, somewhere where it will not destroy the effect that would last weeks in the garden and but a few days in the house.

In the offing, foxgloves will cover the ground with their rosettes of broad, soft green leaves, for few plants ask so little in the matter of attention and give so much in return for garden space, and spring without foxgloves would not be spring at all, would it?

Yours till May Day,

Edna Walling

MAY, 1 9 4 3

Dear Gardeners,
It is with the utmost pleasure that I recommend to you the grouping of the following plants for an early autumn picture: *Aster* 'Silver Spray' (you may remember, my Faithfuls, that I once said rather rude things about *Aster* 'Hon. Edith Gibbs' because she doesn't come up to 'Silver Spray'. Well, she doesn't—not by a long chalk!

The American golden rod is the next plant, and to my own surprise, too, for in the past I have regarded it with somewhat slight favour. The blue salvia, *Salvia azurea* (no, I believe it's *S. uliginosa*)—at all events it's the pale blue perennial that is most common in our gardens, extremely hardy, seeming to revel in a hot summer, and disliking too much disturbance; if you pull it to pieces as you sometimes must to increase your supply, as well as to rejuvenate the old clump, it may sit back for the first year, and flower rather miserably, but all will be well for the following three years or so.

But I mustn't stop to give cultural directions for each individual member of this flower group, or I'll absorb all my allotted space, PS and all! Oh, and by the way, some of those PSs are not mine, you know, they're the Editor's, and when he says things that I wouldn't have said myself, I go purple with rage (like the man who had waited for his wife for three-quarters of an hour. 'Have you seen my husband anywhere about the store?' she asked the shop walker. S.W.: 'Well, er ... I don't know, Madam; is there anything distinctive about his appearance?' 'Well, I should say he would probably be purple by now.').

The next plant is *Gaura lindhelmeri*, which has soft sprays of white flowers with rosy calyx tubes. All three grow fairly tall, from three to four feet, at least, and need most careful staking; that is to say, the supports should not be visible, and the sprays should look natural. This mauve, blue, yellow and white picture really is a delight, and entirely trustworthy, for they are all so hardy.

The Australian Landscape Beautiful. (If there is anything that makes me positively ill it's an adjective tacked on to the end like that).

Came home almost crying with rage the other day. 'My goodness! Sparks seem to be flying,' they said. 'That remark', I replied, deedily, 'is more fitting than you may suppose'. 'Tell us all about it', they urged, and I thought I caught a twinkle in someone's eye. I begin to suspect that they egg me on in these outbursts of fury. 'Well, I've just seen the most glorious piece of Australian landscape I think I've ever seen, and some wretched purveyor of plants, whose advice was sought, has daubed this beautiful canvas with golden cypress (groans from the audience), *Cryptomerias* (shouts of derision), golden poplars ...' 'Oh, no; not that!' 'Yes, hundreds of them.'

'Well, what do you think should have been done?'

'Very, very little.' Some shelter for the cattle was needed, which could have been achieved with sturdy and more congruous native trees and shrubs; but for the life of me I can't see why it was necessary to plant anything along the drive except perhaps an occasional clump of native trees that were ecologically suitable. I've seen so many country properties ruined by these 'ribbon borders' of exotic plants enclosing the drive from the moment it leaves the highway until it reaches the residence, and the cost of labour and material necessary in fencing in these plantations of such doubtful virtue could often be expended so much more wisely. A drive that runs over the landscape in easy sweeping curves, following as natural a track as possible where the cattle and sheep may graze right up to the very edge of the roadway, generally fits into the landscape much more harmoniously than one that is laboriously planted and maintained. There are, of course, exceptions where a great boldness in the planting has given a certain magnificence to the idea; again in the rare cases where a straight approach proves the best line to follow, the idea of an avenue may not only be tempting, but desirable, there being no particular attraction in the contours of the native growth on the property. It must be remembered, however, that to achieve sufficient boldness it is necessary to give up a considerable area of the grazing ground on either side of the driveway.

The mauve-flowered daisy bush of Australia—I wish I knew where you could get this lovely little shrub which I have often referred to as *Olearia dentalta*, but is, more accurately, *Olearia asterotricha*, I believe. It is just as attractive as the prostantheras, but has not yet been brought to the fore by nurserymen. Of course, like most of the natives, it grows a little spindly if neglected in the matter of pruning, and then gets the sulks if you hack into it because you HAVE neglected it in the past ... don't blame it. It is

heartening to know that this and many other natives of great charm grow very easily from cuttings, and if you like to send a shilling towards the Prisoners of War and a 2 ½d. stamp to Sonning, Mooroolbark, you shall have some cuttings of this olearia, and there is also the native white fuchsia *Correa alba* (same price), which is a marvellously hardy little shrub of three to four feet for arid positions. Oh, and by the way, there is some seed of tweedia at 1/2½ a packet—not much, so hurry if you want it.

PS (all my own)—I have received five postal notes for 2/6 from some anonymous donor which I take to be for the P.O.W. Many, many thanks. And I still get the other shilling. You are dears!

PS (not my own): Sorry that I posted a photograph of *Olearia asterotricha* too late for inclusion.

Edna Walling

J U N E ,   1 9 4 3

Dear Gardeners,

There's so much to tell you that it's hard to know where to start—with the Russian cranberry jam; with the fun I'm having taking cuttings of everything in the garden; (everything with a reasonable chance of striking anyway); with the joy the medlars have been this autumn, and the *Cornus kousa*, a dogwood that has outdone the pink flowering *Cornus florida rubra* in leaf colouration this year.

Then there's the thrilling news of the £85 that went into the Red Cross last month from Sonning. The Croydon branch of the Red Cross Society and I thank you very much for coming when the garden was open, and hope you will come again in November, when we hope to have a treat in store for you. Given suitable weather, it is planned that the stage will be used for the first time and it will be something good, you can rely upon that, and if there are not plenty of foxgloves in flower it certainly won't be my fault, for they are being planted by the hundred. But I shouldn't have said that. Nature has such a way of playing tricks upon one, she likes to put on her own shows without any interference, and just because *I've* decided 'foxgloves,' *she'll* decide on something else and do something to the foxgloves so's they won't spoil her show.

Ambrosia

The Mistress of Lynton Lee said, 'Smell that!', handing me a jar containing some dull red berries. 'Glorious, how do you describe that?' 'Ambrosia', she said dreamily! She had gathered them from her Russian cranberry (which is *Eugenia ugni*, a little evergreen shrub from Brazil). In the evening when she came over to share my fireside she brought me a small pot of jam. It was certainly food for the gods; I can only describe the flavour, and the fragrance, as a cross between pineapple and sweet peas. Grasping secateurs the next morning I toured the garden, taking cuttings from every specimen of the little eugenia I could find, and now hundreds of them are rowed out ready for the onslaught we expect when others get to know about this luxurious fare.

Autumn Colour

The medlars have really been staggering in their autumn colouration this year. Their bold foliage grouped with the more delicate leaves of the birches makes a very satisfying picture. Can't quite decide if they'd grow from cuttings, but think we will have a smack at them. One gets such surprising results in propagation experiments and all good gardeners should do some propagation each autumn and winter so that the plants we love may be increased, or replaced. How to grow trees and shrubs from cuttings seems to me to be part of everyone's education.

NEGLECTED BRANCH OF EDUCATION

It's most interesting to read of all the new ideas for education in the future, but I'm still mystified that trees and timber and landscape gardening are never included, since without trees we would be unable to live. We couldn't endure the cold, we couldn't endure the heat, and we would have no soil, and we would have nothing to build our homes with, and yet few take the slightest interest in the timber which helps to shelter them and to provide them with chairs, tables and beds!

And landscape gardening? Yes, of course that's a necessary part of everyone's education, too. It's the normal thing that we should all have a garden just as we should all have a home and just as there is no excuse for architectural ugliness, so there is no reason for the display of ignorance in the development of the landscape, whether it's a tiny backyard of a civic park, or a traffic highway. Up to the present we've put up a pretty good display and it's time we took a little more care with the good earth. We don't hang mediocre pictures in our national galleries, and it seems equally imperative to guard the landscape against fifth-rate, pseudo-landscape gardeners. Enough!

ANOTHER DOGWOOD

The rough-leaved dogwood (my goodness, I am good to you, here have I been hunting for a common name for *Cornus asperifolia* for what seemed to be hours) is one of the best very late autumn-foliaged shrubs, but I think it is a matter of very little or no water with this plant as with many others. So often I hear: 'That doesn't turn with me.' 'You're too kind to it, perhaps', is the usual reply. The Sonning plants are all in those parts of the garden that get no water but that which drops from the skies, and the soft pinkish foliage in early winter never fails to please us. This shrub throws up occasional suckers which may be planted out, but cuttings are going in, too, so that there will be plenty to plant out later and some for the Prisoners of War Fund.

'Of course what is wrong is that there should be twins of you', said a visitor who came when I was in the midst of doing four things at once. 'Twins? No, quintets you mean, I could keep them all going!' I haven't told you a thing yet, have just been burbling. Well it's your own fault really, you shouldn't write me such nice letters. But I'm glad you do!

And so till next month, goodbye—

Edna Walling

AUGUST, 1943

Dear Gardeners,
It's one of those overwhelming mornings and I'm literally quivering with excitement. I just can't get over all there is to see, and to do. It started at the breakfast table. From there I have a prospect that never fails to please me and this morning the *gold* of the silver birches made me almost forget my breakfast!* It's a morning that glistens with sunlight and the light caught the handle of the white china jug on a blue and white check cloth, which is our habit to spread on the end of the kauri bench. The sun was on the little cloth too, and on the paving stones, and upon the edges of the funny old broom (brought all the way from New South Wales because it looked like our back door) and so I bolted the last mouthfuls of breakfast and flew into the office for my camera, duly recording this precious scene.

HEATH AND ROSEMARY

It's really winter now (June 15) with a vengeance and any pictures in the garden are more than ordinarily to be appreciated. When I observed how charmingly prostrate rosemary and *Erica darleyiensis* (that very low-growing and extremely good-natured little heath that makes such a marvellous ground-covering plant) were flowering together, I nearly left the fort (which was manned with spades, yes, spades, for I like different weights and sizes when I'm on a job of work; one minute you may be working amongst some closely spaced plants and the next you're attacking a worn out or undesirable tree with all the vigour necessary for its removal, vigour that would soon snap in two a light spade; then one must have a shovel ... when I hear anyone calling a spade a shovel I involuntarily squirm, to allude to forceps as pliers seems little worse). Oh! yes, prostrate rosemary and things like that (sorry, Editor). Well, *Eriocephalus africanus,* (I'm sorry about that too, for I do think a simpler name is needed for this little greyling) is also in bloom as I continue this effusion (still June 15), but note that the birch was golden (not bare when this letter began) and its strange little white flowers with reddish-brown centres are most useful for tight little bunches for the dinner table or one's desk. It is particularly sweet with the pale blue flowers of rosemary.

Another thing I love amongst the winter-blooming shrubs is that very old-fashioned erica which has little spires of tiny white bells, *Erica arborea*. How scornful will be the *Erica* fans, but it's very sweet all the same, and an extremely useful shrub which is more than may be said of some of the more showy varieties which sulk shockingly if they don't get exactly what they want in the matter of soil. Amongst this little bunch of flowers two or three blooms of that delight of delights, *Felecia bergeriana*, have been added and this clear blue daisy has given just the depth of colour that the pale grey-blue of the rosemary, the dusky pink of the *Erica darleyiensis* and the greyish-white of both the *Erica arborea* and the greyish-white of both the *Erica arborea* and the eriocephalus appeared to need.

A Word for the P.O.W.

I hope all of you received your cuttings safely; it was a grand response and the P.O.W. Fund profited considerable.

Now we have something really useful to offer you, and that is seed of the tree spinach. You probably know the New Zealand spinach which grows along the ground. Well this grows erect on a single sturdy stem to about four feet in height, and you merely cut the leaves as required.

For four 2 ½d. stamps you may have a packet: P.O.W Fund, of course. Will you enclose stamped addressed envelopes in this case? It would save me a lot of work and you will receive them more promptly; incidentally, the whole 10d. would go to the fund!

Edna Walling

*This letter from Sonning arrived too late for the July number, which explains why the birch was a golden glow and not a tracery of bare branches when those lines were penned.—Editor.

SEPTEMBER, 1943

Dear Gardeners,

I've just put some paper in the typewriter to write some important business letters and this most insubordinate of machines promptly starts 'Dear Gardeners', and I am undone! I must admit I was thinking, 'Must remember to tell them about that group', which made the business letters become so tedious that temptation got the better of me ... never mind, let's hear about the group.

It is composed of a white-stemmed birch, the silver red cedar (*Juniperus virginiana glauca*), the tree heath (*Erica arborea*), *Eriocephalus africanus* (from South Africa), and the Meyer juniper (*Juniperus squamata meyeri*). I think it's the most pleasing winter picture in the garden. In fact, it looks well the whole year around, but in winter its value increases tremendously; then the foliage of the birch has fallen, and the white bark, together with the delicate tracery of the slender twiggage, makes a better foil for the junipers than when the birch is in leaf.

THE ART OF GROUPING

The silver red cedar (cedar is a misnomer, of course, the true cedar family being a small group consisting of *Cedrus atlantica, Cedrus deodara* and *C. libani*). At all events this juniper is next to the birch, about eight feet away, or less. It grows fairly rapidly and eventually reaches a height of 20 feet, I believe, which makes this particular one rather close to the birch, perhaps. However, it is a tree with an open and rather loose habit, and does not appear that it will be in conflict with the birch as a more compact and rigid variety might have been; too-wide spacing might have produced an effect of 'Specimens' and have missed the idea of a natural group.

Next to the juniper and a little to the front of it comes the heath with its spires of tiny white flowers looking so lovely amongst the silvery-grey of the juniper; this is from four to five feet away, and about the same distance from the Meyer juniper, which could be either forward or slightly back of the heath. Incidentally, the heath could be a little behind rather than forward of the red cedar, in which case the Meyer juniper would probably be best forward of the heath. Do you get the idea? The more low-growing, coarser-leaved Meyer juniper would then appear to be in closer association with the tall-growing red cedar.

Of course, so much depends upon where the group is to be made and the shape of the border in which it is planted. One can't give rigid rules for the making of garden pictures with trees, and shrub, and ground cover, since no two sets of conditions are ever the same—or very rarely so.

Growing to only 12 or 18 inches in height, the eriocephalus is obviously for the foreground, but no, I shouldn't have said obviously, because these low-growing, ground-covering plants should frequently run back in drifts amongst the taller-growing species to give the best effect and to avoid that dreadful habit of 'bordering' a group of trees and shrubs with some edging plant. Really it's as bad as putting a row of stones around a bed or border.

To return to the eriocephalus, it will fit in anywhere in such a group, where the colouring is simply grey and white, but it might be advisable not to allow it to hide any of the effect of the birch trunk, which is always so beautiful right to the ground. Nay, even loveliest just here, perhaps and so for ground cover around the birch you need something very low indeed, like the silvery-

grey *Thymus serpyilum* var. 'Lang Hall', or *lanigunosa*. It's an awful humbug
trying to get ground-covering plants to grow when the trees have become
established and have become accustomed to having all their own way with
the ground round about them; so you must get your low-growing planting
done at the same time as you plant your trees. That is, you must COMPLETE
your picture or you'll find yourself battling most unsuccessfully later. Give
plants an equal start and they will grow up happily together, providing the
association is a reasonable one—we all know the propensities of some plants
for smothering everything within reach.

A Superb Apple

Quite by accident I have run to earth the correct name of that loveliest of all
flowering apples, so long catalogued as *Malus augustifolia*. It seems to be a
recently introduced form of the prairie crab. It has been given the name of
the 'Bechtel Crab', and is botanically known as *Malus ioenisis*. I believe I've
mentioned this apple before, but don't think I had this information then. It's
an American, with rather rigid branches beset with numerous short lateral
thorn-like spurs. The soft pink flowers are much larger than all the other
apples, and being double, they are rather like balls of very pale pink cotton
wool. It flowers after the more familiar varieties are over and has a fragrance
that is exquisite! When I think of the autumn foliage of this little tree I
remember I have told you about it before. It is distinctly good in autumn.

And a Fairy-Like Shrub

For the first time I have seen a plant of *Viburnum fragrans* flowering really well
and I gasped with joy, it was such a surprise. We were walking around a garden
I'd planted several years ago, and on turning a corner of the house there it was,
covered with the daintiest little bunches of white flowers, faintly flushed with
pink, and as we drew nearer the fragrance was positively inebriating! I'm sorry

I don't seem to be able to keep off birches, but you must know that a birch tree in the offing did greatly enhance its beauty ... it's their devastatingly beautiful silvery-white bark, isn't it? I'm going to have the most glorious time planting out dozens of them this season. They have been rowed out in the nursery for a year waiting until we had that slope ready for them, and now we have ... No, really, I *must* go back to those importunate business letters.

Yours till October,

Edna Walling

OCTOBER, 1943

Dear Gardeners,

It's cruel, I'm afraid, to tell you about a *Prunus mume* I know you cannot get, but there's always the chance that you *might* locate it. Then I become sorry for the nurseryman who has to listen to a deedy description of the only plant he can't supply! On one occasion I accompanied a friend to a nursery in search of a climbing rose 'that holds up its head'. Yes, that was the qualifi-cation; she didn't want anything that 'hung its head'. Well, the tour began, and during the tour we were shown, and we discovered, many delightful plants, from herbaceous perennials to forest trees, sprinkled with the species ROSE, which was the object of our visit, of course. The friend was a much keener gardener than I am and much more knowledgeable; consequently she asked searching questions about each treasure—rather intimate ones, I thought: whether it 'becomes a nuisance', for instance, and whether it was 'fussy'. We came upon many roses and several times were on the point of making the momentous decision when the question would come: 'Does it climb?' 'Oh, no, this is a bush rose', and on we would go again. On, until we were shown another rose that was obviously a climber, already throwing itself about in the most self-assertive fashion. 'Does it hold up its head?' that poor man was asked. 'Ah! No, I'm afraid it doesn't.' (What a man!) On, on, and the next stop is at a shasta daisy (the variety 'Chiffon'), described so poetically that we both purchase a plant. 'Does it thrive as well as the old variety?' the nurseryman is asked. 'Yes, and it holds up its head and climbs!' he replied!

Oh, yes, the *Prunus*. It has large double white flowers—that is, larger than the ordinary white one, and it's fragrant, of course. I must give some buds to a nurseryman so that it can be distributed.

THE BEAUTY BUSH

Kolkwitzia amibile! (The beauty bush). It does seem a pity about the name, doesn't it? But there it is! I don't think there *could* be a sweeter shrub. The arching sprays of pale, pale pink flowers in late spring please everyone that sees it, and it most obligingly surrounds itself with rooted pieces (suckers, if you will) that enable one to share them with one's friends and increase one's own supply of beauty. I shall never forget seeing this shrub with rhododendrons one year. It was a lovely combination, lightening the somewhat heavy effect of the rhododendrons. I must say I don't enjoy a *mass* of the hybrid rhododendrons; they seem to be so much more effective when grouped with other shrubs and trees, and yet I suppose that's why people mass them— for an effect. Well, I'm afraid I don't like a *show*—perhaps that's it.

A THYME I COVET

I make no bones about it, for I definitely covet *Thymus carnosus*. Who wouldn't covet a little plant that is described as being 'rather like a miniature poplar, slow-growing, compact, with long pure white flowers'? It was the 'pure white flowers' that completed my downfall, for I do love white flowers and find it difficult to make further conversation with those who declare their dislike for anything with white flowers.

Another thyme that I'm ready to leap upon, if it ever comes within my ken, is 'Pink Chintze'. Heavens! What a dearth of these delights there is in this country. In the *Gardener's Chronicle* of May 29, 1943, recently received from London, I read with delight the leading article on 'Thyme', and particularly remarked the following:

A fit playground for fairies which are said to love thyme-decked banks for their revels, although we confess we have never been so fortunate as to see even one.

Of all the periodicals I subscribed to in pre-war days, this and *My Garden* have survived the economy campaign. *The Chronicle* I find indispensable for those editorials (and I have never yet written to the Editor to say 'Thank you') which have such an appeal, regardless of the country in which one lives. Until I read this particular article I did not know that thyme not only makes food more palatable, but more digestible as well. But did you know that *Thymol*, the antiseptic so reminiscent of the dentist's chair, is much more powerful than carbolic acid, much less toxic, and, of course, of much pleasanter flavour? Apart from its usefulness, the common thyme, *Thymus vulgaris*, is a most attractive early summer-flowering plant, the soft pinkish-mauve flowers making a marvellous setting for flowering shrubs such as the hybrid brooms. Both plants enjoy the same conditions, rather on the arid side, and so here's your ground cover for that spot where 'nothing will grow'.

Goodbye till November,

Edna Walling

N O V E M B E R ,   1 9 4 3

Dear Gardeners,

Of all the fairy-like shrubs, could anything be more fairy-like than *Spirea thunbergii?* It seems strange that a more appealing name has never been given this gem to offset its botanic appellation—with all due respect to Mr Thunberg! There are drifts of it all over the garden, but we need still more. A little later *Spirea arguta* follows with equally fairy-like flowers; it's really sweeter, if anything, but then the point about these two pets is that they don't cramp one another's style. That's rather nice of them, I think. It's almost as though *arguta* looks around at *thunbergii* (Oh! I do hate that name!) and says 'Finished?' and when it's quite sure, it bursts forth with all its specialties. It is just divine with that variety of forsythia I find quite the most pleasing, in spite of its rather golden foliage (no, I don't like golden foliage much) which goes by the name of *Forsythia vitillina aurea.*

22.9.43

This delayed action sort of letter has its advantages; it is now the 22nd and here follows all that is in flower at the moment: right bang in front of the office window is *Malus sonningiensis* at her very best. My word! She's a bold lass, with all the richness of colouring of *Malus eleyii* (one of the best of the wine-red varieties of the *floribunda* type of apple, but later in flower). This chance seedling that came up at Sonning certainly knocks the old *floribunda purpurea* clean out of the running, it pales so miserably before this 'blousy' beauty. I'm ashamed that there isn't a single *floribunda* (the Japanese flowering crab) to be seen; my sole specimen the possums took to with tremendous gusto, and I've neglected to plant numbers of this most delightful of all the crabs, to my great discredit. When ordering, for heaven's sake don't let them send you *M. floribunda purpurea*, which is entirely different; *floribunda* has bright red buds, opening to white petals, and therein lies its charm. *Purpurea* has petals of a washed-out red.

Ceanothus rigidus is flowering as never before, and the almost navy blue flowers are simply exquisite with a foil of forget-me-nots; a few white Germanica irises are in the offing, and a clump of prostrate rosemary leaves nothing more to be desired in this particular picture.

Some adorable very dwarf flag irises are just finishing, their flower stems are but six inches high, and often even less. *Iris marginata* is surely no more than three inches in height, and of a most exquisite shade of amethyst and blue. I regret that I have no name for the lovely clear yellow variety of five or six inches which provided such a welcome patch of soft yellow among the thymes at its feet last month. There you are! I've wandered away from that list; how untidily long-winded some people can be!

Viburnum carlesii, and could anything be lovelier? You can all safely plant it, because I've never heard a single person have anything but praise for this deciduous flowering shrub with its pink and white fragrant blooms.

Cytisus praecox, that earliest of the brooms, is very charming in its pale yellow, or deep cream dress, and that it is not one of the lusty growers makes it useful for small gardens, and excellent for drifts in large ones.

Exorchorda grandiflora (commonly called the pearl bush, because of its very round white buds, I suppose) makes a stately shrub to group with the flowering apples, it is a cloud of white at the moment; and another white flowering shrub of the same large growing proportions is the shad bush, *Amelanchier canadensis*. This is at its best when only half in bloom, the soft grey buds of the unopened flowers make such a delightful setting for the expanded petals of the more precocious flowers. In the fall the foliage turns most beautifully, in places where the water supply is not too lavishly tapped.

Rhododendron racemosum. My goodness! I better not let myself go on that one: it's just smothered with tiny pink flowers set off with the quite small greyish-green foliage. Another native of western China is a perfect delight with its pale mauve flowers and very tiny foliage, it is evidently *R. impeditum*, but I'm not going to be sure after all I've recently read about these small-growing species. If I ever break my leg and can have an uninterrupted session with an encyclopedia, etc. I'll be able to straighten out a lot of things and shall write it all down for you.

I shouldn't like to be without *Armeria alpina* of the Pyrenees, I much prefer it to the sea Pink of England so often called 'thrift'. The flowers are paler and less aniline in tone; they are also shorter in the stem and larger of bloom. The white form of *Armeria maritima* (the English thrift) I love, and cherish the sweet fresh greenness of its foliage drifting along the pathway's edge.

One of the brightest and gayest of the rock plants at present in bloom is *Aethionema*, there are dozens of varieties of the species, but the one known as 'Warley rose' seems to be the only one available here. This is a bright pink—very bright!—and as gromwell (*Lithospermum prostratum*), with its gentian-blue vividness is in flower, too, some considerable distance is needed between these two colours of no uncertain tones if violent contrasts are to be avoided—unless you're a glutton for colour!

I've nobly refrained from saying I think we should all be planting timber trees instead of rock plants. Heaven knows we'll need 'em before we're done! Nine hundred trucks of firewood a week! And that's not to mention the hundreds of truck loads of building timber which go into Melbourne steadily as well. Ah, well, goodbye.

Edna Walling

Dear Gardeners,

It seems ages since I last wrote to you, but there has been no urgent, 'where the so-and-so is your letter?' from the Editor; perhaps he is saying 'I'll learn her, I'll publish the paper without it', I feel like grabbing my hat and starting to run, not stopping till I reach his office, falling into a chair exhausted—it's 20 miles so I probably would be exhausted—but I'd manage to pant 'Oh, Mr Editor, *please* wait for little me; I know I'm unimportant but THEY are important to me and they might, they just *might* be disappointed if I don't write.'

Goodness, wouldn't I cut a funny figure in the old white helmet used for lawn-mowing and vegetable gardening, the old and very patched blue shirt, jodhpurs of an even older vintage, blue- and white-striped socks (very special favourites, donned this morning to put me in the right mood for writing to you) ... No, I think I'd better risk his vengeance.

I've promised someone, who wrote one of the sweetest letters I've ever received and shall always keep, that I'd say something about pathways this

time. It's rather strange, because I had already made a note to do so. They are so very important. You know how I LOVE concrete! Well, the reason I'm so against it is that it so cruels all one's efforts at making pictures in the garden right from the outset, and if we are not striving to make pictures what *are* we doing? Of course some people grow plants just for the joy of the individual specimen, or the thrill it gives them to look upon a blazing mass of one particular species. Paths to them never mean anything more than merely a dry footway from one part of the garden to another; that they should be permanent, clean and entirely free of maintenance is all they ask. For those concrete is all very well, so long as 'we' can't see it! However, here am I slating something that we jolly well have to use sometimes for lack of the real thing.

In districts where paving stones are unprocurable and in places where gravel is undesirable—and by gravel I mean interesting things like limestone toppings or crushed rock, which is the fine material used for surfacing country roadways—we sometimes have to set to work and make flat stones, but there is no earthly reason why they should take the form of those awful outsized postage stamps which I have never yet seen looking anything but silly. 'But that's all one can buy', some will say. *That's* why you must make them yourself.

One of the things the war has done for us is to make us less helpless. I hope I haven't sounded too snappy when perfectly well and strong people (unused strength) get, 'Do it yourself!' in answer to their complaint that they can't get a man anywhere. I haven't had the pluck to say it to those beautiful ladies who have never stooped to pull out a weed in their lives, having no previous experience with fainting ladies. Heavens, I'd love to see them mixing concrete!

REALLY CRAZY PATHS

Anyway, here is the 'infallible recipe' for making stones for paved pathways: mix three or four parts of coarse sand (rough stuff with little stones in it would be all the better) with one of cement. Mix it thoroughly in the dry condition then add the water by sprinkling, not flooding. On a piece of hard-swept ground dump shovelfuls, some small, some large, of the mixture and roughly pat them down to one-and-a-half to two inches. When set, about 48 hours, turn them over and behold your 'stones.' Rather rough ground will give a more natural surface than too smooth, which gives that artificial evenness which is so distasteful. The stones will be sufficiently uneven in shape to make it unnecessary to endeavour to make them more crazy, except perhaps for a little push now and then so that they will not be of a uniform roundness. These are set in the earth. There must not be a fraction of a root of couch or of other grass of a similar creeping nature underneath them. It is really not a good idea either to sow grass in the joints. Mosses and other tiny plants will soon come; meanwhile, keep it clear of coarse weeds by hand weeding. Don't disturb the earth by raking between the joints with some scratchy tool, thus discouraging the mosses, etc.

Paved pathways trickling up to the front door are very inviting, and when they are laid with not too much care as to line they are much more charming than when they follow a perfect curve. Of course, if it is to be a straight pathway it must *be* straight, and a brick-paved path paved with old, old bricks running straight from gate to doorway can be very alluring—no that's not the word, that makes us think of a little track running through trees and shrubs to no-one knows where; fascinating little paths that may be just of earth or just sprinkled with gritty sand or inconspicuous gravel.

QUITE CRAZY

Once I visited a garden where they had spent so much money that there was not one spot in all those acres where nature had been allowed to make her own incomparable pictures. At last we came upon a little earthen track running through a thicket of trees and shrubs and we breathed a sigh of relief, only to espy at the other end workmen busily laying down crazy paving. 'Crazy!' we muttered with one accord.

Broken bricks that have been roughly trimmed into little squares make dear little pathways. I never see a heap of such 'rubbish' without the desire to set to work making a little path or paving a little with them.

One thing I have noticed and that is that expensively laid pathways are nearly always ugly! Isn't that encouraging? Take wooden plinths and other forms of kerbing. They're all expensive and all ugly. Even if they do keep the earth back, I'd rather wait until plants do it and have them wandering about hiding up the hard and unsightly man-made lines. Nothing in the world is prettier than a pathway trickling through borders of 'Shepherd's thyme' (*Thymus serpyllum*). Never, never, never should these be trimmed. You see we walk upon the most precocious shoots and thus restrict them; besides it wouldn't really matter if they crept right across, it would be all the lovelier to walk upon. Would YOU rather walk upon thyme or something hard that wears out your shoe leather and jars your nerves?

I must go and hoe after that lovely rain. My system of managing this rather extensive garden is to wait for the rain and then go for my life! It's a very pleasant system, for when the ground is hard and uninteresting I always say to myself, 'Well, don't do it, wait for the rain!' However, I'm working towards the perfect system, which is to eliminate all activity but the mowing of grass. That is, I'm feverishly covering the whole place with mulch as fast as I can rake it up; hay in the paddock makes up the deficiency in lawn cuttings. Where the weeds have overtaken me I just stamp them down and throw the mulch on top!

Goodbye,

Edna Walling

FEBRUARY, 1944

Dear Gardeners,
I think I've mentioned once before that I have a reputation for harping, and frenkenia, that adorable little native of England, where it is called sea heath, is probably a note on which much harping has already been done! Well, you see, it is in flower now and I don't think there *could* be a sweeter little plant, and if you've ever longed for a thyme with pink flowers, as I have done, you need not any longer, for nothing could more closely resemble such a—such a—what *is* the word to use for something you desire very much? It doesn't seem to mind a fairly hot and dry position, so long as there is a bit of body in the soil.

Of all the flowers that are most satisfactory in times when only a few may be grown because of the necessity for food-growing surely the perennial lupin must be one. Apart from its generosity in giving a succession of bloom it is a legume, and that means that it is quite likely to be a soil improver as well because of its capacity for gathering nitrogen from the air. Of course this theory might be refuted by those much wiser than I, but legumes *do* store up nitrogen. You have only to pull up a lupin to see for yourself. There are the little white bags right enough. Save the seed of the best of them because although they are perennials it is necessary to have young plants coming on as the old ones fade out.

I have just read a most enlightening article in the *Gardener's Chronicle* (England) on carrots and carotene. Apparently carotene, which is the precursor of vitamin A, still persists when the chlorophyll in leaves fades away, giving place to chromoplasts, to which the yellow and brown of autumn leaves are due. There! You've probably often wondered. But there are several carotenes it seems, and the one most readily, or most effectively, utilised by the liver in its manufacture of vitamin A is known as carotene B. And here's something to confound past theories: although carrots contain exceptionally large quantities of carotene (hence their characteristic colour) the absorption of carotene from carrots in man is low, whereas practically all the carotene and vitamin A in butter is absorbed by our bodies.

Green vegetables are also rich in carotene; cooked green peas, for example, are worth twice as much as spinach—and much easier to grow! The article ends by saying:

We shall not look down on the carrot, for in spite of any carotene shortcomings it has plenty of other virtues: it keeps well in storage, gives abundant yields, looks nice in the herbaceous border, and is a pleasant food if you do not have too much of it. All the same, we shall rely as much as possible on butter and cod-liver oil and green vegetables for giving the children the material for making vitamin A and only fall back on the carrot when these other helpers fail.

The photograph is of *Ceanothus edwardsii* trained as a wall shrub. I've come to the conclusion that is the only way to cultivate this unwieldy plant. One must prune it just as frequently, but the effect at flowering time repays one's attentions in this matter of constant snipping, much more liberally than when it is a large, buxom shrub displaying two-thirds of its beauty to the sky.

There is one thing about the plant pictures which I prescribe—you may always be sure they are practically foolproof for, as you've been told before, I'm no gardener, and if a plant thrives in my garden it's a pretty good-tempered piece of plant life! Two such plants are *Hypericum cuneatum* and *Campanula porcharskyana*, whose soft yellow and mauve flowers group so charmingly in summer when so many other rock plants are past their best.

I'm extremely interested in the hardiness of *Daphne cenorum*, a quite small shrublet with pale pink flowers and a fragrance all its own. A plant in my mother's garden has withstood many searing summers without water other than the rains that fell from heaven. It is sometimes called the garland flower, and is a low-spreading shrub of no more than a foot high with downy branches thickly clothed with leaves. I have said the flowers are pale pink but they are really a rosy pink. It is a native of Central and Southern Europe.

Another daphne, very unlike the familiar variety we all know so well is *Daphne genkwa*, a deciduous shrub probably three or four feet high, sparsely

branched with silky-grey shoots bearing lilac-coloured flowers on the naked branches in November. Unfortunately this exquisite little shrub from China is short-lived, but I fancy it would not be difficult to propagate.

Aethionema, 'Waverley Rose', is seeding fairly freely this year. One of the most delightful pink-flowered rock plants which we might cultivate more freely perhaps. It always seemed to be asking too much that it would strike from cuttings easily, so I must cherish the seed and experiment with it or give it to someone who will.

Sonning, 24/12/43

Edna Walling

MARCH, 1944

Dear Gardeners,

Goodness! Boys are lucky. I've just read an announcement to the effect that they may go to the Creswick School of Forestry for a two- or three-year course (I've forgotten which) free of charge, and I think that includes their board. They must have their 'leaving' and I believe they have to pass a simple exam and a medical test, of course. Until recently, I had the idea that a University course was essential, and in my anxiety to start a certain boy (who was unable to pay the fees) upon the road to a forestry career I wrote to Canberra asking was there no other way in which he could commence, and was informed that they were afraid there was no 'back door entrance to Forestry'. It seems a pity we did not know of Creswick at the time, it's such an attractive life and one that many youths do not think of until well on the way to another career, in spite of its immense possibilities.

GARDENS OF THE FUTURE

'I don't want to spend all my Saturdays and Sundays mowing and watering lawns and weeding and planting flower beds.' Yes, and what a number of other men kick at that, too. I don't blame them! It is not at all necessary, of course, it's merely a matter of planning. Actually some quite small gardens need not have any lawn at all. Paving of stone or brick with plenty of creeping thymes to provide softness (and Irish moss, too, where it is too shady for the thymes) will present a much more interesting effect than the conventional grasses and demand no labour beyond the occasional removal of weeds. Now don't complain of that. If you do there's nothing for it but concrete from house to street ... Yes, plenty of paving, that's what I would advise for those who would rather rest in their gardens than work. The little treasures you grow in between and at the edges of the paving will find a cool root run beneath the stones, and a rinse down of the paving now and then will be all the watering they will require.

A garden comprised of [comprising] one fairly large shade tree, a birch, a liquidambar, an American hornbeam (or the English one, which grows much bigger), a pear, a plane or an apple tree—unpruned, of course, if you're after shade and beauty—with some wall shrubs to conceal the boundary fences and the ground covered with bricks or paving stones, can become a veritable outdoor living room. A very low table made of two or three wide planks clamped together, and some canvas chairs and a stool or two, will make you breathe a sigh of relief and pleasure immediately you enter the gate, instead of hissing, 'Curse that lawn!' Any irresistible plants might be grown in pots. But that means daily watering. It doesn't take long to water a few pots, but if you are going away it's a nuisance unless you are good at those Heath Robinson contraptions which provide a steady drip over a given period.

A MINIATURE AUSTRALIAN

Brachycome graminae is a harsh name for one so sweet as this little native daisy. I mention it now because it is in full bloom in a coloured cement pot (Jan. 24th) and its cherry mauve half-inch high blooms are particularly enjoyable on that account. Few other rock plants are in bloom; there is a flower or two on some young plants of *Dianthus*, 'Little Jock,' a great favourite of mine, and *Thymus serpyllum coccinea* and *T .s. alba* are abloom.

If I hunted about no doubt many other little treasures would be holding up their faces to be taken notice of, but I'm grass-minded rather than flower-minded just now, owing to the prevalence of bushfires. How very industrious and how very tidy we shall all have to be, for we just can't continue to get away with long inflammable grass. Fires start in grass and rubbish, and so pottering about growing this and that isn't really permissible if we have not cleaned up our boundaries and made our own neighbours' properties safe from fire.

There's a terrific task ahead of me in a two-acre bush paddock, but when the telephone rang this morning a seraphic smile spread over my face as I listened to an offer of a day's work from two of the best workers I know, and so three instead of one pair of hands will reduce that particular fire hazard considerably. Both these men have their own properties. That's life, isn't it? Help always comes from the busiest ones.

People with country estates might adopt the idea of having raking parties, and hay-making parties, too. It's ever so much more fun doing something all together than just lolling about. Moreover, if we are to save this country from these everlasting fires we shall have to do a lot more figure-reducing work, for its no use speaking about the lack of labour if we're not going all out ourselves. In the West there are few fires because you are bound by law to cut your grass, and keeping grass cut means keeping blackberries and other noxious weeds down, too. I wonder why Victoria is so far behind the other

States. That we have not followed W.A.'s lead as regards the compulsory cutting of grass is a piece of gross negligence when one views the devastating results.

Perennial Beauty—Sixpence a Packet

Not really perennial, of course, compared with trees, but with many years' flowering confidently to be expected of them; and the flower is the perennial lupin. We have saved a quantity of seed, some of which may be had for a stamped addressed envelope and six penny (or four 1½d.) stamps; proceeds to the Prisoners of War.—Yours,

Edna Walling

MAY, 1944

Dear Gardeners,

The other day I decided it was time that I bestirred myself to action, instead of talking so much about the alarming elimination of gum trees in this country, and as the trees about here were bearing seed at that time, there was nothing to excuse me from gathering and sowing it. Of course, one had to turn a deaf ear to all those other things that were crying out to be done, and, with no assistance at all at the moment, I found myself literally stepping over the things that would claim one's time, in my path to the potting shed. However, the result is that the little trees that are now nearly six inches high, were sown on November the 20th. Not bad for 11 weeks is it? I look fondly at these little fellows, musing upon their importance; for one day they, or their offspring, will make good timber, fuel or paper pulp, incidentally they will provide us with beauty for years before the time comes for felling them.

MADAM, IT'S UP TO YOU!

Asked why I had not planted a forest a little while ago, I replied with studious calm (in order to conceal the exasperation which burned within me) that such joys seemed to be denied those fully occupied in furiously tidying a country property in order to prevent it from being overwhelmed by noxious weeds or fire, and that it might be that those living in flats or boarding houses had more opportunity for doing this national work of reafforesting the odd corners not dealt with by an apparently already overtaxed Forest Commission. Whereupon the lady looked at me as if I was something that offended her delicate nostrils! It was clear that she saw no obligation upon herself in the matter of tree planting, so I continued, warming to the subject of timber planting as a social obligation. 'Have you ever stopped to realise that every hour of the day you are dependent upon wood in some shape or form?' No reply, which meant she hadn't. 'And that you take your frequent walking and camping expeditions where you may enjoy the trees natural to the countryside? And have you ever done a single

thing about their preservation and propagation, or have you just taken all you can get, including the wood to boil your billy, the health, and the priceless mental refreshment, not to be gained in such proportion by any planting of 'ornamental' trees? Because you derive so much from these expeditions, do you belong to the Forest League? If so, are you an active member? Has it ever occurred to you that for quite a small outlay you could acquire an acre or two on which there are no trees, and without absorbing even half the time given to just walking, you could plant from six to seven hundred trees to the acre? And have you the vision to imagine the thrill of pride that is in store for you not so many years hence?'

We looked down towards the meadow at some lovely little conifers. 'No, those are not Roman cypress, they are your own native 'Victorian cypress', *Callitris cupressiformis*, and they were grown from seed gathered from some grand old specimens near the O'Shannassy water course at Mt. Evelyn. It is rather pathetic, isn't it? We know the Roman cypress so much better than our own!'

And after that I went straight to the potting shed and sowed some gum seeds! She had certainly put me on the spot, but I wasn't going down without a struggle.

Gathering the Seed of Native Trees

I suppose most people know what the seed capsules of gum trees look like; but it's amazing how many don't realise that you don't sow the whole thing. Not that it would matter, of course, for the seed would eventually trickle out and come through the soil, no doubt. However, it is customary to place the capsules in a box, and, in a day or two, the fine, almost dust-like seed, will have dropped out; this is sown in a pot of sandy loam just in the same manner as you would raise any other seeds. When about two or three inches high, they are potted into three-inch pots, where they remain until they have developed a sufficiently compact mass of roots so that the earth does not fall away when knocked out of the pots for planting out. Since starting this letter, I have potted out a number of my baby trees, and hope to be planting them out into their permanent positions in about May. By the way, the capsules must be examined to see that the seed is still there, also to see that it is not too green. It doesn't take much imagination to judge whether it is ripe, and certainly none at all to discover if the vessel contains any seed. You merely have to peep into the little holes in the top; these won't even be open if the seed is still there; if they are open it is hardly likely to be there.

The seeds of callitris are contained in little cones which spread open in a day or two after being gathered, shedding the rather flat seeds peculiar to this species. Being much larger than eucalyptus seed, they need more covering ... about an eight or three-sixteenths of an inch. Eucalyptus seed requires but a dusting of soil. Callitris seed seems to take a good many weeks to make up its mind to appear. In one pan of these seeds, two little trees appeared fairly soon, and were half-an-inch high before the rest of the seed showed through. I certainly did not expect the belated ones, and was registering slight annoyance and bewilderment, because I had gathered the seed myself and knew it to be fresh.

I suppose this is all very irritating to those with no earthly hope of ever being able to put such ideas into practice; but if you simply can't do it yourself, you can inspire others to do so, and try to get children gathering the seeds of gum trees, instead of looking upon them as something to cut down. Grown scientifically, as they are in other countries, they are an inspiring sight, but we rarely, if ever, see serried ranks of the beautiful timber trees of Australia because the forest has receded so far from the cities' boundaries, and we have not yet adopted the policy of planting all wastelands and worn-out farms with native timber trees; moreover, we have suffered from the delusion that *Pinus radiata* is a better tree to plant than the native timbers. It makes me so hot around the collar that I had better stop right now! And I promise I won't say a word about gum trees next month.

If I have missed a month, I can only plead 'reduced capacity', probably due to no holiday; it just didn't come off, nor did it last year. This holiday-at-home idea doesn't work. Perhaps the Editor will print this over-long epistle under the circumstances, and even include the picture, which has been especially asked for. If we do nothing else by building these 'picture postcard cottages', as one amused person dubbed them, we produce a good laugh from the exponents of the boot and corset box type of architecture. I may be wrong, but in a climate where living on the roof is not as appealing as in a rainless and continually hot one, I do not think the flat roof has come to stay.

I hope no-one minded receiving their lupin seeds in used envelopes. Saving paper becomes more and more essential, I am told. And thank you all for the nice little notes of appreciation of these letters.

Edna Walling

JUNE, 1944

Dear Gardeners,

Two of the loveliest plants in the garden at present are the manna ash (*Fraxinus ornus*) and the American blueberry (*Vaccinium corymbosum*), which is a deciduous shrub growing to—well, from four to 12 feet high, apparently! You see my particular plants are not more than three-and-a-half feet, and I have not seen any larger, but according to Mr. W. J. Bean, in his fascinating volumes *Trees and Shrubs Hardy in the British Isles*, we have it that it grows from four to 12 feet. The autumn colouring is simply exquisite, and to my great joy I discovered it grows quite readily from cuttings rowed out in the open ground, and so this year I shall have a real party grouping them about with ash and liquidambars, and the large-growing maples, *Acer saccharum* (the sugar maple, as you probably know) and the English maple (*Acer campestre*), which turns such a glorious clear yellow and has such fascinating small, rather blunt-pointed leaves.

Where these will go there are already two rather good specimens of the shad bush, *Amelanchier canadensis*, which have coloured such a rich red this year, in spite of the season, and their position, which is far removed from a tap. One does have fine autumn colouring when the trees are not coddled, but enjoy a heavy mulch of leaves and grass cuttings ... well that is coddling them, of course; far more so than pouring the water on as though that was all the Board of Works had to do—conserve and convey to us water to be poured onto plants we have been too lazy to mulch!

CASCADE CHRYSANTHEMUMS

I'm beginning to think that no late autumn border is complete without cascade chrysanthemums, and for indoor decoration they are simply delightful. At the moment we have a huge white pottery jug full of these pale pink and white chrysanthemums which look rather like outsized perennial asters (Michaelmas daisies). A few branches of that rarely seen variety, *Aster trinervis*, which is the latest to come into flower with its rather bright purple, yellow-centred daisies, are very sweet with the chrysanthemums. This aster has a leaf that is distinct from those of the other more familiar varieties, and is usually to be found only in very old gardens where it has been fortunate enough to escape the energies of the ruthless digger. The broad, rough leaf makes it very easy to distinguish in the winter when the flowers have passed, and anyone who calls it a pest because it increases by underground stems is talking through his hat, for it is quite easy to control. The fact is that many very delightful plants have been 'controlled' out of existence, just because they take up a bit of ground space if we've been neglectful in the matter of attending to these most useful and desirable perennials. However, we are learning now, being sick to death of the expense and labour of growing annuals; not to mention the nightly raids upon that horrid nudist, the slug.

THE DOYEN OF TREE LOVERS

Since starting this letter I've been to see Mr St John—twice! Do you know I can't get over it when I have to explain who Mr St John is? Why? Because he is one of the most interesting men in Australia. Small wonder that, in one of his books, Ambrose Pratt called him 'The man with the marvellous memory'. What is so enthralling about listening to his answers to one's endless queries is that he tells you so many intriguing things of the plants that you ask about ... Oh! That's funny, I was just saying to myself, 'Now, don't talk about gum trees ... you promised you wouldn't' (and it was going to be difficult because Mr St John is *the* authority upon them, you know) when the mail came and with it a letter from Mr Editor, in which he says, 'Don't be late this month (!) and you can expatiate a bit more on gum trees if you like'. Whereupon I threw up my hat, crying 'Oh, Boy!' (most unseemingly), planked my typie upon the desk and prepared for a really good time.

Well, as I was saying, Mr St John is one of the most interesting men in Australia, but much more than that, he is one of the most valuable men to this country, for from him we can learn best about the most useful commodity in the land, namely the eucalypt, or gums if you wish.

You probably know that it is to Mr W. R. Guilfoyle that we owe the design of the Botanic Gardens. I regard it as one of our everlasting losses that Mr St John did not succeed him as Director, for no-one had greater knowledge or so great an appreciation of the art of picture making on the landscape. Sir Ronald Munro-Ferguson (later Lord Novar), Governor-General of Australia at the time, spent every available spare moment with Mr St John, whom he used to whisk off to the forest and enjoy hours of instruction from 'The Father of the Eucalypt'. It was Miss Francis Taylor, whose untimely death was such a loss to the journalist world, and to the cause of the Australian trees, who gave that title to Mr St John. That Lord Novar should have been made Forester-General of Australia was a suggestion that Mr St

John put to many, for he knew him to be not only an expert forester, but that the timber industry was the chief interest in his life.

Another person we hear practically nothing about, who edits one of the most educational little books in Australia, is Miss Thistle Y. Harris, of New South Wales. *The Junior Tree Warden* is a book that should be on every bookstall. To think that the country spends £200 a week on the publication of a radio weekly when there is a person in our very midst who could produce a most informative, practical and readable periodical of undeniably greater value! In my exasperation at the thought I nearly forgot to mention that Miss Harris is the author of *Wild Flowers of Australia*, a reference book I would not like to be without.

There! Now I've talked all about people and have no space left for trees after all; but never fear, it will follow! Besides, if we get to know more about these people we can't help getting to know more about trees, too. Meanwhile, I am gleaning all I can from Mr St John who, even if he were not ill, has insufficient self-assertiveness to make his knowledge more fully available to us ... how often this is so; meanwhile we suffer the half-knowledge of many so-called 'experts'. No more brickbats for now!

Edna Walling

JULY, 1944

Dear Gardeners,
The other day I returned to a country property to which I had been called a year or so previously, and on the long drive from the boundary fence to the residence I glanced across at a favourite hill, to my utter dismay saw that all the drifts of bursaria that made it so lovely had been removed! The tiny

foliage of this fragrant shrub is so shiny that it reflects the light and gives an airiness to the landscape which constitutes an extremely valuable component of the natural scene.

Not being spectacular this, with many another delightful native shrub, is all too frequently slashed down and consigned to the fire as 'scrub'. I wonder what those who so wantonly destroy all that is not positively showy imagine the landscape would look like without these lesser jewels—this material that forms the setting and the shelter for more delicate things! I don't suppose they *imagine* anything ... that's the trouble. On my own particular property I value the common tea-tree and the self-sown blackwoods as much as if not more than the exotics, about which I feel quite shame-faced at times. Of course, if we understood and appreciated ecology (also see 'oecology') a little more, this matter of plants in relationship to their surroundings would save us from making so many stupid mistakes.

Erosion

We stood looking across at a steep hill lightly timbered, and on being told they intended to clear it except for shelter belts, I had meekly asked, 'Aren't you afraid of erosion?' and with not the slightest hesitation came the reply, 'Oh, no, it's too wet here'. (E.W., *sotto voce*: 'Heavens!') This from what would be regarded as an otherwise intelligent person. Evidently the *Daily Press* is the place—and the only place, because everyone reads that—to publish facts and pictures showing cattle tracks becoming grand canyons, tiny rivulets forming vast washaways. I have never understood why so many vitally important matters are published in the Weeklies and left out of the Dailies. If they cannot appear in both it would seem more beneficial that they appear in the latter. However, it is nice to know that at least two people in the same district are about to plant hundreds and hundreds of gum trees, having decided that timber-growing is more profitable than grazing.

ONE OF SPRING'S SWEETEST GEMS

We have become so inebriated with the beauty of thryptomene (not even objecting to its botanic name!) that another native of this country sits quietly in the background unknown to many to whom thryptomene is quite familiar; it is *Calythrix sullivani*. Mr St John tells me that *C. tetragona* is even prettier, but if you cannot get *C. tetragona* you won't be disappointed with *C. sullivani*, which is a bush covered with tiny pink buds that open to white star-shaped flowers. I should say that it needs an open situation. Oh! And have I mentioned *Leptospermum rotundifolium*? It's a glorious little thing; quite my favourite amongst the pink flowering tea-trees.

PREPARING FOR WINTER

'Taking castor oil?' said my inquiring friend, sympathetically, upon seeing the familiar deep blue bottle. 'No, I'm not taking it, I'm wearing it! I wear it on my feet—my boots, to be more precise, because it's the best way to waterproof 'em, and when the greasiness has worn off a little they take a marvellous polish—preserves the leather, you know, and prevents it from cracking.'

I don't believe I told you what a lovely bowl of colour and form we had a few weeks ago by gathering several varieties of crab apples. Veitch's scarlet crab was the most vivid. *Malus eleyii* was a light mahogany, 'La Trobe' was red and yellow, and *Malus florentinus* was the most exquisite yellow and slightly long in shape; yes, I'm afraid you are going to have a job to get that variety, it's very like the large-fruited *M. floribunda*, but it is distinct and I would not hesitate to say *florentinus* if asked to choose between them.

So with this note on autumn decoration I'll say goodbye until next month.

Edna Walling

SEPTEMBER, 1944

Dear Gardeners,

Threading my way for 12 miles across the eastern suburbs in a bus the other day, I came to the conclusion that gardens play quite an important role in the community. Not only do they soften the architecture, but when there are trees they screen the lack of it! But for the gardens the monotony of the design of the dwellings would be appalling. Because there is a merciful variety in the horticultural ideas of the owners, there is a consequent relief in the general effect. There surely isn't any law, is there, that insists that the pitch of all roofs should be the same? And it is so unfortunate that it is such an uninteresting pitch. In a discussion recently, a builder alluded to it as the 'Australian' pitch, giving the number of degrees, which I didn't register, though I should have ... even to avoid it!

CHILDREN AND GARDENS

To expect any but the most exceptionally 'horticulturally' minded child to take an interest in the average suburban garden is asking rather much, I think, and I can't help thinking that more would be attracted if they were shown how to make pictures with mossy boulders, little blossom trees, very small shrubs ... the Kurume azaleas, for instance, tiny alpines such as the very compact *Dianthus* species, the various thymes, and so forth, (I've used the word 'alpines' for fear of giving the wrong impression by saying rock plants). The alacrity with which the average mind jumps to succulents when you say 'rock plants' simply terrifies me, and if you DON'T remember to add, 'I don't mean succulents', heaven knows what you might have started.

If we would sometimes take the children into our confidence, we would probably have far more interesting gardens than those that are handed over to the gardening contractor and handed back to us in deadly stereotyped

form ... just something to be maintained. How children love a little bit of wilderness. I always feel that we have achieved something if a child likes our garden, and so why not say to the children: 'What shall we do with this?' when surveying the uncultivated ground surrounding the new home. You are missing a lot of fun by turning to the pink pages in search of a gardening contractor to whom to hand the problem.

It's not a problem, really; it's an exciting adventure, and when you have thought it all out is the time to ring the contractor. Then you can say: 'We want you to do this, and this, and this', and stick to your guns! Even if it is unconventional ... (and let's hope to goodness it will be), it couldn't be worse than thousands of gardens in Melbourne.

You know, I don't think it is exactly fair not to give a child a little grounding in garden design, because they are going to have gardens of their own one day, and a good mother sees that her daughter knows something about cooking, house management, and interior decoration.

Walks into the country are the best lessons on landscape gardening. Notice how the trees are naturally grouped, how the ground-covering plants grow in drifts of different species round their feet, how boulders help to make up the natural scene, and how little tracks ... made by cattle, perhaps ... wander about in lines that are never straight.

Don't imagine for a moment that you can't make little pictures on the average suburban allotment of 60 feet frontage, for you can. You wouldn't use gum trees, of course, any more than one would use elms and oaks in a small English garden. These are forest trees, and out of scale in the small garden, and there are plenty of smaller trees from which to choose without resorting to the same genera or species as those which made up the natural scene you may wish to recreate. Nurserymen will always help by telling you how big certain species grow, and always remember that trees take up less room than shrubs. Several people may sit under, and enjoy, the shade of a tree, but a large-growing shrub may absorb quite a big area of the available garden space, and yet give a small proportion of shade for the amount of ground space it demands.

The Country Garden in Australia

Drifts of *Podycarpus alpina*, spilling masses of *Leptospermum rupestrine*. Sheets of *Brachycome multifida* and *B. graminae*. Groups of callitris, and woodlands of the spotted gum (*Eucalyptus maculata*). Misty clouds of mint bush (*Prostantheras*), glades of olivewood (*Bursaria*), masses of fringe myrtle (*Callythrix*), soft, pale pink clouds of *Boronia muehlerii*. That is what I expect visitors hope to see when they come to this country; but alas, alas! Ah, well, perhaps we shall learn.

What marvellous opportunities present themselves in the proposed green belt that is to surround Melbourne, but will it be woodland scenes? Or will it be specimen trees and meticulous lawns all over again, with automatic sprinklers to make it always too wet to enjoy the grass? Grass that is a little wild is ever so much more restful than a well-kept lawn in areas of any extent. We have so much to learn in the matter of our places of recreation, and it is so hard for gardeners to succeed with that which should be something of the forest, and something of the meadow.

Yours,

Edna Walling
Sonning, 25/7/44

OCTOBER, 1944

Dear Gardeners,
Ah! That's what it likes, 'a light soil and plenty of sunshine!' I've been browsing through *Ornamental Flowering Trees and Shrubs* (edited by F. J. Chittenden) to see what they had to say about the Italian crab, *Malus florentina*, and came upon my old friend Bechtel's crab, *Malus ioensis*. I have often mentioned this double-flowered form from the central States of North America, with very large soft pink flowers and the most heavenly fragrance, like the scent of Parma violets; but I have never been able to tell you that

it does not flourish in very heavy ground, because I didn't know! My ground is not very heavy, but it certainly is not light, and that accounts for the rather slow progress they have made, no doubt; some gritty sand must be incorporated around their roots.

However, it's the Italian crab that I wanted to tell you about. It is quite charming in the spring when in flower, but in the autumn the clear yellow fruits (about the size of a cherry) with rather pronounced calyx are really lovely. We had a bunch of them in a crude little white bowl and it was one of the sweetest of table decorations. Having only one tree I became nervous of losing it and put some cuttings in last winter, and to my joy some have struck. They had to weather last summer's terrific heat and dryness, for they were in that part of the garden where there is no tap, so I'm lucky to have two little trees out of ten or so cuttings; under more favourable conditions the percentage might be better. *Malus florentina* was formerly know as *Pyrus crataegifolia*, and it was under this name that I purchased it many years ago.

Whilst we are on the subject of flowering apples, I would like to suggest that *Malus floribunda purpurea* be abandoned forever, in favour of the much better varieties, *M. 'Aldenhamensis'*, *M. eleyii*, and *M. sonningensis*. *Eleyii* is usually later in blooming, and is useful on that account, but for grouping with the pinkish-white flowers of the small growing *M. floribunda*, *sonningensis* and *aldenhamensis* are definitely superior to *purpurea*, which is a washed-out looking affair in comparison. Of these three wine-coloured and dark-foliaged varieties the fruits of *eleyii* are slightly larger and more colourful; all are purplish red, of course.

Finally a word of warning. The frequency with which *M. floribunda purpurea* is supplied when *Malus floribunda* has been ordered is infuriating to those who know the vast difference between these varieties, and disastrous to those who don't! Just imagine visiting a garden five years after advising the owner (over the phone perhaps) to plant that adorable little Japanese crab (*M. floribunda*) with its rose-red buds intermixed with the pinkish-white of the open flowers, only to find a lusty specimen of *Malus floribunda PURPUREA*, which is so utterly different and has none of the fairy-like grace and sweetness of *floribunda*. That it is so difficult to get *floribunda* and so easy to secure *purpurea* is exasperating, for in comparison it is not worth garden space.

Considering the endless number of varieties and their usefulness for garden purposes it seems strange that the pears from southeastern Europe are never, or hardly ever, available. I know only one source, and that a very remote one. Nothing could be more picturesque than the grey-leaved *Pyrus amygdaliformis* with its narrow grey-green leaves and rather stiff boughs. It is an excellent tree for a windy spot, and in autumn the foliage turns to the most delicate shades of pink and red.

Another tree that will thrive in a windswept site is the English sloe or blackthorn, both the double-flowered and the purple-foliaged forms.

How extremely useful the ericas are for winter blooms. Amongst a tight little bunch of flowers brought in for the table in late June there were five varieties: *Erica darleyiensis* (one of the most amenable of the heaths and a very dwarf grower), *E. mediterranea*, *E. daviesii*, *E. arborea*, and *E. regerminans*. To these, the omnipresent *E. melanthera* could of course be added, but for the fact that it refuses to include Sonning in its omnipresence!

I don't miss it much, however, charming and all as it is, for the reason, no doubt, that any plant that you see in every alternate garden is inclined to pall; *Malus* 'Gorgeous', for instance, almost makes me sick! I'm perfectly certain that no self-respecting nurseryman would leave it out of a list of 'choice' shrubs. The term recalls an occasion when I was called in by a gentleman with oodles of money.

'I want you to select me some choice shrubs', he said deedily, whereupon my mind became a blank.

'Now what does he mean by that?' I wondered. Was I to take it that each one must cost a lot of money, must be bright of hue, must never lose its foliage (I've observed that quite a lot of people are prejudiced against deciduous plants, regardless of their exquisite blooms). In a moment of perverseness I longed to write down all those old darlings that had served me so well in the making of pictures—plants that many an 'expert' gardener had dubbed rubbish as I happily grouped them together.

Choice! What an awful word to apply to plants, and yet when I appeal to my 'Concise Oxford Dictionary' it says 'carefully chosen; exquisite', The difficulty in my mind seemed to be what we were going to do with these choice specimens when we'd got them. To have the jewels without the ring, so to speak, for the garden was as bare as a board! You see, you MUST first create a setting for your 'choice' specimens just as you must have the ring for the jewels. But we were talking of ericas! Goodbye.

Edna Walling

PS: On September 24 (of course that will be past when this sees the light of print), but again on Saturday, November 4, Sonning will be open to visitors, and any *Home Beautiful* readers will be doubly welcome. The entrance shillings and the proceeds from jams, preserves and other 'homemades' will go to Red Cross funds.

NOVEMBER, 1944

Dear Gardeners,
Walking around the garden this morning (yes, I know I should have been working, but never mind about that just now) I came upon a most beautiful flowering shrub with small softly-grey foliage of graceful and rather open form and exquisite clusters of white flowers, with the most adorable silky buds crowding around them awaiting their turn to bloom. The effect on the

tips of the branches was a symphony of grey-green and white; although the individual flowers are but three-quarters of an inch across, there is an architectural beauty about them that is absorbing when you closely examine them and you find yourself murmuring, 'There is nothing lovelier!'

What is this shrub? It is merely the swamp or woolly tea-tree, *Leptospermum lanigerum*, a native that will soon disappear if those who are fortunate enough to have it growing on their properties do not guard it assiduously and see to it that young plants are encouraged, not obliterated. If these are not forthcoming, seed should be gathered and the resulting young seedlings planted in some damp corner. Admittedly this may not be an appropriate plant for the average suburban garden, but it is very much more suitable for many a spot in a country garden where an exotic is eking out a miserable and most lonely existence because the planter has not

realised that some native plant might not only be happier there, but would present a much more restful and pleasing effect.

Much as I was enjoying the various exotics that abound with bloom at this time of the year, quite involuntarily I stopped next at the Australian snow myrtle, *Lhotskya genetylloides*. No, I won't have it said that I am a fanatic where native plants are concerned; I could not manage without many, many plants that come from other lands (Westmoreland thyme, for instance!) and much as I believe that in certain places we should studiously exclude the exotics and strive to recreate the natural scene—not a simple task—I think it is neither necessary nor desirable to consider where a plant comes from for the average home garden so long as we enjoy it just for itself and so long as it harmonises with its neighbour's foliage and flower. Some plants, no matter how beautiful, look so dreadfully uncomfortable in their setting and it seems so unfair not to consider them in the matter of the plants with which we force them to associate.

Sorry, I'm rambling again. It was of lhotskya we were speaking. This needs a Reginald Farrer to describe it! With a limited vocabulary I can but tell you that it is an extremely dainty shrub with tiny starry flowers very, very lightly flushed with pink. I put in some cuttings this winter in a pot of washed sand and they look quite promising and so shall hope to be able to plant out a drift of this medium-sized shrub in the future.

Cuttings of *Calythrix sullivanii*, another of the myrtle family which grows more robustly and bears a fluffy mass of pink and white stars, also look hopeful. This shrub is positively inebriating! It is really bewildering to think how these plants of such great beauty are so comparatively little-known and so seldom propagated. Goodness! Great sheets of them should be in our public gardens and on our highways. Oh, no! Don't say people would strip them. We only need to legislate, as they have done in New South Wales, to stop the picking of wildflowers. You just wouldn't dare then. Of course, I don't think it is as bad to walk into someone's garden and pick the flowers as it is to pick them from the roadside ... you're depriving thousands from seeing and enjoying what is taken from the roadside against a mere handful of people who see those in a garden.

We planted some cypress pines (*Callitris cupressiformis*) on the roadside where it was rather bare and uninteresting. The group was just beginning to show their beauty when one day the mistress of Lynton Lee saw some 'lady' bending down outside the gateway. She wondered what she could be doing but did not think of the callitris at the time. Several days later it was discovered that one of the best trees had gone. Of course it would die; they loathe being moved when once established, but in any case isn't it despicable? If only people would stop to think how utterly selfish it is to remove for their own private gardens something that is making the public highway beautiful. Scene-shifters, that's what they are. The funny part of it is they never take anything out with them to plant on the roadside, not unless it is some rubbish they're glad to get rid of: an overdose of montbretias, for instance, or something equally incongruous, and undesirable, amongst Australian flora.

The brooms—although they do not last in good condition much over 10 years, and often less, they are so quick-growing and are so easily propagated from seeds or cuttings that the brooms, or cytisus, are amongst the most satisfactory of garden shrubs for planting amongst permanent slower-growing shrubs that will later require the space the brooms occupy. The habit and size make that charming little fellow with cream flowers, *Cytisus praecox*, a delight for small gardens and for grouping beneath the larger-growing varieties which are a little cumbersome in restricted places. *C. Praecox* has been in flower for some time when the other hybrids begin to bloom, but it remains in flower to take a part in the colour scheme if the deep red *Burkwoodii*, 'Dorothy Walpole', etc., are in the group.

Hope you'll be able to come to Sonning on November 4th. This time buses will meet trains at Mooroolbark railway station at 1.30 p.m., 2.00, 2.20, 2.45.

Yours till December—

Edna Walling

DECEMBER, 1944

Dear Gardeners,

Do you know I suffer agonies when the conversation turns to gardening; how such and such a plant is 'doing' and what happened to some other specimen; how to produce something monstrous in the horticultural arena, and so on. Perhaps they think 'we'll talk about gardening, that'll be safe'. Well, it isn't really! I'm liable to break every convention and behave like a very ill-bred person. And yet during a recent journey of several hours I sat beside someone with whom I chipped about plants and gardens almost all the way!

'What a charming little fellow is *Anthemis aeizoon*', he said, right out of the blue. Goodness, I thought, if he likes *that* I'm sure he must be nice, and off we went hopping from this little ground-hugging chamomile to some towering tree. I was ashamed of him, for not knowing *Callitris columellaris*! Of course there IS only one in Melbourne, against about five thousand Roman cypresses, so all that has been said about the planters of our public parks and highways has been more than justified for their utter neglect in the matter of planting native trees—some of the most beautiful in the world, as instance this glorious cypress pine. I shall go on harping, however much it offends the friends, relations, and wives of the guilty ones.

GARDENS AND GARDENS

Funny things, gardens. I think they like to be *discovered*, not shown off. I shall never forget being shown a collection of gardens by the proud designer. His pride one could forgive him, but the halting at the given spots just simply produced an irrepressible desire to giggle. I found myself outwardly expressing hollow words of praise, but inwardly irreverently wondering where he procured those wonderful English corduroy slacks. Coming home, I resolved that I too would have my halting spots ... the bad spots! Then the visitors could have a really good giggle ... they might even be moved to extend some suggestions.

No, tempted as one may be, I think it is better to refrain from pointing out the pictures, and hope for the best. Of course in some gardens you don't have to point them out. They scream at you! It's one big splash of colour, except when the frenzied changeover from spring-flowering annuals to summer-flowering ditto is taking place.

I always think it's rather indecent not to ring down the curtain or something during those periods ... it seems so crude that they have to change their costumes under the very gaze of the public eye. Of course the owners rush in the manure and rush over the digging in an amazingly short time; it is all fairly straightforward, but for one or two specimen shrubs and trees, there is nothing in the way of perennial ground cover to hinder one's spadework. Once the annual crop has been removed (frequently in the very heyday of its bloom because it is time to put the next lot in), the area presents the appearance of a miniature wheat field which has been ornamented with 'a pound's worth of shrubs'.

I don't know whether this is a 'Garden' or an 'And Garden', but I do know that I, for one, prefer the type of garden where as much permanent ground cover as possible clothes the earth; wherein, when it is once established, a spade rarely appears; where there are little surprises invented by Nature, patches of self-sown foxgloves, little colonies of that adorable alpine violet, which will so obligingly clothe the pathway's edge and run back under the trees and shrubs if encouraged and unrestrained in its wanderings; columbines coming up in the least expected places and many other delights that await the one who gently hand-weeds her garden, steering off all who would help her 'clean it up'.

Once upon a time there was a very pretty garden owned by a busy woman who really didn't realise how lucky she was to live in a setting where nothing beyond mowing the lawn, and the removal of the occasional thistle, was necessary. One day she said, 'Flossie is going to do the garden for me, isn't that kind of her?' 'Oh yes, very,' I replied. 'But what is she going to do?' (There was a man who mowed the lawns.) 'Oh, I don't know,' she answered quite impatiently. 'She's a very good gardener, you know.' 'Then heaven help the garden!' I said with warning. 'Well, I can't offend her now, what do you suggest I should do?' 'I don't know, but I'd rather offend her than the garden.'

The next time I called a dismal sight confronted me where once was a restful scene. All the thymes had been thinned out, now resembling tiny islands in a sea of dirt. Around the back there was a great heap of thyme and other fragrant carpeters waiting to be incinerated. For the life of me I couldn't imagine what she thought she had achieved. The owner was out (mercifully for her!) so on her desk I left a little note: AND WHAT DO I THINK OF YOUR VERY GOOD GARDENER?————!!! Here, I felt, was the justifiable use of the great Australian adjective. For pity's sake don't let's *worry* our gardens so much.

Being the most satisfactory plants for landscape effects, the spireas might be brought to the fore more than they have been of late years. This year they have been exceptionally enjoyable at Bickleigh Vale (of which Sonning is a part, you know) and in autumn we know we shall have excellent autumn foliage from all the varieties, whatever the weather may be. *Spirea* 'Van Houtee' and *S. reevesiana* are billowing masses of white clouds in spring, a lovely foil for the more spectacular performers.

Edna Walling

1945

Dear Gardeners,

I have secured for you a photograph of a venerable tree which lives at Mooroolbark. It is a yellow box, *Ducalyptus melliodora*, and it is one of the most beautiful trees I have ever seen. It is so old that the top seems to have been blown out of it. It must have been a tremendous height (for a box tree) in its prime. Now its chief beauty is in its trunk. The pattern of the bark is fascinating beyond description and I live in perpetual terror of its being cut down for firewood. I can just imagine someone walking up to it with an axe and saying, 'That's a good tree', meaning good for firewood! It is too, of course, but I hope they spare it all the same at least until there isn't another tree left.

All around it there is a healthy little family of its children, but as they are growing in a grazing paddock they will, no doubt, be cut down as 'brush' (horrible thought), unless the property falls into the hands of one who sees in them the much greater value than the small area of grass they occupy.

Our Crying Need

This natural reafforestation from mother trees makes all old and mature trees extremely valuable in this country—in any country for that matter—but particularly in the one where the percentage of forest is as low as two per cent. If we could only get THAT into people's heads, TWO PER CENT! The time might come when every sapling would receive due consideration before being cut down. At present the value set upon naturally-grown seedlings on some of the finest timber trees in the world is, to the average Australian, *nil*! In consequence, down come hundreds upon hundreds of saplings often through the sheer joy of clearing. 'Clearing' has been a national sport for so long that it is going to be hard to stop it now. 'Burning off' is another sport ... a most exciting one, but they are two most devastating practices. Some of it has been done in the interest of the community to prevent the spread of bushfires, but the damage which follows by the destruction of the most valuable thing in the country (yes, much more valuable than gold which, we can't eat!)—namely humus, which produces the soil, which in turn produces our food—makes it clear that these methods will have to be supplanted by more intelligent ones. Let us stop and think before cutting down trees (even the tiny ones) and burning off undergrowth. Sometimes we shall decide it need not be done.

It Should Grow Bigger

I have received the 1944–45 number of *The Junior Tree Warden* from Thistle. Harris, B.Sc., the Editor, and again I am sad and worried to think that this most valuable, interesting, and extremely attractive little book reaches so few. Of course it's marvellous to know that the New South Wales children have the benefit of it, but there are thousands of grown-ups who would enjoy these beautiful pictures, and who would, I feel sure, be more thoughtful for our beautiful roadsides, after a perusal of these little books, and they would certainly be less ignorant. It is simply packed full of information, 96 pages of it! And although it is written for children I, for one, don't feel like skipping a page of it. Always the illustrations are good, but this year they are lovelier than ever, and they make you want to fight like blazes to protect and recreate the beauty of Australia. There! See what you have started, Miss Harris!

But I can't expect you all to be as interested in all this as I am, and some of you will be impatiently waiting for me to leave the open road and get back into the garden.

On 1 November, I made a note of *Azalea occidentale*. When we say *Azalea occidentale* we really mean *Rhododendron occidentale*, as the genus is now generally accepted as including those formerly known as azaleas. Somewhere in the recesses of my mind I dimly remember seeing this biscuit-coloured beauty referred to as 'honeysuckle' in America. I wonder why? Perhaps it's the fragrance; it is a little suggestive of that familiar plant. To see this growing wild in the American woods and on their highways would make one almost leave home I should think.

Added to the fragrance and beauty of *R. occidentale* in November was that of the Himalayan species, the most familiar, but not necessarily the best, being *Rhododendron fragrantissima*. When one thinks of the extent to which that rather dull species *Azalea indica* is planted to the exclusion of many that are so much more captivating, it has to be admitted that our horticultural status is rather low. However, if vast quantities of varieties of this 'azalea', and of hybrid rhododendrons are propagated to the exclusion of some of the most interesting, but almost totally unknown, species it does make it a little difficult for the public. What seems to be needed is a firm that will set out on an entirely new course that will provide us with all the delights for which we are so hungry.

What amuses me is that in Australian and New Zealand catalogues much space, and great effusion, is lavished upon the leathery-leaved hybrids having their flowers in 'large round trusses', and upon the *indica* azaleas with which all civic gardens abound, and in a very small space at the back of the catalogue you discover 'HIMALAYAN SPECIES AND VARIETIES,' which include some of the most desirable shrubs in existence! Ah well!

Goodbye once again,

Edna Walling

F E B R U A R Y,   1 9 4 5

Dear Gardeners,
Well, I think I've got the hang of vegetable growing at last. Apparently you have to do a little messing around in the vegetable garden every day, or at least every other day. If you don't, they sulk! As you know mulching is a subject on which I'm inclined to harp but until now I had thought that a clean surface so that the cultivator could be pulled through easily was the best system with vegetables. Now I can't get the mulch on quick enough! As fast as I can gather up the manure and grass in the paddock it goes in between the rows of carrots, parsnips, red beet, potatoes, in fact everything; and though it means a good deal of hand-weeding, the luscious growth that follows well repays this work. Actually it is less work than the continual hoeing and it's simply grand to have the ground continually moist.

It is obvious, of course, that in a climate which treats us to such drying winds and scorching sun the continual mulch is imperative, but of equal importance is shelter. I was talking to a research worker on the Erosion Control Board the other day and was most interested to hear her say, 'We need hedges to stop the wind'. Of course we do. When you think of the miles that the wind can travel in the wheat-growing country, and on sheep runs unchecked, it's positively terrifying. One can't help thinking that smaller paddocks enclosed by protecting hedges will perhaps be one of the best ways to reduce the devastating loss by fire and wind erosion in this country. At all events it is interesting to note the greenness that persists in sheltered pieces of landscape compared with the scorched up wastes that have been denuded to all trees and shrubs.

Rock Plants and Rock Melons

Another thing I have discovered about vegetable gardens is that a little colour is a great help to one who finds being methodical not only tedious, but a quality most difficult to win. For instance, if that little Pixie says, 'Don't go down to the vegetable garden this morning, come to the rock garden!' I can now say, 'But there are rock plants in the vegetable garden, too!' That's fixed him! I've started edging the paths with prostrate rosemary, *Hypericum coneatum* and various thymes, and today I straightened my back and beheld the sweetest picture composed of the golden blooms of this hypericum, and the quaint little white daisy flowers of chamomile. I just love chamomile. The very finely dissected, softly green foliage is almost velvety in appearance, and those darling little daisies are so perky. I most ardently desire a chamomile lawn, and I'll have it one day, even if it's in my toothless old age. Up to the present, all that has been achieved outside the vegetable garden is a patch a foot square planted where few grasses will thrive, beneath a candle bark gum. At least it has proved itself there and made me long all the more to be able to walk across a whole sward of it. It appears that it would take most kindly to the mower and would, I imagine, demand far less mowing than grass (husbands, please note). For the country garden with no water it should prove a boon. It's an *Anthemis*, of course, but I'm blessed if I know which one.

'ROW AND SPECIMEN' SYSTEM OF PLANTING

The other day I was summoned to a huge window to admire a new landscape scheme that had been worked out on the distant boundary. The ground was undulating and all about was one row of Lombardy poplars, one row of cryptomerias, and one row of Japanese maples. I was winded and unable to peak, and so was treated to a word picture of the scene. It seemed to me like explaining a blackboard with nothing on it! It does seem better not to do any planting at all until we can do better than that. But no! With the most amazing confidence trees are assembled, and marshalled on to the landscape much more often in military than in picturesque formation. And yet when you boil it all down ... this landscape gardening business ... it is chiefly a matter of observation. Walk along a country road ... one that hasn't been meddled with, of course, and observe how nature groups her trees and shrubs; how some of the trees come right to the fore sometimes and some of the shrubs are right at the back. It's all so simple. Yet we go on with these awful rows, these awful regularly spaced specimens. A suitable idea for street tree-planting and straight avenues may be, but rarely, if ever, for gardens and the open landscape.

THE NATIVE CHRISTMAS BUSH

This, of course, is a different species in every State! But it is the Victorian Christmas bush, *Prostanthera lasianthos*, which is in bloom now that I'm about to eulogise. Actually it is only suitable for country gardens, and for roadside planting, because like many another native shrub it is a little leggy and not particularly attractive when not in flower.

The flowers, which are in lovely soft bunches, are white, tinged with mauve and it really is a beautiful cloud of bloom. Planted amongst gum trees and cypress pines its grace is all the more noticeable; it appreciates the shelter of these trees, too. Like all the other prostantheras, it grows amazingly quickly from cuttings taken in winter, rowed out in the open ground; in a sheltered spot naturally. There is a little dwarf prostantheras growing in the Grampians that should be a delightful thing for small gardens. However, I'll have to tell you more of that later when I've found out its name and more about it.

Yours, till March,

Edna Walling

MARCH, 1945

Dear Gardeners,
Yesterday we went up to the Mount on a strange and amusing mission. Usually I am on business bent and although one subconsciously takes in all the lovely scene that Mount Dandenong provides, one's mind is generally on the job of work ahead, as one pelts along the highway. However, this time I was merely the driver, and waiting outside sundry residences afforded opportunities of surveying the landscape leisurely.

Sad to relate I did not see one building that had added to the beauty of the landscape. Oh yes, there was an exception—the little stone church; *that* is very lovely. Yet, what do you think they've done to it? They've dotted all sorts of exotic trees around it and lined the track with stones of an even size most meticulously! Of course it's spoilt it. It would have been better, far better if they had done absolutely nothing at all, just kept the rough grass mown. You see there is a background of the most glorious native mountain ash (*Eucalyptus regnans*, I suppose they would be) and all this horticultural flotsam and jetsam in the foreground detracts from the beauty of the little church so tragically.

IMPORTANCE OF THE SETTING

There is such an art in the setting of such pieces of construction, whether they are homes or churches, and the chief necessity is restraint. In this particular instance it is clear that only most carefully chosen native plants, quiet in effect, would suit. None of your red flowering gums and waratahs (they wouldn't grow anyway, but no doubt some other flamboyant Australians might). *Podycarpus alpina* would probably have enjoyed life immensely there, and what a lovely effect it would have produced with its small dark green foliage! Drifts of *Olearia gunniana*, both the white- and the blue-flowered forms, would have been heavenly. The creeping tea-tree, *Leptospermum rupestre*, could have clothed the ground in places, and I doubt whether anything could have surpassed the effect of an entire carpet of that sweet little mauve-flowered mountain daisy, *Brachycome multifida*, with perhaps nothing to break it but one or two enormous mossy boulders.

THUMBS DOWN TO CRYPTOMERIAS!

How terribly pompous we can be at times in imagining that we can do better than to re-establish the most desirable of the native flora peculiar to the district. Those dreadful cryptomerias made me want to gather them up and ship them straight back to Japan. I know these particular plants would be children of the children of original Japanese parents but I'd like to send them there all the same! They look too silly in the vicinity of this little church, however lovely they may appear elsewhere. In any case they have been done to death by now, so let's hope some fell disease will descend upon all the future progeny of this pink-painted prodigy of the order Pinaceae.

This particular piece of landscape planting is only one of the many others which might serve to warn us what NOT to do in the future. Here it is on the highway for all to observe and study. It is a serious reflection upon our sense of the fitness of things that we have not yet begun to realise that the recreation of the natural scene is the only way to deal with quite a considerable amount of the landscape work surrounding any city. Sooner or later we will overcome the specimen-spotting habit and realise that for the setting of beautiful architecture, and for the planting of the open highway, we do not want the type of plant that shrieks at us with gaudy blooms, except when they are natural to the district. Soft, restful foliage is the first consideration; colour can always be added if desirable and necessary.

A NATIONAL DUTY

You may say, 'What has all this to do with us?' Well, don't you think that gardeners, of all people in the community, should take the trouble to find out something about the landscape work that is being carried out in other countries? At present it is appalling how few people know if a newly planted park is good, bad or indifferent work. Quite frequently it is judged upon the amount of money it cost to develop—favourable if it cost a lot, of course, although it might be all the more gruesome. Now, in the future development of Melbourne, indeed of all our congested capitals, there will be extensive planting projects in which a considerable improvement upon the ideas of the past decade will undoubtedly be displayed. Those who have done a little research on the subject of landscape architecture, as it operates in countries where it is a university course, and where the landscape architect does not deal only with horticultural problems but with locating of buildings and driveways; where they work closely with engineers and architects, will be able to follow the work much more interestedly. Moreover, he will be in a position to express an intelligent opinion instead of either walking past it as though it had nothing to do with him (although it was his money that helped to pay for it), or applauding something that is actually an example of the type of work that went out with bustles. It will be most interesting to see just how they will tackle it all. One would imagine that a tremendous scheme of propagation would be the first step, for a landscape architect must have plants with which to make pictures, and he would need materials a great deal more interesting than the plants available at present—and masses and masses of them, too.

This all sounds very deedy. I'll promise to write of the more intimate side of gardens next month, but I do feel that we should develop a broad vision, take an intelligent interest in civic landscape work and refuse to be content with the mediocre. Nothing but the best is good enough for Australia.

Yours till April—

Edna Walling

APRIL, 1945

Dear Gardeners,
I've just had a ring from someone who lives at Preston complaining bitterly of the wind there. It was strange because I had been thinking of those windswept places and the tremendous urgency to do something to reduce the velocity of the wind and also produce more shade and greenness in these hot and arid suburbs of Melbourne.

I know the first thing I would do would be to surround myself with a brick wall and a good seven-foot-high one at that. Yes, I know they cost money but so do fences, and brick walls don't blow over; nor do they need any maintenance. Moreover, a walled-in garden is always delightful: One built of old secondhand bricks is the most lovely background to any garden. Once we built a wall of old bricks, some of which had whitewash on them. It was intended that the wall would be painted white, but the effect of the pink bricks with the flecks of white here and there was so charming we left it as it was.

Actually, when the garden wall is of brick it is better not to be too meticulous about the brickwork. One that is built of new bricks with joints that are 'pointed' is most difficult from the aesthetic point of view; lime mortar is also softer in effect than cement mortar and cheaper.

Tall trees which provide shelter do, of course, shade the garden also, and therefore those that are deciduous are generally the most desirable when the area is restricted. Oaks are ideal for town gardens because their roots are least troublesome, and if only we could get it, the upright form of the English oak *Quercus robur fastigiata* would be splendid as a windbreak. I was given some acorns a few years ago and now these pyramids of deep green foliage are a distinct and most satisfactory note on the landscape. Far lovelier than Lombardy poplars and with none of their distressing habits. Frankly, I'd rather have the wind than the poplars!

The English maple, *Acer campestre*, seems to be as hardy as the Japanese variety is delicate, but there again, can you get it? It all makes trying to be a help *très difficile*; all one's brightest ideas are nullified because you can't get the darned plants! Well, you can get birches ... or you could, and they're tough when once you get them going; but they haven't the 'body' of the upright oak, of course. Oh! Isn't it irritating to be so restricted in the choice of plants? Goodness! I hope the end of the war will see a tremendous difference in our nurseries, and I'm sure it will; as I've said

before, it's up to the public just as much as it's up to the nurseries ... if the demand is there they'll soon follow.

Lower-growing trees are not so difficult for there are hawthorns in great variety to be had: the well-known Washington thorn, *Crataegus cordata*, for instance, and quite a host of others, all of which are quite able to withstand the wind and provide good foliage, and fruit in autumn. The grey-leaved *Crataegus tanacetifolia* is especially to be recommended, and since some evergreen would be an advantage even if it does reduce the sun in winter, this particular variety is a good companion to the Arizona cypress, *Cupressus arizonica*, and also the Roman cypress, *Cupressus sempervirens stricta*.

In the country, walls of adobe or pise make excellent garden boundaries, and there is many a country property that would be infinitely more livable with a pise wall separating it from the fierce blasts of the hot winds in summer and the icy winds in winter, which make life so trying in some districts. Actually, these walls become imperative, for many homesteads were saved from fire by their high garden walls—mostly stone, of course—during the devastating fires last year.

Walls made of adobe bricks are very much simpler to construct than those of stone. Anyone can build them. A foundation of concrete, stone or brick, is advisable, but if none of these were available, or the wherewithal not forthcoming, the mere removal of the top soil to provide a firm bottom for the mud bricks will suffice for a garden wall, since dampness is of no importance here. In a light iron mould, bricks of a size convenient for the job, perhaps 12 inches x 9 inches x 6 inches, for example, are very quickly turned out; one slim girl turned out 160 a day! Why in the world more country houses are not built this way is beyond my comprehension, but that's a pet subject I'd better keep off! It does make me fume, though, to think of all those frightful little hot-boxes that pass for homes on the Australian countryside when they could be living in cool, thoroughly comfortable and infinitely more attractive abodes. Such a large percentage of our soils are ideal for the purpose, a fact not generally appreciated; the climate is ideal but there, the climate is unimportant, some of the oldest buildings in all parts of the world, including England, are of earth. Ugliness resulting from the removal of the top soil for building the walls need not be if forethought is given; it can be taken out in a neat trench that could form a surface drain, or the area from which it is taken can become a future pool, lade, dam, or site for out-buildings. There is really no worthwhile argument against pise, even the one that it is primitive; it seems much more primitive to roast in summer and freeze in winter in the erections that are supposed to be less primitive.

Yours,

Edna Walling

MAY, 1945

Dear Gardeners,

Perhaps it is just as well it's not easy to get unusual plants here, for I can see I would become a 'collector' ... a collector of penstemons. I've just been looking up *Penstemon ovata*, to see if there was such a plant and if it is likely to be the low-growing species that was so gay a little plant in my garden last spring; quite a lot of seed was saved, which will benefit the Red Cross funds.

VARIETY IN PENSTEMONS

Well, there is one called *P. ovata* (which is the nearest to the name under which mine was originally purchased', but it grows two to four feet; this one never exceeds one foot. However, until it is identified, just ask for *ovatus* when writing. It is delightful near mossy boulders and in the foreground of taller-growing perennials. The flowers are a clear mauve and the leaves roundish. It does much better with me than the blue-flowered species *P. heterophyllus*, which is fairly familiar here.

Another species that is a perfect little gem flourishes under the name of *Penstemon pygmea* in this benighted garden but is not in Bailey's *Encyclopaedia* as far as I have been able to pursue it. (When I break my leg I will go right through the seven columns of species to see if it appears as a variety of one of them.) Meanwhile the hasty scanning has revealed numbers of the most alluring little penstemons, mostly in mauves and blues, and for the great part indigenous to the United States. *Pygmea* is so dwarf that it is easiest enjoyed in a pot perhaps, but a crevice in the rock garden or the top of a retaining wall of stone will provide happy conditions for it. It needs a few stone chips and a miniature lichen-covered 'boulder' when grown in a pot, not being of those plants generally accepted as 'pot plants'—begonias, geraniums and so on ... plants that would never tolerate the idea of being treated as *incidents*; oh, no, they must be the whole show and have the whole pot to themselves. Come to think of it, one never thinks of planting a typical pot plant anywhere but bang in the middle of the pot: planting it to one side to make room for a mossy stone and perhaps some other little plant for company seems most inappropriate and would probably look dotty!

I should have said at the beginning that those bright-coloured tubular-flowered bedding and border penstemons are not what were in my mind when the 'collector' feeling swept over me as I delved into the *Encyclopaedia*. Not that I dislike them, but they are utterly opposed to the little low-growing, soft-coloured species that I pounce upon whenever a fresh species heaves in sight.

WALLS AGAIN

Ever heard of a Ha-Ha wall? Legend has it that on seeing one for the first time a certain English man burst out laughing and they've been called Ha-Ha walls ever since—unfortunately. I've done a little sketch to show you how they are built. The idea originated from the desire of some Englishman to enjoy the distant scene of sheep and cattle grazing in the meadow, unbroken by the discordant effect of a fence. Actually the low shrubs and trees shown in the sketch are not necessary, and if a continuous effect of turf is desired they would be inadvisable, of course. If the stones are reasonably large, only one thickness of stone is required to face the earth bank and a batter of from two to three inches in three to four feet will suffice. Well-and-truly-laid stones should not require mortar, and so the job is quite inexpensive when stone is present.

Ever since I mentioned that little greyling, *Anthemis aezoon*, with its two-inch-high daisy-like flowers, I have intended suggesting *Veronica prostrata* as a companion in the picture. On top of a dry-built stone wall, at the edge of a pathway or nestled into the rock garden where they will have plenty of sun, are all places where this picture of blue and white, like little patches of blue sky and white clouds, could be planted.

The reports of *Malus toringoides*—a variety of *M. transitoris*, apparently—that I've read from time to time have not been such that one would be tempted to acquire it, and yet this year it was loaded with the prettiest little waxy apples of a warm yellow with cerise cheeks. It was quite the prettiest little tree in the garden in the early autumn.

At Lynton Lee a section of the foundation planting around the foot of the whitewashed stone wall is very satisfactory. The prescription is: one large bush of rosemary, a sizeable clump of the Scotch harebell (*Campanula roundifolia*), and a bush of *Ceratostigma wilmotii* ... Ah, that just reminds me of a little score. I had occasion to write Stephani Bini the other day (a letter which she didn't acknowledge, of course!). Meeting her later, she 'acknowledged' the letter by saying, 'Yes, I did receive it, and I took it straight to the chemist and had it made up'.

Yours,

Edna Walling

PS: Touching those *Penstemon ovata* seeds I mentioned in opening, if you like to send a shilling and a stamped, self-addressed envelope, I will post you a packet. The Red Cross will profit.

The address is Sonning, Mooroolbark, Victoria.

JUNE, 1945

Dear Gardeners,

What a pity it is that there isn't a Society for the Prevention of Cruelty to Landscapes. I've just heard that a shelter for 'bus passengers is about to be built on one of the prettiest corners in Mooroolbark. That's all right, but the proposal is that it shall be a 9 feet x 4 feet lean-to, built of cement sheets. That's barbaric, and if it gets smashed to pieces by kids taking pot-shots at it, I, for one, won't mind! It's high time we took a two-fisted stand in this matter of defiling the landscape; it's just not intelligent and quite unnecessary. Here in this district could be found material to build the whole thing; yes, roof and all, for shingles could be split from local timber, and the walls built of logs. We don't even lack the men capable of doing it!

Down on the fringe of Lake Wellington, in Gippsland, I saw some picturesque small trees with small dark green foliage, which turned out to be the tall-growing form of *Bursaria*, commonly called 'Sweet Bursaria'. This particular species is *Bursaria pantoni*, and is one that we should certainly cultivate; in the vicinity of some massive, lichen-covered boulders, it would be most picturesque. What is needed is someone who will propagate all these delightful natives that are so pleasing (but not necessarily showy), who will have in their make-up the artistry to make them into pictures on suitable sites. Many a country home could enjoy an exquisite setting of Australian plants; that doesn't mean a 'collection of native plants'; it may mean that only three or four species would predominate as a setting to some more colourful and floriferous types.

I have mentioned the sorrel tree, *Oxydendrum arboreum*, before, but this is certainly an occasion to mention it again, because it is looking simply marvellous! Some of the toughest of the trees have lost all their leaves in this drought stricken autumn ... all the worse for being preceded by a damp

summer, but the sorrel tree hasn't turned a hair ... looks as if it is thoroughly enjoying itself, in fact. It is only six feet high, as yet (it grows from 15 to 60 feet), and actually has never been planted out into a permanent position. However, I wouldn't dare move it, any inharmonious neighbours will have to be removed from its lordly presence. It is of the heath family, you know, and that it has done so remarkably well here is a great surprise to me, especially without the slightest attention, and it has never known what a hose or a watering-can looks like. In Julia Rogers' *The Tree Book*, in which she is always concise and ever delightful, she describes it thus:

Flowers: June or July (Dec. or Jan. here), in panicles 7–8 inches long, of racemed white bells, narrowed and frilled at the tops. Leaves: Alternate, deciduous, membranous, oblong or lanceolate, entire, 3–4 inches long, smooth (I find them rough, however). Preferred habitat: Moist woods.

(H-m-m! What an accommodating plane, for here the habitat is ... well, not exactly moist; and certainly not wood-like).

Distribution: Pennsylvania, Ohio and Indiana, Florida, Alabama, Louisiana and Arkansas. This little deciduous tree, whose sour-tasting twigs and leaves temporarily assuage the thirst of the hunter lost in Southern woods, is beautiful in its bronze green spring foliage, and its long compound racemes of tiny, bell-shaped flowers, and, later, in its autumnal robes of vivid scarlet. It is a heath in all its characteristics, recognisable by its prim little flower bells and the dry capsules that succeed them.

One of the most distinctive of the brooms, and one of the most charming of dwarf shrubs is *Cystisus purpurea*, which grows but 12 to 18 inches high. It is a native of central and southeast Europe, and is most distinctive on account of its mauve flowers and dwarf habit. It is an admirable ground cover under taller-growing, spring-flowering shrubs and trees. There is no difficulty in propagating it, as it strikes readily from cuttings, and also grows easily from seed. There is a white-flowered variety which I would very much like to possess, and also one with more rosy flowers, *carneus* or *roseaus*, which must be the pink form that has been puzzling us for so long; it's a little washy, but of good form and useful for its low-growing habit. One never seems to be able to get sufficient really low-growing shrubs.

If I lived by the sea, I should secure and plant cuttings of the native sea-box posthaste. This, of course, is *Alyxia buxifolia*, which is the most fascinating ground-covering native plant I know. The rich, deep green, leathery foliage is quite architectural in effect, and the small white flowers are like little stars all over the plant. To see people battling with plants that simply loathe being near the sea, when there are so many beautiful ones that love it, always amazes me.

For a small evergreen tree, *Myoporum insularum*, or the so-called *Bubiala*, is most satisfactory. It is sometimes called the tempest bush—that suits it well, for it grows and thrives right on the sea, taking all the winds that blow. There are many places along the coast where it is very picturesque in effect, being a deep, rich green, with a well-rounded head and a rugged trunk. This also grows quite easily from cuttings, and is one of the best and quickest shelter plants for seaside gardens.

Yours till July,

Edna Walling

JULY, 1945

Dear Gardeners,

Last month I mentioned the need to consider scale in the matter of planting, to consider whether the shrub or tree you are about to plant will, when mature, be too large or too small for the area in which it is to be planted. Not only the actual dimensions of the whole plant, but the size of the foliage is a point, too; big leaves tend to bring the plant closer to the observer, thus reducing the apparent extent of the garden. And so you see that by using plants with small foliage, you give a texture to the pattern of your garden that tends to enlarge it and to create a greater sense of distance.

There can be no hard and fast rules about this ... in gardens there rarely can be (thank heaven!), but it is one of those little things that we observe in order to make our gardens more interesting, and more satisfactory. The garden is generally seen, or approached, from one direction more than another. We, therefore, deal with the pictures from this observation point. If it is possible to do so, the broad and large-leaved plants should be kept nearer the eye, or closer to the house, but not until you get the feeling of this idea will it be wise to adopt it, and it would be better to ignore it altogether than practise it slavishly, with ludicrous results.

Again, the amateur landscape gardener who considers his planting effects from the ecological point of view—that is, the study of the natural association of plants—will make better landscape pictures (and even in the tiniest gardens we can make these pictures) than those where no thought has been taken for this matter. This is the reason why palms look so ridiculous in association with birches—to mention but one frequently-seen example. 'I hate palms', or 'I hate cactus', or 'I hate dahlias', are remarks so often heard, but it is really where and how they are used, or abused, that we dislike, and so when you are going to plant a certain tree, some thought for its associates is necessary for an entirely pleasing effect, and it's very interesting to do a little fossicking to find out what the tree looks like in its natural habitat.

Before I forget, there is a correction about the 'Scotch' harebell (*Campanula rotundifolia*) mentioned in the May issue; it should be English harebell. For this I am indebted to a reader who was kind enough to write and draw attention to it. According to this reader, it is known in Scotland as the bluebell; it is, however, quite distinct from the English bluebell, which is a bulb—*Scilla nutans*. And, speaking of ecology, the English bluebell is a perfect carpet for birch trees.

Here's something else noted to include in this letter to you, of a very different nature: 'A 10-inch rainfall over a eucalypt forest is equivalent to 30 inches over a pine forest.' Makes one think, doesn't it?

Hunting through the garden for something in the way of a berry that the birds hadn't already devoured, we came upon *Crataegus durobrivensis*. Amongst the great number of these American hawthorns which have such attractive large fruits that they are often mistaken for crab apples, this scarlet-fruited species, which is allied to *C. Coccinoides*, is quite distinct, the fruit being perfectly round and hanging in bunches on the bare branches. You can imagine it is quite one of the most attractive of the ornamental thorns of the northern United States. It grows from 10–16 feet high, and has white flowers that are larger than most others of the species. It was discovered on the banks of the Tennessee River at Rochester, New York, in May, 1900, by a Wm. J. Dunbar.

A most useful and delightful low-growing shrub known sometimes as *Hebe hartiana*, and at others as *Veronica hartiana*, is one I have been intending to mention for a long time, but have fought shy of it because these hebes and veronicas could really drive one batty! I started going dutifully through the veronicas in Bailey's *Encyclopaedia* in order to give you an intelligent description of it, where it hails from, and so forth, but heavens above (it's terrific). A friend had just dropped in—a research-loving sort of friend, so the book was flung at her with a peremptory, 'see if you can find *Hebe hartiana* under the *Veronicas*, will you?' 'Could you make up your mind?' she enquired, sweetly. 'Well, no—it could be either.' Five minutes later she replied, 'Well, it's neither—it just isn't'. Nevertheless, in the catalogue of a Melbourne nurseryman there appears '*Veronica Hartiona*, bright green foliage, very attractive mauve-pink flowers in Spring, of trailing habit; nine inches ... 1/6'. Just like that! Of course, it would take a Reginald Farrer to describe this adorable trailing shrublet, and it is Mr Farrer who says:

Veronica has overflowed into Australasia, and there developed (besides rock-jewels) a new, most perplexing family of wholly different aspect— repellent leathern bushes with hard, dead-looking foliage, often of a metallic, cast-iron look.

You, who have all travelled on the Victorian Railways, know them. Don't

imagine *hartiana* is anything like THOSE, for it isn't.
Yours till August,

Edna Walling

AUGUST, 1945

Dear Gardeners,

Someone from Beaumaris (whom I do not know) has just phoned and asked: 'Can you do anything to stop them destroying all the tea-tree?' Of course I can't, but I can sympathise with them. It is so amazing that the authorities don't start on cypress trees if they feel they must hack out something in order to reduce the fire risk. They will permit people to go on planting highly inflammable cypress hedges and cypress specimens whilst they are laying low all the coastal tea-tree they can lay hands on; and this the chief feature of our waterfront suburbs!

I know that one of the first things I would do if I lived near the sea would be to plant coastal tea-tree. It's a splendid windbreak; it's one of the most picturesque native trees in the country, and it has to be ignited before it will burn. Certainly out-of-doors smoking where dry grass surrounds the tea-tree, is looking for trouble; it is, almost anywhere, in the vicinity of growth that is not continuously watered in summer, and almost without exception, fires start in long grass. This, then, is the first fire hazard to attack, grass, not tea-tree. When the authorities cut and remove the grass and weeds from all vacant allotments, from all neglected fence lines, and from all open spaces, it won't be necessary to remove the tea-tree because the seat of the trouble will have gone. Everyone knows that long dry grass is the greatest menace in summer and yet only in Western Australia is it compulsory to mow it!

Scale in planting, as I have mentioned before, is a matter we must consider in all gardens large and small; if we don't study it in the large garden the effect may be ludicrous, and in the small garden, disastrous! But apart from the necessity of remembering that large shrubs are often too bulky for small gardens, dwarf-growing shrubs enable the owner to enjoy a greater variety in a limited space. It must be realised, too, that a tree takes up less ground-space than a shrub, it requires less elbow-room; in many places where you daren't plant a shrub you could safely plant a tree, on the edge of a pathway, for example. When it reaches maturity a medium-sized shrub could make the path impassable but the tree will grow up and out of the way. A stray branch or two may have to be removed, that is all. The effect of very low-growing shrubs under trees (flowering apples, almonds and so on) is delightful, whereas larger shrubs may clutter up a small garden too much. That most satisfactory of winter-flowering shrublets, *Erica darleyiensis*, growing beneath a flowering apricot (*Prunus mume*) is an excellent illustration of this.

Amongst the brooms (*Cytisus*), many of the varieties take up too much space in the small garden and it is unfortunate that those that are really small-growing are not easy to secure; *Cytisus purpurea*, the only mauve-flowered variety, is quite low-growing and a most shapely and delightful little shrub of about 18 inches in height. *Cytisus praecox* is about twice as high but still suitable for the limited garden and very soft and sweet in effect with its pale yellow flowers and greyish-green foliage, if you can call it 'foliage'.

The Kurume azaleas, are, of course, quite perfect in scale for small gardens. Some are extremely dwarf whilst others grow a little taller, and the colours are from white and the palest mauve to the brightest rosy red; the most extensively propagated varieties are the latter, and that's a pity when you happen to desire the softer, cooler shades.

How extremely rarely one sees a daphne bush doing a real job of work in the garden; always the poor thing is expected to be a 'specimen', and yet used in a group with the winter-flowering almond spreading over its head it is much more interesting. Somehow the brightness of the daphne flowers seems to need the softening influence of the almond blossom. No, not the flowering almond, the fruiting almond, which has such exquisite blossom, is the one I have in mind. This is less bright than *Prunus pollardii*, the flowering variety.

One of the loveliest low-growing shrubs of all is *Baeckia ramossisima*. This is a native shrublet which is covered with white flowers about the size of three pence; it is just flushed with pink. Years ago it used to grow in glorious drifts at Kinglake and may still, but when the appreciation of one person was such that he took a nurseryman friend to the spot, where they thieved 300 specimens of it for sale in the city, one falls to wondering. I believe it grows quite readily from cuttings, so without resorting to the thieving method of distribution to the public we may be able to secure it one day. The better-known *Baeckia plicata* is also a dream of a shrub with tiny pink flowers in clusters along the stems. It is incredible that great drifts of it are not seen in large gardens and at least a sprinkling in suburban gardens. Goodness me! What IS wrong with us that none of our public gardens have masses of these exquisite natives gracing their shrub and tree borders?—Yours,

Edna Walling

SEPTEMBER, 1945

Dear Gardeners,

Of all the booklets sent to me recently quite the most interesting have been those on New Zealand forestry. On meeting a New Zealander I expressed a desire to know more about the timber trees of that country, with the result that this busy person has forwarded the most informative material, and what is more, some ten samples of wood! As yet I've not got past the purring stage; there has not been sufficient time to really enjoy them, nor to peruse all the pamphlets, amongst which the 'Monograph of the New Zealand Beech Forests' in two parts bids fair to keeping one up o' night. Of these New Zealand beeches the one with which we are most familiar is, of course, the red beech, *Nothofagus fusca*. To see a forest of them is a pleasure yet in store for me, and dipping into this book is most disturbing!

The more one reads of forestry the more one realises that trees grown in forest formation could be one of the most enchanting features in the landscape treatment of extensive country properties. Confronted with several acres to be planted we always seem to be at somewhat of a loss, and frequently end up by dressing up the whole area with specimen trees and lawn, and it's so frightfully dull. To be able to wander off into a little forest somewhere would be much more romantic, and if we can't be romantic in the development of our gardens we might as well be dead. And that reminds me, a certain person called in on a property on which I had planted a little forest of American oaks, actually the only worthwhile feature on the place (except perhaps the little formal rose garden which the present owner wrecked for no conceivable reason). The past owner (the caller) swept a majestic glance at the oaks and said, 'I always said she planted them FAR too close', I'm still puzzled, for if anything they're a little wide to be really effective as a forest. What her idea was is not disclosed, but 'a collection of isolated specimens' is what I fear. Anyway she has a knowledge of alpines and herbaceous perennials quite above the average, and tree planting and gardening, in the general acceptance of the term, rarely go together; we might as well accept that.

UPS AND DOWNS IN A GARDEN

The latest blight upon this garden is the dictum that a well-developed and quite healthy juniper is to come out, and you know how they hate being moved. It is growing against a pearl bush (*Exochorda grandiflora*) and it so happens that the owner has a pash for the pearl bush (but not for the juniper, apparently!) There is the funny part of it of course, when gardens pass from one person to another all these different pashes are apt to lay the whole thing low in time; the next owner might adore junipers and have a rooted dislike to pearl bush ... unpleasant memories of childhood or something like that, you know ... goodness! How our poor gardens do suffer! And what is so amazing is that they suffer so often at the hands of those who are otherwise quite above the average in intelligence, or more than ordinarily artistic in other matters. I know one person whose taste inside the house is beyond question. Outside, it runs to rockeries around the flowerbeds; rockery-encircled 'lakes' with rockery islands in the middle; the cultivation of all those plants that only thrive when draped with sacking (because of the frost in winter or the heat in summer); are surrounded by timber (sawn in the form of stakes) to support their unwilling heads, or are pruned to the bone until all natural form is quite satisfactorily destroyed. Ah! me, poor gardens!

But to return to the juniper. I'm sorry that this pleasant foil for the glistening white flowers of the pearl bush is to be lost forever, more especially that the house is at present rented by one who has the artistry to appreciate it. Never mind; at least the incident has refreshed the memory, and I can recommend to you the combination of these two plants which make such a charming picture.

Why Not Gaiety for the Vegetables?

Today I have been working in the vegetable garden ... always worthy of note ... and I must admit that no little time was spent in, no, not sowing seeds for our future sustenance but in planting irises in spare corners, cuttings of alpines and various thymes along the pathway edges and collecting herbaceous perennials from other parts of the garden for the herbaceous border I've always longed to have in this part of the garden. 'How absurd!' someone will say no doubt, and I'm sure that person who remarked, 'I don't know how they publish such rubbish!' will say it again, if she can't think of another way of putting it. What I am looking forward to one day is an article by her: she must have a dickens of a lot to tell if only she would get to work and do it, but if it's that person who walked off with the prize for the best potato at the local show because the man who planted them for her applied the fertiliser that did the trick instead of that he was told to use, well perhaps ... someone is calling for a saucer of milk for pussy. Well, it does make me furious when people don't pass on what they know, but grab and read (critically) what others have written. The rub isn't in the criticism, that can be enjoyable and even helpful, it's the superior attitude and their laziness, plus the refusal to lay themselves open to criticism.

Edging the beds in the vegetable garden with prostrate-growing plants is a practical idea anyway, and that's a good thing because I like doing it ... in fact I like doing it much better than filling up the centres with eatables. Keeping that strip at the pathway's edge free of weeds is a waste of effort when thyme, prostrate rosemary, violets, gromwell (*Lithospermum*) and any other plant of similar habits will do it for you and make the area a more pleasant one. If your kitchen garden is only two by twice, you just can't spare the space I know, but the country plot is generally of ample-enough proportions to make the idea an entirely practical one.

Edna Walling

OCTOBER, 1945

Dear Gardeners,
Well, that bus shelter is up and it looks just ducky; I won't tell you what one person said it was reminiscent of. Someone else quoted from Sir Arthur Helps:

> *A thing of ugliness is potent for evil. It deforms the taste of the thoughtless; it frets the man who knows how bad it is; it is a disgrace to the people who raised it—an example and an occasion for more monstrosities.*

Anyway, I'm not going to stop and pick up anyone till the novelty wears off and they stop asking questions that I can't answer such as: 'Why didn't they make it all weatherboard instead of a bit of plaster sheet around the top?', 'Why don't they cover it with brushwood?', 'Why did they put it *there*?', 'Why didn't they put it *there*?' The last person was so vehement he poked a hole in my side curtain in the enthusiasm of indicating *his* site. Now I am more annoyed about my side curtain than I am about the bus shelter, which is a good thing. But for heaven's sake, let's talk about gardens.

To Climb or Not To Climb
Lonicera caprifolium is a honeysuckle with greyish-green foliage and bunches of pink and pale yellow flowers. The rather deep dusky pink is on

the outside and therefore before the flower is fully open it is distinctly pink. The fragrance is unlike any other honeysuckle; it always reminds me of *Lilium auratum*, and so you may judge it is very lovely. If I had the position I would certainly train it as a wall plant. However, it makes quite a good shrub of eight feet or so, and is excellent in a hedge made up of missed flowering shrubs. What is more, it does not twine all over everything else like its dreadful cousin, which strangles all in sight and invites the bird to do a little propaganda by means of seeds which come up in the remotest corners of the estate (and in other people's gardens, too). I'm sorry I can't find its name to warn you, but it's the one with yellow flowers all up the stems instead of in clusters, and TWINES! Strangely enough, the rather similar variety with dark and rather purplish leaves and rosy-red and yellow flowers never seems to become a pest, though it is definitely a climber, and the seeds are evidently unpalatable or infertile or something; at all events, you won't be troubled with more than one plant of it, and it is glorious on an old shed, being a rich bronzy-green in foliage and producing the loveliest fragrance. I think it is *Lonicera japonica* var. *Halliana*. Clifford Bottomley, whose exploits as a war photographer you may have read about, took this picture of *L. caprifolium*, which shows the form and disposition of the leaves which is a guide in getting the right variety.

ANOTHER PICTURE-MAKING CLIMBER

The other day I saw an exquisitely lovely picture in a small garden composed of the thin trailing branches of *Jasminium grandiflorum* with its glistening white flowers against a background of a weathered grey tea-tree fence made of the heavy sticks, not brushwood. What a perfect foil such a support does make. I do love green, grey and white in the garden.

The deep rich green of English box, the soft silvery-grey of Spanish cypress, of Arizona cypress, of Australian gums and that superb resida green that is the Tasmanian cypress pine; all this makes one wonder why so many crave so ardently for colour that they do not see the greens! It is all a matter of values, I suppose. Look at the colour there is in a lichen-covered boulder; could one desire for more?

One of the Australian timbers that thrills me most is tallowwood. It gives me infinite satisfaction to rub my hand over the silky wood, which takes on such a lovely soft polish by merely rubbing it. The natural greasiness prompted the simple name tallowwood, I suppose. I do hope thousands of this species will be planted in the drive for the replanting of devastated forests of this country.

PROGRESS?

Incidentally, we've just started a Progress League. Seems funny to be deedily concerning ourselves with further comforts when so many need all the time and money we can give to making and sending overseas a few vital essentials. A nice prickly person *I* shall be on that committee. I don't like the way Progress Associations usually 'progress'; they seem to suburbanise the country instead of protecting it from a metropolitan invasion, and I'd be much more interested if it was that league I suggested the other day—a Society for the Prevention of Cruelty to Landscapes. I know exactly what it will be. So much earnest chatter about electricity, etc., and afterwards community laundries and community this and community that, that my little squeaks about preserving the beauty of the roadside and acquiring for preservation tracts of natural country will be brushed aside as so much nonsense. Then I feel that every member of Progress Leagues should have read 'The Culture of Cities,' and I've only dipped into it.

Yours till November,

Edna Walling

N O V E M B E R ,   1 9 4 5

Dear Gardeners,

I *do* love *Vinca minor,* and who would ever want to call it anything else; it sounds so chirpy, doesn't it? And it IS a chirpy little fellow with its bright little snow white faces covering the ground and sprawling over nearby boulders. I often wonder why some people do not regard white as a *bright* colour; actually, it's the brightest colour in the garden on a moonlight night; a heaven-sent blessing to all who would make photographic records of their gardens, and a perennial delight to those who like restful, cool and quiet effects. That's what I think of white flowers!

What is *Vinca minor?* Well, it's a small periwinkle, and I suppose this one is *alba,* for I'm sure we once had a blue one but I'm not going to look it up after my last encounter with Bailey's *Encyclopaedia* ... I've forgotten what it was, now, but the last time I shut the tome with such a bang that the dog shot out of the room and the cat flew up the stairs believing their last day had come. Not that there is anything against this admirable and indispensable book of reference, except perhaps that it is SO thorough.

THE GENTLE ART OF SNIPPING

I'm not very keen on planting on top of double walls—that is, those that are not mere retaining walls—but a dry-built wall does, perhaps, permit clothing it with verdure instead of capping it with coping stones if one is so disposed; to discourage the planting of nasturtiums and other annuals that never looked right I once suggested *Vinca minor*, not knowing whether it would do but feeling it was worth a try. Well, it thrived in spite of the conditions and no watering in summer, and soon it was hanging down in graceful little festoons almost to the ground looking perfectly adorable. Not long after someone came and said (rather dramatically), 'They pruned it back'. 'What?' I asked, in an unsurprised voice. 'The *Vinca minor*!' they replied. I knew it was the wall, because it was only the day before that we had admired this little picture as we came home. What an awful habit this *snipping* habit is in the garden. Secateurs are unsafe in the hands of so many. How they could prune off those lovely tresses of foliage that softened the harsh stone wall is beyond me.

A RARE SOUL

Today someone came to cut wood for me. I don't mind chopping wood but I pale before a foot-thick log of dry black wattle, it's like iron, and when I went over to the wood heap by the lemons I gasped at the mass of 14-inch logs that awaited a mere touch with the axe to split them into stove wood. 'And I got all that for a pound!' I found myself murmuring, some men do work. At afternoon tea we looked about us and found the natural bush very pleasing; he just can't understand men who see no beauty in it; and to explain it he said, 'I didn't plant that they think, I suppose, and lay the axe at it!' That's just it, I thought; what they haven't planted they don't value. It's pathetic; and what follows is those awful 'beautification schemes'. Goodness! It's time we woke up.

TESTING THE GARDEN

Until the other day I thought that the test of a garden's beauty and appeal was a camera. By that I mean, did one feel impelled to go and get one's camera? Now I know there is another test. Does one, upon entering the gate wonder which way to turn, all directions being so enticing. I had driven someone home and he said, 'Will you come and see the garden?' Now, I was struck with that phrase. Why? Because he didn't say, 'Would you like to come and see the garden?' I often long to say, 'No thanks'; one gets enough of them when its one's job. Well, in we went and my eyes fell upon some stone steps that were just as right as they could be. 'Do you like them?' he asked incredulously. 'Of course I do', I assured him. 'But I did them myself.' Perhaps that's why I like them,' I explained. There's always something about a garden built by the owners and this one certainly had that 'something'. Once up the steps I found myself trying to go in two directions at once because both were so tempting. The plants were nice and thick, the ground was well covered, and there was an air of wildness about the garden. It was the sort of garden in which you could garden if you wanted to but if you didn't it wouldn't matter. That's my idea of a garden.

Yours till December,

Edna Walling

DECEMBER, 1945

Dear Gardeners,
I've just returned from Phillip Island (Victoria) and the thing that struck me most down there—at least, the thing most vital to us all—was the rye grass growing right down to the very water's edge thereby, stabilising the sand wonderfully and providing good fodder as well. And, strangely enough, I've just opened a copy of the *Christian Science Monitor*, in the magazine section of which appears an article upon stabilising shifting sands. Apparently in America when the sand dunes have been levelled they are seeded with grasses; a two-inch layer of straw (requiring from five to seven tons an acre) is then spread, and to prevent it blowing away it is tucked into the sand by rolling— the roller might have blades on it or something. The grass, protected by the straw, soon sprouts and is not blown away as it would be without this protection.

THINGS IN FLOWER JUST NOW

I agree with the person who said they liked white in the garden because it 'Tells out!' Perhaps the shad bush (*Amelanchier canadensis*) does not 'tell out' as much as some, for it is distinctly off-white rather than a clear and gleaming white, and this dusky whiteness is one of its charms. As we came up the drive after an absence of ten days shad bush, a mauve native daisy (*Olearia gunniana,* var. *coeruelea*), and masses of Westmoreland thyme greeted us with all they had to give, and these three did make a lovely picture. Just as if to add a little extra brightness to the scene—and it did need it—a vivid splash of gromwell (*Lithospermum prostrata*) was there, too.

THE GARDEN OF A GARDEN DESIGNER

You know what they say about the cobbler's children—how often they are badly shod—well, this garden is a little bit like that, but I do fluke it sometimes, and that drift of deep cream *Cytisis praecox* is quite good. They are just behind a young tree of black peppermint (*Eucalyptus amygdalina*), and the dark sepia trunk and graceful head of this tree make a lovely foil for this low-growing broom, which thrives in the poor, dry conditions.

One other piece of planting that is quite good here is the group of five liquidambars. I must have been in the right mood the day those went in. One *MUST* be in the mood for planting, at all events I must, and when I say I don't like gardening it is not a pose (as so many will insist), it's just that it is worrying except when one gets inspirations. Perhaps it's conventional gardening that I don't like! But the reason for mentioning these two plantings is the lesson they teach; in both cases the success of the picture is in the grouping of several of one species instead of one of this and one of that.

What to do in the Garden at Christmas

Find a shady tree, a comfortable chair, a low bench for your books and light refreshment and don't do a thing! (Just remembered you'd probably receive this at Christmas time.) We work far too hard in our gardens—or not hard enough, as the case may be—and the best greeting I can think of sending you is a few suggestions upon how to reduce weeds, and thus work!

In the first place, there are many odd weed-producing corners where forget-me-nots would be quite willing to take the place of weeds. They have those sort of smothering leaves that let few other plants survive. Occasional clumps of grass need to be pulled out, but this doesn't take a minute, and the sheet of pale blue in spring repays you for this small service. Baby's tears, *Erigeron mucronatus*, is another smotherer, and the small pink and white daisies are very sweet. *Ajuga repens* is a little plant that will carpet the ground charmingly. Even the native *Ajuga australis* is better than rank grass or bare ground.

I do think that full marks should go to gromwell, otherwise *Lithospermum prostratum*, for its all-year-round effect. The deep green foliage always looks

good and the intense blue flowers rival the gentian in blueness. I've turned to Reginald Farrer for the perfect description as usual, and this is what he says:

The plant occupies Northern, Central and South-Eastern Spain, indifferent, it would seem, to lime or granite though its best masses are associated with sandy and non-calcerous gardens. The wild types, so it is said, grow with the passionately lime-loving Daphne Cheorum *among the limestone blocks about Biarritz.*

Well, that's not exactly a description but its a help, and its the end of my space, so goodbye.

THE GENTLE ART OF SCYTHING

My final greeting in this Christmas letter to you is that those of you who have places in the country and are worried about long grass should buy yourselves a scythe for Christmas and practise the gentle art of scything. It's really fascinating, and for exercise it surely leaves no muscle untouched, untwisted, unstretched, unjolted, and unexhausted ... in short, unemployed. I defy an osteopath to execute a more thorough job and at the same time protect the countryside from fire, make the landscape look nice and tidy, and produce a useful crop of hay. What to do with the hay? Well, you should know that by now. Use it for smothering sorrel, couch grass, dock weed, or some other troublesome weed and, incidentally, improve that particular piece of ground.

A merry Christmas, and you should be sylph-like after this one!

Edna Walling

Dear Gardeners,

It's May 13 and the birches have put on their golden dresses (dear Elawheelerwilcox, if you remember her). But I'm an adorer of birches and ... aren't we all? (quaint Dion Boucicault; you can't have forgotten him!)

Around the garden there are several little spires of gold that are pyramid birches; who would ever want a troublesome Lombardy poplar after seeing this tree? For that matter there are numbers of fastigiate trees, that is those that grow in an upright manner, that are most useful for growing where there is little space for the spread of branches; there is a form of the common oak for example, with the manner of the Lombardy poplar, *Quercus pedunculata fastigiata*, this is commonly seen on the Continent; then there's the Guernsey elm, *Ulmus stricta Wheatleyi*, which is most interesting.

Personally, for a driveway, I like to drive through a tunnel of trees, with branches arching overhead. These pyramidal trees are not always the wisest for driveways, however narrow they may be. They are, however, delightful as accents in the landscape garden where they provide an interesting skyline for enframing a building and occasionally grouped. I think that is the way Roman cypresses are at their best, and also the common juniper, *Juniperus communis*. Groups of five, seven and so on of the last two mentioned trees, planted on a stony hillside, with various species of cistus, prostrate juniper and sun roses (*Helianthemum*) produce a fascinating landscape effect.

THE PROBLEM OF TERRACING

I've come to the conclusion that I do not like a collection of terraces (there are exceptions, of course); they always look so fussy, so expensive, and so ... well, often so silly! And now you are going to remind me of some divine garden in Italy, or France, or somewhere else on the Continent where the proportions and the execution of the work is so exquisite that a series of terraces becomes the most beautiful thing.

It seems that terraces need to be individual. That is, each one needs to be *different*, different as regards their width, their character and design, and their planting; each an entirely separate garden in fact. Witness the Italian garden composed of terraces. Each terrace is a separate garden; one may be a parterre, one a maze of tall clipped hedges, one a lawn or paved area, and yet another a setting for water features.

Terracing demands a special skill in designing, and it's a little risky to indulge in a 'series of terraces' unless you have that skill. Of course, a lot of us think we have and bog in! But those of us who don't like to become laughing stocks had better think twice about making their hillside gardens a 'series of terraces'.

There is nothing more monotonous than a set of stone walls equidistant up and down a hillside, nothing that can spoil that hillside more, and I can tell you there is nothing that exercises the imagination more than working out a garden imagination scheme on a steep slope that looks like a tilted-up table! One formal terrace near the house is generally fairly safe, and after that some of the ground might be left with its natural grade and planted with low-growing shrubs and perhaps a few trees, according to the area. Through this, informal steps of stone or a winding path might lead down to another levelled area cut into the hillside and retained by large boulders (preferably mossy), amongst which rock plants might find a home to their liking.

As regards 'succulents' in such a position it is, of course, a matter of taste, but don't imagine they've got to be succulents, or that one means succulents when one says rock plants. On the contrary, succulents are futherest from my mind. I loathe them and that's flat! To see such a position usurped by prickly, juicy, hot-looking plants that might have been a sheet of gentian blue of gromwell (*Lithospermum prostratum*); of the glistening white *Phlox nelsonii*; of the silvery-blue of *Campanula isophylla*, and the radiant white that is *C. isophylla alba* just makes me want to bolt before becoming personal ... before revealing one's prejudices, which is worse.

ON THIS MATTER OF TASTE

Actually I think it is a good thing to mix with people of opposite tastes. As someone most aptly remarked, the only difference between a groove and a grave is a matter of depth. But in such mixtures a sense of humour is a most necessary ingredient ... to prevent bloodshed; 'But how do you know you're right?' someone once shot out; 'I don't', I replied, 'I don't even think I am, *but I still don't like succulents!*' It is obvious that prejudices are frightful obstacles in all walks of life, and if you are prejudiced against certain plants it just means that you won't use those plants when they are clearly the most suitable for the conditions and the most appropriate in effect.

Yours till July,

Edna Walling

POSTSCRIPT

Another unanswered letter on my desk asks for suggestions for a cheap and attractive cottage, and the answer might be pise! Obviously neither the space nor the time permits more than a few remarks and the mention of 'Sleep-out' starts one off. The outsized meat safes which we attach to our houses and name 'Sleep-outs' are frequently uglier than sin; the worst thing about them is that you can't see out of half of them. I know about the rain driving in and all that sort of thing, but I still think one should be able to see the garden (if any) whilst lying in bed—to say the least, it's one very good reason for going on lying in bed. It seems that if one must sleep out it would be best to make a stone, brick or tile-paved porch into attractive sleeping quarters with the sort of covers that look right in the daytime and movable weather screens rather than those boarded up affairs which we have clung to for so many years. A room with plenty of casements that may be flung widely open is my preference.

The usefulness of verandahs could never be denied, but the wooden-floored type that shoots to right or left of the front door is not the best of planning; so often they darken some living room and are most unimaginative in appearance. The type we have to walk across to get to the front door is not always a success, and it seems a very good thing that it is one of the building habits that is being dropped in favour of paved porches accessible from the living room by glass doors.

JULY, 1946

Dear Gardeners,

American Plants for American Gardens by Roberts and Rehmann is a
book I've probably often mentioned before; it's a title that may tend to
restrict the book to the American public, whereas it is of great value to
all who have gardens where these American plants thrive. Actually, until
we have studied such books on plant ecology, we haven't much chance of
getting on to the right track with plant grouping, unless we travel afar
and see the plants growing in their natural associations (a rather more
expensive method and not so comfortable as the fireside with a book). It
was the chapter on 'The Juniper Hillside' to which I turned today, and I
wish I could quote it in full. It is delightfully written in words that paint
the natural scene they describe as vividly than any photograph could
do—perhaps even more so. In addition, through the whole book runs the
subtle lesson the landscape has to teach all would-be landscape
gardeners. In this chapter it is *Juniperus virginiana*, the red cedar, which
predominates, and the following passages will give you some idea of the
charm of this book:

The black haw, Viburnum prunifolium, *grows in small groups close against
the cedars ... The scrub oak and the choke berry are found here and there.
And roses, sweet fern, bayberry and blueberry cover the fields and drift
downwards into the hollows. The sumachs, too, gather in wide-flung
masses in the lower and less sterile spots. Besides, bitter sweet and Virginian
creeper climb into trees and shrubs, tumble over rocks and clamber over
stone walls. And the common barberry,* Berberis vulgaris, *grows there
singly or in small clumps. It is really a European variety, introduced years
ago, that found this situation so congenial that it became naturalised.*

It is the junipers, grey-toned in spring and deeper green later on, that make the foil for the seasonal effects of these shrubs and vines. Their evergreen sets off the black haw when the numerous sprays of white flowers make the one telling flower display of this association. And they make a background for the striking colours that the autumn brings ... The irregular spaces of seemingly barren ground between the juniper

groups and the shrub masses are covered with low herbaceous plants. The outcropping ledges are veritable little rock gardens. Mosses and lichens spread them with soft greys and greens. Tiny rare maidenhair spleenworts and other small evergreen ferns spring up in many a little nook. The grey rosettes of saxifrages fill every crevice, while the slender stems of the airy columbines rise delicately above their groundwork ... Later, the golden rods are in flower. And with the golden rods come the asters. Aster cordifolius *and* A. prenanthoides *have blue flowers,* Aster vimineus *has small white flowers, and the white slender sprayed* A. ericoides *is the daintiest of them all. This intermingled white and gold and blue is scattered lightly over the fields and as it fades the silvery-white everlastings show against the browned autumn-dried flowers and fawn-colored grasses.*

That's a very long quotation, but it tells us so much. I can never bring myself to cut down the fluffy soft buff and brown seed heads of perennial asters until well into the spring. The early frosts make fairyland of the garden where herbaceous perennial stems still remain, and quite a lot of autumn colouring is sometimes provided by the leaves.

THE GARDEN IN EARLY WINTER

May is one of the loveliest months in the garden if it is a woodland garden. The tracery of the branches of those trees that have lost their leaves, against the sky and against white buildings; the delicacy of the thinly foliaged birches; the small and fragrant pink and white flowers of *Viburnum fragrans* against white birch trunks; the soft red of the small-leaved rowan, *Sorbus discolor*; and the strange suffusion of red and yellow which the creeping euonymus (*Euonymus radicans*) assumes in winter, and the spireas, most of which are invaluable for early winter colouring.

EDUCATION?

It would appear that botany is one of the most essential of all subjects, and yet Public School students in Victoria are allowed to drop this subject in favour of others. Here we have a subject that gets to the very root (the pun is not intended) of life. Without plants we cease to live, and yet an astonishing number of Australians know little or nothing about the herbage that is fodder and all essential ground cover, nor about trees which provide timber, paper and an increasing number of essential things to man. On the question of nomenclature we are positively childish, except, of course, if it's a chrysanthemum, a dahlia or an ageratum. The other day a doctor (of medicine) asked the name of a shrub. *'Abelia'*, she was told. 'Oh, yes, but what's it's common name?' she replied with some impatience.

A chemist who was also present said, 'What's the common name for vertebrae?' 'Thank you', I said.

Yours till next month,

Edna Walling

A U G U S T ,   1 9 4 6

Dear Gardeners,

I would say that *Ornamental Flowering Trees and Shrubs* is the best book on this subject. It is edited by F. J. Chittendon, F.L.L.S., V.M.H., and published by the Royal Horticultural Society, Vincent Square, S.W.1, London, 1940.

Here is a guide to flowering trees and shrubs it would be hard to surpass; in it you have the considered opinions of those who have specialised in the growing of those trees and shrubs that we have all come to love, to cherish and to desire—viburnums, cherries, plums, apples, brooms, lilacs, rowans, magnolias, philadelphis, spireas, serberis, and a number of other familiar species.

I picked it up just now to see what they had to say about the tansy-leaved hawthorn, *Crataegus tanacetifolia*. Actually, I was wondering what I might group with this grey-foliaged hawthorn (but this was not the book to tell us that). However, here are some interesting facts about this delightful tree. It is one of the azaroli group of thorns native of south Europe and Asia Minor. It grows up to 35 feet high (though I'd call it a small tree), and has downy globe-shaped fruit of a soft red colour, and practically no thorns.

ECOLOGY AGAIN

As a guide to the grouping of our plants we can indulge in the reading of some of the most delightful travel books by Capt. F. Kingdon Ward, author of *From China to Hkamti Long*, *The Romance of Plant Hunting*, *The Riddle of the Tsangpo Gorges*, and his latest book, *Assam Adventure*.

Amongst the plants he mentions is the small-leaved and small-flowered rhododendrons that I covet most. Just listen to this:

... in the silver fir forest the rhododendrons were a magnificent sight, most beautiful of all being R. concatenens, *a slender, pyramidal shrub, its branches arched and drooping with countless carillons of crystal orange bells. The leaves of this shrub are small, of a delicate glaucous green, and do not interfere with the display of the flowers. We climbed another thousand feet, and everything changed once more. The forest of silver fir remained, but a fresh tide of rhododendrons was flowing. Now came into view the tubby, round-leaved* R. campylo-carpum, *whose innocent pale primrose bells one can imagine giving*

out a silvery tinkle, in contrast to the metallic clang emitted by the red-hot bells of R. Thomsonii.

I'd better stop; this quoting is becoming a habit. Just two more lines:

The country was quite open, bare of trees, and the rocky ground dabbled with the crimson heads of the little aromatic-leafed R. anthopogon *and the crushed-strawberry of* R. fragariflorum, *on which we walked as on a springy carpet.*

What a joy these smaller-leaved species would be in our small gardens!

FRAGRANCE

Prunus mume in early winter is the loveliest sight, and added to that is the exquisite fragrance. A double white form with flowers with a little more body than the pink varieties seems to bear the most scent. I have gathered up the seedlings growing about the two that I have, and shall watch them carefully. Some will surely come white and the rest be quite desirable no doubt; one of the best pale pinks in the garden came from a chance seedling, which all goes to show!

MORE OF THE BEST NATIVES, PLEASE

Considering the extraordinary ease with which some of the most desirable and delightful native plants may be grown from cuttings, why, oh! why do we not see more of the fringe myrtle, *Calytrix lhotzkya*, Baeckia (*Micromyrtus microphylla*), the mint bushes (*Prostanthera*), and thryptomene? The last-named is perhaps the most familiar, but baeckia is no less beautiful. Of late years a little mint bush called *Prostanthera incisa rosea* has been on the market in fair quantity. It is quite attractive, but no more so than *incisa* itself, which is mauve, of course.

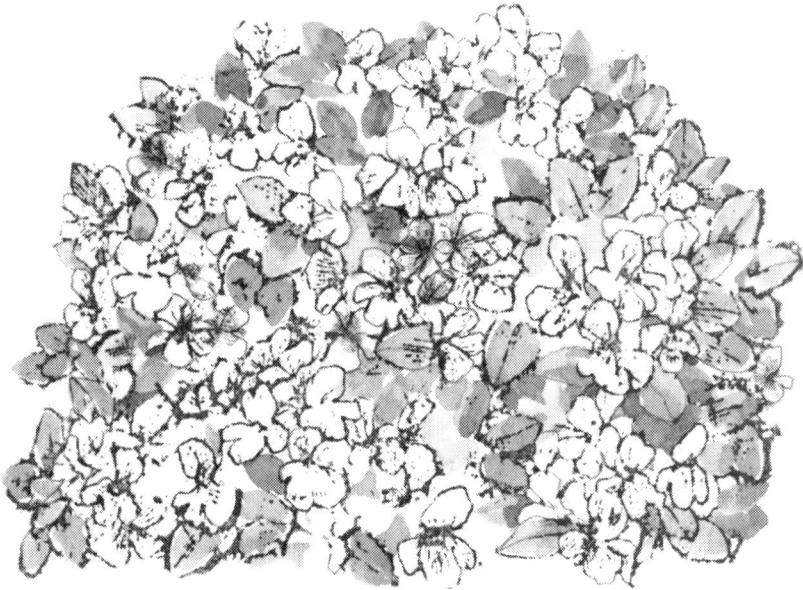

A TREE FOR COURTYARDS

Last night I called upon someone living in a most charmingly situated flat.
I ascended the stairs, and stood upon a little balcony at the entrance
doorway that overlooked an enclosed courtyard softly lighted by simply-
designed lanterns. Everything was right except the trees. They were
bolleana poplars. Even if one did not know what those roots were one day
going to do with the drains, the choice did not seem the best, and I found
myself unable to think of anything but almond trees—not the rather
sprawling flowering *Prunus pollardii*, with its rather too blatantly pink
blossoms—but the fruiting almonds which soar up and bear faintly pink
blossoms that 'tap on the window panes', as Katherine Mansfield said.
Their lovely picturesque forms when left unpruned, and the rather thinnish
growth make them most desirable trees for courtyards.

The picture of the gateway at Sonning has often been requested, and so here it is with my best wishes to you all.

Yours till September,

Edna Walling

JANUARY, 1947

Dear Gardeners,

We've just returned from the Grampians and how could I write of anything else! I don't mind admitting that when we came upon the wildflower garden on top of that mountain behind the Bellfield Hotel, tears rolled down. They call it Wonderland Range, and I was trying to avoid saying it. Wonderland! It sounds so like St. Kilda. Surely some day that will be changed and some lovely Greek word will take its place.

Wandering up and up the mountainside you begin to wonder where the wildflowers are, not that you're not enjoying the little familiar violets and innumerable other plants that brighten the climb, but you know it is going to be something to take your breath away, and that every step is bringing you nearer and nearer. Suddenly we see a baeckia (yes, I know it's really called *Micromyrtus*) and then more and more of them, and we think we are there, but go on wandering along the track of washed sand which is so lovely to walk upon, and skirting a mass of sandstone boulders we come face to face with thousands of baeckias and the shell-pink *boronia* (*B. polygalifolia*). I just sat down and gazed and gazed. To have seen anything so exquisitely beautiful before one dies seemed to be all that mattered! I shall never forget that soft pink cloud of flowers amongst the lichen-patterned, rosy-hued sandstone.

How friendly those rocks are, how unaustere. That's what I loved about the Grampians, for all their magnificence they're so friendly. On and on we wandered, threading our way through a veritable sea of baeckia and boronia that covers the plateau at the top of this mountain. I didn't know it was going to be like this. I didn't know this glorious garden would be on top of the world. It's so remote, and you are so glad, for somehow you feel it's safer up there! It was a dull day, mountain mists drifted over us, and though we wanted photographs (had we not come to the Grampians especially for pictures?) it didn't matter, we were so terribly lucky to be there. And now the thought of some day seeing it in sunlight makes the next visit all the more exciting.

I loved being on top of Mount Rosea, to which we hauled ourselves up, after a day gathering strength to do so. It was so still and silent, and the little glades and glens so surprising. These glens are made and shaded by huge sandstone masses, and the leathery foliage of banksia and alpine gum, and an occasional small tree of cypress pine. There are very few of these soft-textured trees and I viewed with delight every tiny seedling, wondering if I should one day return to see them as grown trees.

Just to make it harder to guess, the coast banksia here appears with leaves that are not serrated, a beautiful tree against the background of sandstone, and the mountain correa (*Correa lawrenciana*) gave lovely foliage effects in this rocky setting, too. Such light and shade, such undappled paths I had not expected.

We walked out of this glade of tree and boulder onto a treeless plateau, and looked down upon drifts of the rosy bush pea and crimson kunzea. The colour effect reminded me of the pinkish-mauve of English moors, with the heather in full bloom, but these shrubs were taller and with flowers on a larger scale, but certainly not 'rosy' and not 'crimson', we felt. I should never attempt colour descriptions, but would call this rosy bush pea, which is *Pultenaea subalpina* (*rosea*) by the way, a rosy purple, and the *Kunzea* (*K. parviflora*), a rosy mauve, but I'm willing to be corrected. Mount Rosea is the only place where this rosy purple variety of pultenaea has been found, most of the other forms are yellow and orange, I believe.

I know so little about native plants that one has to be most cautious when writing about them, but I never want to become a fanatic as regards Australian plants, and shall never attempt anything beyond a knowledge of those I really love.

Everywhere we came across plants of the most decorative white flower tea-tree I have ever seen, the flowers must be as large as a shilling. It was surprising to learn that it is *Leptospermum lanigerum* var. *grandiflorum*, for it isn't nearly so woolly as the riverbank woolly tea-tree and the leaves are so much larger and more leathery. It was covered with seed, and the little corms or whatever they're called that I brought home have now opened up and shed the fine seed, so we will sow it immediately, before the weather gets too hot.

The big umbels of the mountain conosperm (*Conospermum mitchellii*) I should think (what fun those who *really* know are going to have with this letter) were as decorative as the tea-tree, but not at all like it, of course.

I could go on for pages and pages but I've gone on too much already for the Editor's liking, and am hoping I can squeeze the little violets we sat amongst having our lunch somewhere between Ararat and Ballarat. It was the first time I had seen a pure mauve violet in Australia (wild, I mean) and

I nearly burst with excitement. Digging into Thistle Harris' *Wild Flowers of Australia* for something else, I found this violet so won't have to bother the Herbarium with that little thing. It's *Viola betonicifolia*, though Miss Harris' scientific descriptions are much more readable than most; that this violet is comparatively large and all mauve instead of white and purple, is all that you will want to know, I expect, and that must be the last word, anyway. Here come the scissors!

Yours,

Edna Walling

FEBRUARY, 1947

Dear Gardeners,

For figure and fire-reducing could anything compare with scything? And could anything be more against the earnest creed of the Humic Clubs than the little habit of burning-off? When you want it, hay can be one of the most difficult things to come by and yet because of the difficulty of getting it mown, and because people are impressed with the tinge of green that follows, tons of hay are still burnt off in places where the grass grows rankly, just to get rid of it! It is most dangerous left standing, of course, and it is most dangerous to burn it off, too, because it impoverishes the ground, which is always a dangerous thing to do. Many properties are not extensive enough for a horse mower, requiring a good deal of turning space, and many do not justify the expenditure upon a motor scythe (which runs over £100), and so there remains only the hand scythe. Now in a country where the risk of fire is so great and the need to prevent it so vital one can't help laughing at the frenzied search for men (who can scythe), in which we all indulge on the approach of summer. Summer always (or almost always) comes in the same way ... 'a very bad year for grass fires!' you hear all around, and so one can't help wondering if the art of mowing will be revived, because of the great necessity to get the grass down, and as a result of the ardent exponents of MULCH! Of course, what thrills me about this inescapable respon-

sibility of making one's property fireproof is the effect produced in doing so.

Those who do not know the joy of taking a scythe out for a half hour before breakfast, when the dew is still on the grass (that's when it cuts best), have yet to live. Apart from the perfect exercise—it certainly gets at that waist line—the mowing and raking of rank weeds and grass improves the appearance of any property out of sight and makes it look much more extensive. Scything does need practice, but it's worth sticking to until you've mastered the art. A perfect razor-like edge you must have, and if you're not prepared to master that it's no use starting, but this is easy enough if you use a file instead of a stone. No, it does not take off too much steel, on the contrary the blade on which I have used a file has lasted much longer than those on which a stone was used, for that special rhythmic wrist work required with a stone never resulted in a razor-like edge with me! No, not if I stopped and sharpened it every other swathe, and my impatience at the time absorbed in so profitless a task sent me off in search of a file. Just a few careful strokes with a nice new file (on the top side of the blade only) produces an edge that encourages me so much I just go on and on and on! ... just as I am going on and on and on about cutting grass. Well, I do think we should be made to cut our grass, by law, as they do in West Australia, because most fires start in grass.

An Unexpected Colour Scheme

Drawn by the spires we walked up the hill and stood looking across at the two lovely churches, one on each corner of the main street in Hamilton. One edifice was rather austere, but about the other, shade and softening foliage of trees beckoned us into the grounds—we couldn't get into the church, it was locked and I was rather sorry. We came out from under the branches of an enormous English oak to behold a picture, the colours of which astonished us, for who would have thought that a bright red flowering hawthorn and the pinkish-mauve flowers of *Virgilia capensis* would please one so. I think, perhaps, the grey-mauve trunk of a lemon-scented gum might have had something to do with it, for it seemed to reflect, or absorb some of the red of the hawthorn, and some of the rather harsh mauve of the virgilia, and to blend them together. One thing is certain: that lovely gum was a very important part of the picture, and ecologically so incorrect!

Last evening I made a hurried tour of the garden in search of roses and found but three! I had to have something for the table and I'd set my heart on roses, so I went around again, less critically this time, and into less accessible spots, and came back with a much more interesting bunch than I set out to gather. One of the miniature roses provided me with bunches of little blobs of soft red blooms, a few rather undersized buds of 'Madam Abel Chateney' and one or two full-blown flowers of this old darling next fell to the secateurs, and then the strange mauve-red, crinkly-petalled moss rose joined the still inadequate bunch. I began to walk slowly and disappointedly back to the house when I saw a huge bush of 'Cecile

Brunner' covered with bloom. These were a heaven-sent blessing and I returned quite satisfied with the little bouquet.

'It seems to need a little white,' said the one cooking the dinner. 'Well, *you* find it my girl!' I suggested.

'What about that adorable white rambler with the elusive fragrance?'

It was about half a mile away, but it was worth it. And so one of the sweetest bunches of roses came on to the dinner table.

Until March, goodbye to you all.

Edna Walling

MARCH, 1947

Dear Gardeners,

I now have a file into which go notes of all the little things I'm tempted to talk to you about. It is a good idea, no doubt, but it seems that nothing could make me orderly (and I do like orderly people), because here is a note that should have been written in October!

How I wish you could all see the garden just at this very minute. The grey-white shad bush is carpeted with Westmoreland thyme, the mauve-flowered Daphne genkwa *has a little drift of alpine violets at its spindly feet, and nearby is the strangest-looking weeping apple you ever saw, leaning right over the pool in the rock garden, flowering as it ne'r flowered before, with vermillion buds and almost white petals. Clouds of the clear mauve daisy bush (*Olearia gunniana coerulea*) appear almost everywhere, because I'm always tucking in fresh plants of it, fearing to lose the picture of this short-*

lived shrub. In one spot its legginess has been most satisfactorily concealed by Cytisus praecox, *which remains such a nice little fairly low-growing round shrub, whilst others of its kind race up into such sturdy and somewhat cumbersome inhabitants of one's garden.*

And here is another note written sometime in late spring.

On my desk is the prettiest bunch of flowers you could wish to see, I only wish it could be recorded in colour, just as it is lying there. It is Thymus stricta *and it has just been gathered (though in full flower) for cuttings. It is an adorable little shrublet with its stiff erect branches surmounted by little heads of almost pink flowers. And why did we take the cuttings with the plant in full bloom? Well, because I was afraid we might want more young plants of it than we had provided for in the winter planting of cuttings, and the good rains tempted me to put in more. It is quite the best of the edging plants in the vegetable garden, so good in form, foliage (which is greyish-green) and the abundance of its flowers.*

FOLIAGE FOR THE HOUSE

Some pruning back of a prostrate juniper had to be executed today, and the branches were far too beautiful to cast away, so they came inside and in an old glass battery jar they look very nice. In the summer, branches of oaks and birches or any other green foliage (except gum leaves!) look cool in the house, and I'm inclined to think it is sometimes better to have only one small bunch of mixed flowers, and for the rest cool green foliage on very hot days. Shasta daisies look cool, too, and lavender is refreshing. Gum leaves always make me feel hot and yet the leaves of some of the bloodwoods, which are a darker green and less grey than the other species, are really the most decorative I know. One day I shall find myself using them, no doubt!

EROSION

The possibility of improving the landscape with the help of erosion has been illustrated in an issue of the official organ of the Landscape Architects' Association (America). The sharp sides of a deeply-eroded gully on a country property were broken down and thrown into the bottom of the gully, and the ground then graded to form natural-appearing undulations and sown down with grass. Groups of trees were planted here and there, and in place of the scar there is now a pleasing piece of landscape and no erosion. Herbage is often even more necessary than trees in the control of erosion, and anything that destroys the natural carpet that covers the earth must be guarded against most carefully. That's what burning-off does— destroys the natural carpet under trees. The trees hate it and erosion begins. We just have to find other ways of getting rid of rubbish, and if we must burn heaps of rubbish it is definitely incumbent upon us to protect the top soil, and all the humus and grass seeds contained therein, by stripping it from the place where the burning is to take place and putting it back afterwards. We can't get away with just burning off the grass. I recently visited a country property where this method of erosion control had been practised, but without imagination, with the result that a strange-looking and quite unattractively graded piece of the landscape called forth the same inquiry from all fresh visitors to the property: 'What is it?'

Both sides of the depression had been graded to such a meticulous line that they looked like tilted-up tables covered with grass. It was efficient, but ugly.

BIRCHES

Birches seem to be the perfect foil for so many shrubs. Last spring two or three birches with about eight or ten *Cytisus praecox* growing around them made a picture I shall not readily forget. Clouds of this cream-coloured broom are a delight against a background of Arizona cypress, or some other

conifer with an occasional birch for the whiteness of its trunk. Birches of course are so useful because they are deciduous, but the whiteness of the bark is easily rivalled by the paperbark tea-tree, or myrtle, as it is also commonly called. The sight of two of these native trees in a suburban garden recently took my breath away and rather cut the ground from under my feet, nothing I had thought could surpass the beauty of birch bark! I must go.

Au revoir,

Edna Walling

APRIL, 1947

Dear Gardeners,

I was shopping in Lilydale and had been told of an old brick building which had once been the gasworks. 'They want to pull it down ... say it's an eyesore'; so off I went to see the 'eyesore'. It's anything but an eyesore. On the contrary, it is full of the most exciting possibilities. What a delightful little theatre it would make. The old bricks are mellow, and the structure so good, and it is set among magnificent old trees down near the creek, right in the heart of the township. Nothing that was built up in its place could ever have such charm or such atmosphere. It doesn't look up to much at present, of course, but it doesn't take much imagination to visualise it after some repairs have been carefully effected, and lawn and brick paving set around it. After seeing this we spent the rest of the morning poking around finding fascinating old houses here and there among the modern (I nearly said monstrosities) and we had great fun planning the future of this village (it is a township, but 'village' sounds nicer) so that it would become famous for the beauty of its old buildings and houses, and the thoughtfully-designed new building in keeping with the atmosphere of age.

In between atrocious buildings of this decade one may see old shops built of brick and stone that could be most picturesque if stripped of their plaster and their ill-designed additions.

'But they'd never do it,' my friend said.

'Why not? They might. What about Toorak Village? All but one shopowner fell in with the idea there.'

Inside, the shops are as up-to-date and convenient as anyone could wish. Outside they are so picturesque and attractive that you wish you had your camera when the evening light falls across the small-paned windows.

'Small-paned windows!' I can hear some hard-head say, 'Fancy cleaning them!' Yes, and fancy paying for a plate-glass window that gets broken. That's one of the practical reasons for the popularity of these small-paned shop windows.

'Will it remain like that?' said my friend, as we drove home over the hills to Mooroolbark. 'Will they realise that all the charm will go if they don't preserve every one of those dear old houses that are so picturesque. Will they preserve all the historic value that is there? One can't believe that the home town of so world-famous a figure as Melba will not be preserved and developed along such lines that we shall not be ashamed when overseas visitors come here.'

'You'd think not,' I said, and we were home again, and down to the rock garden to see if it wanted watering.

I water that, chiefly to keep the cabin cool! The cabin is just above it and is used in hot weather for alfresco meals, and an added sense of coolness is given by moist ground without and stone paving within.

MY ROCK GARDEN

Looking down over the rock garden I felt faintly meek about it when one visitor said: 'Your rock garden?' in a voice dispassionate and clear. My rock garden is the one place where birches seem to thrive most happily (one doesn't grow trees in rock gardens!) The 'rock plants' are the very hardiest species such as prostrate rosemary, hypericums, lavender and thymes, and all self-respecting rock garden specialists take one sweeping glance and walk on ... on to the next disappointment.

'My dear, this is nothing,' said one lady on one of our Red Cross Days.

'Why, at "Greensteynes" the rhododendrons are 30 feet high.'

Another voice: 'Personally I'd rather have this little soft biscuit-coloured one ... though it's only three feet high, and that mauve daphne (*D. genkwa*) carpeted with alpine violets.'

It's all in the point of view I suppose.

A FOIL OF GREYISH-GREEN

Again and again I find the Arizona cypress and *Juniperus communis* (the upright one) an excellent foil for some flowering shrub. *Viburnum burkwoodii* with its large heads of white flowers softly tinged with pink is much lovelier against such a background, and this rather thinly growing shrub seems to need the 'body' that a good sturdy conifer supplies. How dull a treeless garden can be. I shall never forget the demand of one client: 'I want you to get me half-a-dozen choice shrubs', he said magnificently.

'Whatever for?' I said, chafing at the confusion of my profession with that of a nurseryman, not that I wouldn't as soon be a nurseryman, both have equal advantages and disadvantages, I should think.

'To plant in my garden, of course', he said snappily.

'What, without some trees to go with them?'

'Trees go too big', he said.

'They don't take up as much room as shrubs', said I, and once again I had to explain this little thing, and before I'd finished, being a man of action, he had decided to have all trees and no shrubs!

'What, no shrubs?' I said, and then I had to explain that I needed some shrubs to make a picture. His energy was fading.

'Oh, do as you like', he said, throwing up his hands.

I made a few rough notes and hurried off to get a ... I've forgotten what it was now, but it was a deserving case.

Yours,

Edna Walling

MAY, 1947

Dear Gardeners,

By the time you get this you will be thinking about the winter planting of shrubs and trees, and a note made on September 11 may be of interest.

One of the most decorative of the viburnums, V. rigidus, *towered above a plant of* Ceanothus rigidus *not yet three feet in height, and at the feet of this deep blue ceanothus, with its tiny leathery leaves, narcissus and freesias bloomed all cream and white.* Lhotskya *and* Baeckia *gave the faintest tinge of pink to a scene which was entirely satisfying. It surely can't be long now before all these things will be easily procured, but I know you are going to have a little trouble about getting them at present. Keep on asking and thus help to create the demand.*

Virburnum rigidus is rather a clumsy thing in anything but a large garden, and yet I have it in a secluded corner of my garden that could be quite suitably reproduced in a town garden of average size. The large heads of bloom might be described as off-white in colour and the leaves are large, rough in texture and of a somewhat dusky green. The ceanothus could be kept within small proportions without detracting from its beauty by continually pinching off leading shoots. It is inclined to grow a little spindly so you will be doing a good thing anyway by 'nipping it in the bud'.

The very small texture of the foliage of *Lhotskya* makes this shrub a delight in any small garden and equally lovely in drifts in a large one. Baeckia, or more correctly *micromyrtus*, is a little shrub one expects to see in every garden, and hardly ever sees at all. Everyone is envious whenever they see onc and it is a wonder to me they haven't compelled nurserymen to propagate them by the million for the sake of peace. But no. We're a strange race—so easily put off.

There are two more pictures flowering in September. *Prunus spinosa purpurea*, which is the purple-leaved sloe or blackthorn, rosemary and *Ceanothus rigidus* again. This is really lovely, for the rosemary and the ceanothus are such a perfect complement to each other. It would be no use supplementing the more familiar *Ceanothus veitchina* or *C. divaricatus* for *rigidus*, both grow so differently, so much more lustily. Besides it is the deep blue of *rigidus* that is so good with the grey-blue of the flowers of rosemary. The sloe seemed to be the perfect little tree for these two shrubs with its small bronze-green foliage and dainty white flowers with pink centres. I like this little tree much better than the double form, which one never feels tempted to bring indoors, yet the single form looks so exquisite in our old glass battery jar.

The other picture was composed of *Malus arnoldiana*, an excellent flowering apple, *Thymus stricta*, an upright little shrublet flowering first amongst the thymes, and *Baeckia plicata* (*Micromyrtus*). They are all different shades of pink and the rather bright, almost red buds of the apple give just that depth of colour which makes the picture.

MORE NATIVES PLEASE

I must say I should not like to start off upon a career of garden-making over again with such a limited collection of low-growing shrubs procurable. One would just have to get to work and propagate some of the native shrubs in sheer desperation (goodness knows they strike easily enough) for use in making landscape pictures. Low-growing, ground-covering plants are indispensable to a landscape designer, and you need them in large quantities for it is not a very extensive garden that requires these small shrubs in half-dozens and dozens of each species in order to form drifts of one kind in place of a messy collection of one of this and one of that.

ADJECTIVES

She's one of those people who speak of plants as 'adorable little fellows', 'this darling little pet', 'this little gem', and so on.

Heavens, I thought, so do I! I felt very inferior in the presence of this great botanist, he is so kind to me, but it was hard not to enthuse, to stuff down those exclamations of delight at the sight of a little boronia with shell-pink flowers hugging the ground and just say, 'Yes, that's interesting, isn't it?'

It is just as hard not to be able to say, 'I think it's simply foul', when some bloated, brilliantly red monster is displayed for approval.

A friend of mine has been visiting a relation, who owned some land in Sydney, where wildflowers grew in abundance, and gathered a small bunch for her room. On the way back to her hotel she was accosted by the police and asked to explain. Her name was taken, and also that of her nephew, who later was called upon to assure the police that the flowers were gathered on his private property. I understand the law is the same in Victoria and it is a very great pity it is not enforced. It is ever more essential here, for we have fewer wildflowers—fewer and fewer in fact!

Yours,

Edna Walling

JUNE, 1947

Dear Gardeners,

Oh! The joy of getting away from conventional gardens, with the same boring selection of exotics, to the exquisite pieces of landscape composed of plant groups so happily joined together, so untrammelled and satisfying. I find I rarely can exert myself to go and see a garden, however beautiful it is said to be, but thrill at the thought of any journey to a place where the trees and natural ground cover are still unspoilt. Nature's garden is never exhausting, always refreshing. You are never conscious of labour and cost and upkeep. Towards those who interfere with natural landscape beauty, my feeling is one of intense irritation. We were looking at a delightful little woodland of young candlebark gums the other day, and someone said, 'But you'll have to thin them out, won't you?' I just wondered what it would look like after they had finished with it; a sorry sight, I fear. 'No,' I said. 'Nature planted this corner and we are very pleased with it indeed and don't intend to interfere. We're so bucked we haven't got to do anything, but I shall cut the blackberries out ...' Two or three small plants were just creeping in, I observed.

Recently, we were horrified to see a woman burning off the roadside outside her property. She was 'only burning the grass'. She also burnt the wild cherries (scorching the big ones and completely killing the young ones), all the young candlebarks, the dogwoods, the bursaria and lots of little ground-covering things.

'It'll come again,' they say. 'And you will burn it again,' we shoot back. The pathetic part about this national pastime of 'burning-off' is that a lot of it is done in sheer ignorance. Restrictions are lifted, they see and smell other people burning-off and they put their books down and decide to spend the afternoon burning-off! Sometimes they have quite a job to find something to set on fire, but there's always the roadside! Some will attend, and listen most rapturously at the meetings of the Compost Society and come straight home and burn-off. It never seems to occur to them that they are consigning to the flames the very thing they have been poetising about in some city hall ... leaf mould, not only from the leaves of trees, but from the leaves of grass.

Reading an article on the Grampians, I came upon this paragraph:

Incidentally the hotel had plans ready and capital available for rebuilding. The intention is to erect a modern brick hotel nearer the road.

No note of exclamation or anything. Perhaps the writer thought it would be a good thing; that the 'modern-brick-hotel-nearer-the-road' would really be a fine idea; that it really did not matter if the quiet charm—almost a farm-like atmosphere—that pervades this particular hotel now, might be destroyed for ever. How utterly sick one gets of BRICK. Where is our imagination in this country, where we plaster it with incongruous buildings which destroy the very quietness people go to the country to seek? Those who want a 'modern-brick-hotel-close-to-the-road' can find them elsewhere without spoiling a lovely peaceful valley with one. There will be no sheep grazing in front of the new hotel, no sound of cows being milked, no rough grass to sprawl upon, and I suppose there might be some golden cypresses in time!

Anyway, how one longs to read something like this:

Necessary additions to the hotel are shortly to be made, but those who love the place need have no qualms, the farm-like atmosphere will still be there. Local stone will be used and probably whitewashed to avoid the hard and showy appearance of some of the stonework to be seen here and there. The roof will be a soft sepia shingle tile, or slate. Brick and Marseilles tiles have been particularly eschewed as being suburban. The proprietors have been much exercised in their minds as to whether to use pise or stone in their desire to be sure of escaping the ordinary in these proposed additions. The old weatherboard buildings will remain and be painted white, as it is felt that they will harmonise well with the stone walls and chimneys (see American magazines) and though old they are too good to be demolished, and the historic and sentimental value is not to be discounted.

And perhaps that is exactly what the proprietors have in mind, and if they have not, this dissertation on 'Discrimination and care in the use of the environment' weighs so heavily on my chest today that, at the risk of the Editor's displeasure, 'hints on gardening' have been sidetracked! Now I feel decidedly better, and will wind up with the following quotation from Lewis Mumford's *Culture of Cities*:

If ever an economic system demands a balance between energy income and outgo, human culture demands a still greater degree of discrimination and care in the use of environment; a more active sense of place-possibility, a more delicately-poised equilibrium between the landscape and the modes of human occupation.

And in my garden this autumn I find there is not nearly enough of those cascade chrysanthemums, whose small single flowers of cream, pink and brown mingle so charmingly with perennial asters. There are not enough asters either, and it's not autumn without these two. For cutting they are both indispensable.

Yours,

Edna Walling

JULY, 1 9 4 7

Dear Gardeners,

I wonder what the honey from the flowers of *Eleagnus pungens* (syn. *E. japonica*) would taste like? Passing a huge bush of this 'Russian olive' just now, I noticed it was swarming with bees. The fragrance of it was everywhere in the garden. For weeks now everyone has been asking, 'What is the heavenly scent?' This plant

is a social climber of no ordinary capacity. From its flexible branches short spurs extend, sloping in such a manner that it may hook itself up on to any object. For those who like to smother an old dead tree with some growth, rather than cut it down, this evergreen will certainly do that. What it is doing in my garden is helping itself up in the world by means of live trees! That is not as to plan, when I planted it, and it is clear that this fragrant and quite attractive evergreen must be viewed in the light of those things which add a mite to the maintenance of a garden. Keeping it within bounds is not difficult nor very time absorbing if not neglected, but it must be done, and the perfect garden, in my opinion, is one that may be left indefinitely, if needs be, without fear of one thing smothering another during one's forced, or desirable, absence. An overgrowth of grass is a mere nothing; that your lawn produces a crop of hay, which in time lies over and rots, will do more good to the ground than harm, and that some hold up their hands in horror at the sight of an overgrown lawn, as though some fell disease had descended upon the garden, always strikes me as funny. Well it isn't funny, I suppose, if you have not acquired the gentle art of scything and can't bring yourself to buy one anyway! There is nothing funny about tackling the lawn with hedge shears.

Autumn Shrubs

Less and less spireas appear in gardens, and more and more I find them invaluable in the building up of a landscape garden! Referring to Rehder's manual of cultivated plants to look up *Spirea aitchinsonii*, there are, I find, about 225 varieties of *Spirea* listed in this book, and there would be more, of course. Perhaps it is because they mostly have white flowers—and small at that—that they are not popular, or perhaps it is that the foliage, on the whole, is fine and soft rather than bold and striking, I can quite imagine that nurserymen may not find them profitable for they don't exactly 'sell' themselves, so to speak; and yet, strip a garden, which pleases you, of all the quieter things that grow in it and all its charm will vanish. Another thing that might account for their unpopularity is that they don't like being pruned much, and some people do like things they can prune!

'When do you prune these?' they will ask, brandishing the secateurs they are dying to try out on something. To the reply, 'Never,' they look disappointed, lose interest in spireas at once, and wheel around looking for something they can prune.

If I had not been put out by the description of *Spirea aitchisonii* in this book you might have been spared the foregoing remarks. The plant I have under this name has pinnate leaves and might be *S. sorbifolia*, it faintly resembles a rowan in foliage (but not height, growing but five or six feet high), has flowers in panicles, and spreads freely by suckers. (Oh! why did I mention that little thing.)

It has been in my garden for years and not until this year have I really appreciated its value. Perhaps I have been a little irritated that it does not always colour. This autumn I like it very much. Yes, it is colouring, but not very brightly, but the saw-edged, pinnate foliage is unusual and attractive.

Another plant that colours well into early winter with the loveliest faintly pink shades is *Cornus asperifolia*. It also suckers ... thank heaven! By means of these suckers it has been distributed about my garden from year to year, and still there is not enough of it. *Viburnum dentata* also assumes these pinkish shades under the protection of large trees. But remember, none of these shrubs colour brilliantly.

THE NATIVE CYPRESS PINE

Being rather dull, I wondered what someone meant the other day when they asked, 'What is the name of those flame trees?'

'Do you mean *Brachychiton*, but I haven't one here.'

'No; those soft cypress-like trees down by the stage that look like the flame of a candle.'

These were Victorian cypress; I had never thought of them in that light before. On a recent visit to the nursery of the New South Wales Forest Commission it was thrilling to see so many varieties of callitris being propagated, and in such vast numbers. It is a glorious nursery where native trees are the chief interest. How encouraging it is to see such a nursery, and to see so many species of eucalypt and callitris planted out in masses (very closely too) on this Forest Experiment station. I long to go back in the early morning with my camera one day. How people can spare the time to go abroad is what amazes me. As I go tottering down the hill I wonder will I be able to see half there is to see in this country before there isn't a totter left. It is not the spectacular view, it's the plants, from diminutive ferns to the towering forest trees, that I want to see.

Yours deciduously,

Edna Walling

O C T O B E R ,   1 9 4 7

Dear Gardeners,

In 1892, Professor Sargent sent to Kew (Vic) from Japan a curious little plant, a miniature *Euonymus radicans*, sometimes known as *E. radicans* var. *minimus*. It has become known in nurseries, however, as *E. r. kewensis*, having originally been distributed from Kew, where it is thought that it may be a distinct species.

The leaves are a dull green with veins of a paler shade. The plant forms low patches rarely more than two inches in height in the young stage. It will, however, climb up the stems of shrubs or, if such support is missing, will form a little pyramid of its own branches.

According to Mr W. J. Bean, these euonymus don't bear fruit or flowers in the climbing or trailing condition, and may be described as like the ivy in character.

Arriving at adult or flowering state, it alters the character of its growth, and instead of the shoots being slender and trailing they become erect and bushy. I love both *E. radicans* and the small-leaved *kewensis* for their foliage.

Quite vivid patches of red appear among the evergreen leaves of the plants of *radicans* at Sonning in winter, but this may be because of rather infertile soil, or the excessive dampness of it in places.

You see, I do not drain my garden. I expect the plants to do that for me— and it is surprising how they will. Trees have made soggy patches quite agreeable places for walking.

But we will talk about drainage when we have finished with the creeping euonymus, for I haven't told you half yet. You won't want to know that 'the branches are minutely warty'. 'Are they?' I said to Mr Bean, rather shocked. 'Well, I won't tell them that, it might put them off.'

But before going any further, here's a warning! Ask your nurseryman for *Euonymus radicans*, and in all probability you will receive not *Euonymus radicans* but *Euonymus radicans* var. *folius variegatis*, or *E. r.* var. *roseomarginatis*.

When my eye lights on one of these, having ordered *E. radicans* and having visualised just what I'm going to do with *E. r*, I put it quietly aside to be given away as a present or something. I have never yet found a spot where these plants (which have the same reaction on me as the variegated *E. japonica*) would be satisfying.

E. radicans has many uses. It will creep over the ground, forming an admirable ground cover in either shade or sun, and it may be trained up house fronts, over walls and fences, reaching a height of 20 feet or more.

It is less trouble than ivy and is used where ivy is not hardy, such as in the New England States.

That is, briefly, what Mr Bean has to say about it. I have not used it nearly as much as I might have done, and have that pleasure in store, especially of associating *E. r. kewensis* with mossy boulders.

I cannot quite see by what means *radicans* climbs up walls, but it seems to do it unaided. If one lifts it gently away, it just springs back against the wall.

Now about this little matter of drainage. What a big matter some make of it!

Clearly, there are times when we must drain the ground, and drain it thoroughly by laying (well and truly) agricultural tile pipes. The 'well and truly' part is most important, for it is a complete waste of money unless the pipes are sitting just in the clay (not *on*, but *in* the clay). It is the cutting of the groove in the clay that matters most. The pipes merely keep that groove open.

For this purpose, a drainage tool is really imperative. It is a weird and wonderful-looking implement which is dragged along the clay bed, making a half-round groove in which the pipes sit nicely. Over the joints of these, tarred paper or sacking is placed to prevent the soil from trickling in. Then clinkers or cinders cover the whole pipe to a depth of roughly two inches or three inches.

The soil (but no clay) then goes back into the trench. Into the groove in the clay at the bottom of the trench trickles all superfluous water. It then goes up through the roughly fitting joints of the pipes and goes away.

There is no doubt about the value of drainage, but there is also no denying that it is often unnecessary. Surface drains at the sides of drives and pathways are, most happily, outmoded.

An adequate number of well-placed catch pits can carry away the water underground before it has a chance to do any damage above ground. Some of the best-kept gravel driveways I have ever seen have no disfiguring gutters or concrete edging.

When appropriate surface drains may be of grass, a softly rolling depression planted with a moisture-loving grass such as woodend bent will carry away a lot of water without the surface being disturbed. At the sides of country driveways of any length this method is most satisfactory, especially where the driveway passes through paddocks where the cattle and sheep keep the grass nibbled right to the drive surface.

It may sound strange, but it is true that drainage work is usually best carried out after the garden is constructed, except, of course, in such obvious cases as protecting the house foundations from seepage when the ground falls towards the house.

Certain alterations of the natural contour and the construction of walls, steps, pools and so on will obviously be done before any drainage scheme with agricultural pipes is carried out.

It is a far cry from drainage to ornamental vines. However, as a picture of the purple-leaved *Vitis vinifera purpurea* is going with this letter, some allusion to it is due. The leaves are at first claret red, later dull purple and finally, in autumn, a soft red. The mauve-blue of the little bunches of grapes and the soft red and purple of the foliage is indeed a delightful sight.

No one, I feel sure, could be disappointed in such a climber when it is happy.

I've been told it does not thrive in sandy soil, but I always believe in trying things out for myself if I want them badly enough.

Yours,

Edna Walling

NOVEMBER, 1947

Dear Gardeners,

Twice lately have I seen the old lemon-scented geranium looking very charming on the landscape. Once it was in an old country garden at Hamilton where this and a mauve-flowered rambler rose were all that remained among the pine trees; and now in my own garden, also under the pines.

To what trouble one might go to have a flowering shrub grow happily in such a place! Yet here is this dainty mauve-flowered geranium not batting an eye, and covered with bloom!

And so I began thinking of a few things that will not only grow, but will thrive, in the most inhospitable piece of ground in the whole of my garden. The garden is not only hungry, but is riddled with the roots of that giant among trees, the Californian redwood.

Here is *Cistus* 'brilliant', looking as if it is getting just what the doctor ordered. It is covered with its huge, floppy, bright (but quite pleasing) pink flowers, and the foliage is lush.

Cistus laurifolius is also perfectly contented and favours us with its delightful, heavy, white flowers.

Then there is *Cistus cyprius*, more inclined to hug the ground than the tall and slim *laurifolius*. *C. cyprius* blooms are also white (single, of course) and everyone seems to like it.

The Italian lavender (*Lavandula stoechas*) is bursting itself with bloom splashed with the clearest of mauves and purple. My first acquaintance with this lavender was in an old, old garden where it was merrily flowering under an ancient cypress tree.

I begged a few seedlings, and by propagating it from cuttings and cherishing the self-sown seedlings, we now have it gracing the hottest, driest, and hungriest places in the garden. Spring in the garden is all the cheerier for its presence.

Grevillea confertifolia, with its particularly pleasing strawberry-pink flowers, is quite vigorous in this patch of awfulness, and the brooms romp away. The prostrate form of *Spartium junceum*, so much more attractive than the tall one that annoys me so much, is a golden mass of bloom, but I think it may one day be replaced by ... well, perhaps, another grevillea with blooms of a softer hue.

Long, low, and broad is a pretty safe rule with steps in the garden. Some of the most charming houses have been spoilt by the addition of steps, and sometimes they are not even necessary.

Once, we raised the driveway at the entrance to a house and built a retaining wall on the outside to make a much more interesting and less tiring approach to the door, replacing six steps with but one at the porch.

Steps coming through a wall look better if they turn and follow the wall down instead of gushing straight down to the lower level. Semicircular steps are all right so long as there are not too many of them.

I shall never forget the ghastly sight of about 12 or 14 of them. You can imagine the proportions they assumed by the time they reached the bottom. It was the most gruesome mass of cement ever seen in any garden. They're still there, I believe. Strange how many ugly things survive and how many beautiful things are demolished!

I have in mind a rather lovely pergola, much lovelier than usual,

whose great big pillars of rubble, roughly plastered, supported an overhead framework of saplings. It was the nearest thing I had ever seen to the famous pergola at Amalfi.

This was pulled down to make room for a house. It could quite easily have been saved and have become a valuable feature of the house and garden with a little wangling by the architect.

Yours,

Edna Walling

DECEMBER, 1947

Dear Gardeners,

For sheer restfulness, Spanish gardens, with their sheltered cloisters, sombre evergreens, paved courtyards, refreshing water features and climbing plants and pot plants (that supply colour with so little labour) seem much superior, much more serviceable, than Australian gardens as a whole. Utterly weary one grows of the gardens in which 'a bit of stonework' has been executed.

I dined with a friend last night who lives in an old house surrounded by such a restful garden of no particular design or virtue. To make it entirely pleasing a few things needed improving, perhaps, but when I was told they were going to have the garden 'done' I grew anxious.

When they added, 'Don't you think a bit of stonework would be nice?' I said 'Good heavens! NO.'

It's so ironic that in some gardens money is spent when it isn't necessary, and when it is essential to face up to a little expenditure you can't get them to part with a penny!

With gardens, it isn't what you are prepared to spend, but what is fitting. If, because of the style of the house, the estimate is more than can possibly be faced, it is so much wiser to carry out the most desirable plan piecemeal.

I just can't get over the mediocrity of some gardens that belong to people who really do know better. For heaven's sake, let us wake up and realise that garden-making IS an art. It does not matter how simple or how humble the garden is, but it does matter if it is in bad taste.

There is one garden in Toorak (Victoria) where no expense has been spared. It is a mass of walls built of all different kinds of stone—sandstone, bluestone, marble and limestone, oh yes! and some ironstone to give it a 'bit of colour'.

Believe it or not, it was designed and supervised, by one of the foremost architects in Melbourne, since dead.

Another garden, owned by one whose taste in the house is impeccable, is extremely dull and boring, in fact, quite ugly in parts. Much money has been spent on it, yet it isn't a patch on one I know of in the same area. In the second garden the only expenditure has been upon the introduction of a few really large mossy boulders and some trees (probably about £25 at the outside). The natural grass was left, mown, occasionally treated with weed killer; a pleasing sward resulted. Why will not those with the wherewithal sometimes think of their gardens as the possible setting for an exquisite bronze figure, or merely as a quiet setting for their home instead of experimenting with all the tricks of the garden-making trade?

After a day of graft in this garden, a friend straightened up and said, 'Let's cover the whole thing with concrete!' and I could not help thinking how nice a paved courtyard with one big tree would be.

You all know what I think of concrete near a garden—even in the backyard—but any form of paving is a blessing. I never see a heap of old bricks without wanting to bring them home, and if ever I have a utility it will rarely be without bricks or stones in the back. Sharp washed sand is another thing it is difficult to pass.

But to return to Spanish gardens, and Italian ones, too. It is really rather amazing that we have copies of the English style rather than the other two, because in this climate protection from hot winds is so essential to intelligent living.

Here in Australia, quite intelligent people continue to live in houses that get hot enough to roast them.

Remarkably few have pergola-covered, out-of-door living rooms. The majority have only two doors, so that to get into the garden you must go to the back door or the front door. Not to be able to bring the garden into the living room on a summer day would be intolerable to me.

To be able to walk out on to cool paving which has just been hosed down and to spread a cloth on a long low table under vines for a late evening meal is not a luxury; it is essential!

Sweeping lawns are lovely, but goodness, the tyranny of them! One can't help feeling that the water they absorb could be more profitably used at times. Come to think of it, keeping quite a sizeable pool or lake replenished with water in summer would probably use less water than the same area of grass.

Yours,

Edna Walling

1948

Dear Gardeners,

Sometimes pools can be an unsightly rather than an additional feature to the garden. You have to take care of a number of things. First of all, you have to find the most suitable site. Then it is desirable that the pool should eventually look like a natural feature, not a reservoir or a tank.

Do your planting on the northern and western sides, so that at the hottest part of the day the pool appears cool and inviting, reflecting the overhanging trees. Low-growing plants of quiet hue, to conceal the edge, and grass running right to the margin in places so that one may walk right up to the water's edge, will ensure a quietly green and softly textured setting for the pool.

Any colour should be most subtly introduced. Blues and mauves create more distance when looking across the water than brilliant reds, pinks and orange.

Construction can be quite simple if the concrete is moulded up the side of the pool without wooden forms, sloping it from a foot thickness at the base to two or three inches at the top. Bevel the top edge back towards the earth, leaving an inch of concrete at the most (less if possible) because no concrete must eventually show or the whole thing is a failure. And don't think you can get over the concrete with 'a row of stones' or anything like that.

A vast amount has been written about concrete, how to build this and how to build that in concrete—personally, I think concrete's the invention of the devil—and so details of construction are superfluous here. Sufficient is it to say that nothing is more fatal to the good appearance of an informal pool than to have any concrete visible, either in the bottom of the pool or where the concrete meets the surrounding earth. A bituminous paint, one that will not kill the essential mosquito-eating fish, will ensure good reflections and will conceal the concrete.

I have confirmed, once and for all, my feelings that sculpture and pottery go hand-in-hand with landscape gardening. For a brief hour we have looked upon the work of William Ricketts. In the forest just off the Mt. Dandenong Highway at Kalorama, up a muddy path is his unusual studio, one that is more out-of-doors than in, and one that is quite perfect. There is not one jarring note in this place where one may see the work of a very great artist in clay. Once again what struck me so forcibly was not only the exquisite delicacy of the figures themselves (Aborigines, with enthralling little native animals occasionally accompanying them), but the buoyant grace in the design of the bases of these figures, and the extraordinarily gifted manner in which these masterpieces are fitted onto boulders, into niches, and by the side of pools.

A little rill of gleaming water flows quietly beside the path through this out-of-door studio to pond and waterfall, graced with native ferns and 'Sweet Bursaria'.

I often wonder why some people are so terrified of planting too many trees. I am not thinking of the suburban garden (though even there it is rather enjoyable to have to fight your way into a house) but of more extensive areas where trees planted closely produce aisles of living green. Closely planted trees give glorious effects in moonlight, cool and restful shade in summer, and shelter and warmth in winter. Compare this with the specimen way—meticulous, unadventurous, and unattractive to the artist, the poet and to children.

Well, you can have your brighter-foliaged *Prunus pissarti nigra* with its redder leaves and pinker flowers. I'll have the old white *pissarti* with its softer bronze foliage and its simple white blossom. Sprays of the blooms of the purple-leaved cherry plum in a large grey pottery jug against the dusky blue plaster of my office walls could only be equalled by the cherry plum blossom, which precedes the purple-leaved form by a week or so in spring.

One of the most enchanting little plants at Sonning is an upright shrublet with grey foliage and mauvish-pink flowers. *Thymus stricta* is the name we have known this by for years, but I now wonder if it is *striatus*, for nowhere can we find *stricta*. Few plants give me so much delight for making pictures with plants and boulders.

Yours,

Edna Walling

FEBRUARY, 1948

Dear Gardeners,
What a number of people there are who have no idea how beautiful a plane tree can be. 'I hate plane trees; they're such an ugly shape', someone replied

to the suggestion of one for a courtyard. One of the things I like about the
Oriental plane is its lovely form, and when I began eulogising about it the
person said, 'But I thought you meant those things that grow in the streets.'
'Well, that is the species I had in mind', I said, 'but unpruned ...that is, not
made into "things", as you call them'.

The plane tree isn't an outsized mop, really; it's a pyramid. It has a central
leader and, if left alone, it is a healthy and beautiful tree. Admittedly,
nothing could be more unsightly than a pruned plane tree, but if you are

fortunate enough to get hold of a young tree that has not already been chopped about with secateurs (and if you are wise enough to allow it to assume its natural beautiful form) you can count upon it to provide you with shade, and beauty, and no troubles.

For years one row of plane trees on Dandenong Road, Victoria, was allowed to grow in all its pristine beauty. This worried 'the experts' for a long time. They used to talk very deedily about it ... it was a little matter of different Councils, I think. Well, everything is all right now, BOTH sides have been pruned, both look equally ugly, and everybody's happy (except me!).

As you know I always thought there should be a Society for the Prevention of Cruelty to Landscapes. Well, there is one—the Australian Wild Life Preservation Society. I advise you all to get their Journal and read what David G. Stead, the Editor, has to say about National Parks and Mr A. G. Campbell's remarks on the Wilson's Promontory Reserve. It's high time we all took a non-active interest in our fast-disappearing national garden, our heritage of natural beauty.

Even as I write, the beautiful gum trees and wild cherries are falling to the P.M.G. Department's axe, at the same time we make an ecological survey (with the patient assistance of the government botanist) of the plant association in this part of the world before they completely disappear, for even though it is not spectacular it is interesting, restful and refreshing— definitely more interesting than the trees planted to replace this natural growth where it has been laid low.

What I feel is this: the smaller our gardens become and the more we live in flats, the more imperative is the preservation of the natural gardens growing along the highway.

I know so little about roses but I love them, and grow them for my round mahogany table. Full-blown flowers of 'Madame Abel Chatenay', some red buds of—oh! any rose that is red, and a white bud or two of 'Frau Karl

Druschki', or any other rose that is white! *That's* how I like roses. I can't imagine how anyone could discard those glorious full-blown ones that look so beautifully blousy. What substance, what a sheen have the petals of a 'Madame Abel Chatenay' when fully expanded! How I hate the moment they have to go, but that they go on to the compost heap is better than into a dust bin. You feel they do 'gently turn their dust to leaves' there.

This is where Edna's 'Letters to Garden Lovers' came to an end. Over the years, Edna continued her work in garden design and often contributed gardening articles to the *Australian Home Beautiful*.